Breaking Point of the French Army

Breaking Point of the French Army

The Nivelle Offensive of 1917

David Murphy

Pen & Sword
MILITARY

First published in Great Britain in 2015 by
Pen & Sword Military
an imprint of
Pen & Sword Books Ltd
47 Church Street
Barnsley
South Yorkshire
S70 2AS

Copyright © David Murphy 2015

ISBN 978 1 78159 292 2

The right of David Murphy to be identified as the Author of this Work has been asserted by him in accordance with the Copyright, Designs and Patents Act 1988.

A CIP catalogue record for this book is available from the British Library

All rights reserved. No part of this book may be reproduced or transmitted in any form or by any means, electronic or mechanical including photocopying, recording or by any information storage and retrieval system, without permission from the Publisher in writing.

Typeset in Ehrhardt by
Mac Style Ltd, Bridlington, East Yorkshire
Printed and bound in the UK by CPI Group (UK) Ltd,
Croydon, CR0 4YY

Pen & Sword Books Ltd incorporates the imprints of Pen & Sword Archaeology, Atlas, Aviation, Battleground, Discovery, Family History, History, Maritime, Military, Naval, Politics, Railways, Select, Transport, True Crime, and Fiction, Frontline Books, Leo Cooper, Praetorian Press, Seaforth Publishing and Wharncliffe.

For a complete list of Pen & Sword titles please contact
PEN & SWORD BOOKS LIMITED
47 Church Street, Barnsley, South Yorkshire, S70 2AS, England
E-mail: enquiries@pen-and-sword.co.uk
Website: www.pen-and-sword.co.uk

Contents

List of Illustrations vi
List of Maps vii
Abbreviations xii
Acknowledgements xiii
Introduction xiv

Chapter 1 The French Army, 1914–17 1

Chapter 2 The Rise of General Robert Nivelle 27

Chapter 3 General Nivelle and his Plan 54

Chapter 4 The French Tank Programme 72

Chapter 5 The Offensive 84

Chapter 6 Reinforcing Failure 106

Chapter 7 The Mutinies 121

Conclusion 149
Appendix: Visiting the Battlefield 166
Notes 169
Bibliography 180
Index 185

List of Illustrations

Unless otherwise stated, images are from the author's collection.

Contemporary portrait of General Robert Nivelle from *L'Illustration*.
General Charles Mangin.
General Joseph Joffre. (*Library of Congress*)
Paul Painlevé. (*Library of Congress*)
General Nivelle at his HQ, 1917.
French troops, 1914. (*SHD*)
NCO and warrant officers on a machine-gun course.
A French *Poilu* of 1917. (*SHD*)
Fort Brimont.
Cartoon from *La Rire* depicting Nivelle.
Cheerful French troops on their way to the offensive, 1917.
Poster depicting colonial troops of the French army.
French aerodrome, 1917. (*Library of Congress*)
Hurtebise Farm before the war.
The remains of Hurtebise Farm in 1917.
Destroyed French Schneider tanks.
Contemporary illustration of a St Chamond tank.
French troops examine German defences.
US troops inspecting a German pillbox.
The Chemin des Dames battlefield.
General Pétain and King George V.
A Renault FT17 tank. (*Library of Congress*)
Jean Droit's 'Les Boues de la Somme'.
General Nivelle on his USA visit.
Christian Lapie's ensemble 'Constellation de la Douleur'.

List of Maps

Maps drawn by Dr Ronan Foley, Department of Geography, University of Maynooth

Map 1. The front line in February 1917.
Map 2. The front line in April 1917 after the German withdrawal to the Hindenburg Line.
Map 3. The BEF area of operations at Arras and Vimy, April 1917.
Map 4. French territorial gains by the end of the Nivelle Offensive in May 1917.

Map 1. The front line in February 1917.

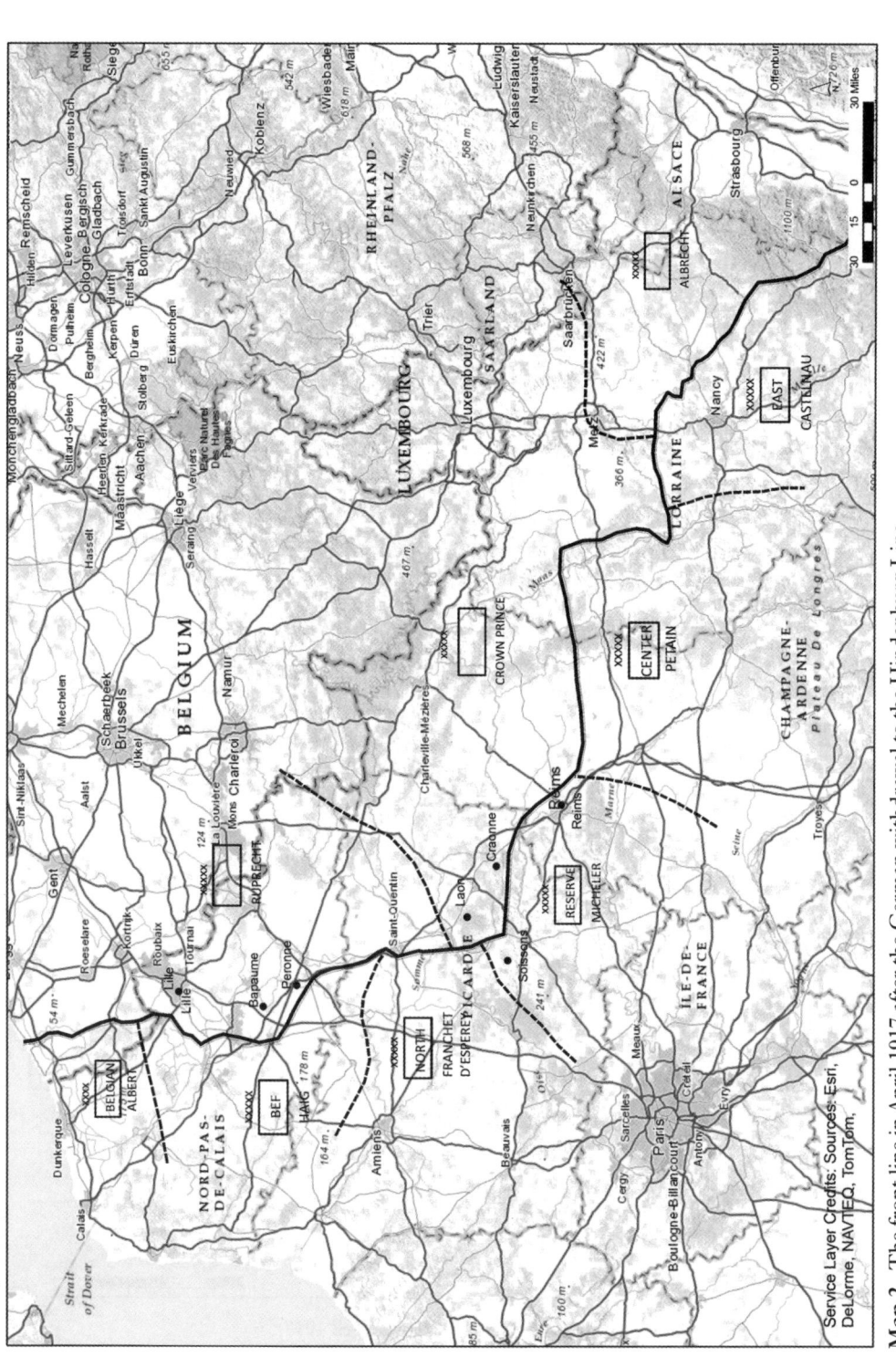

Map 2. The front line in April 1917 after the German withdrawal to the Hindenburg Line.

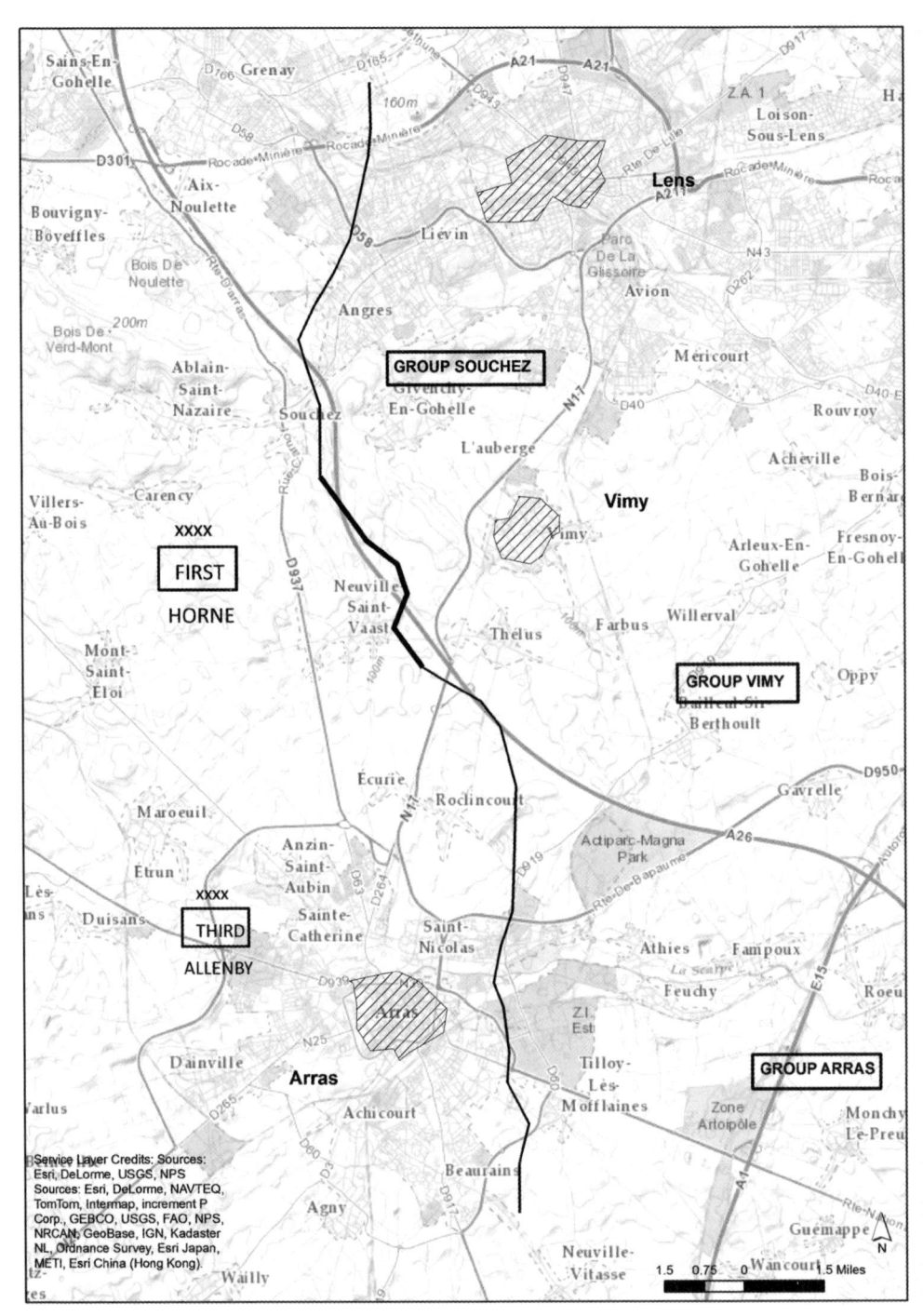

Map 3. The BEF area of operations at Arras and Vimy, April 1917.

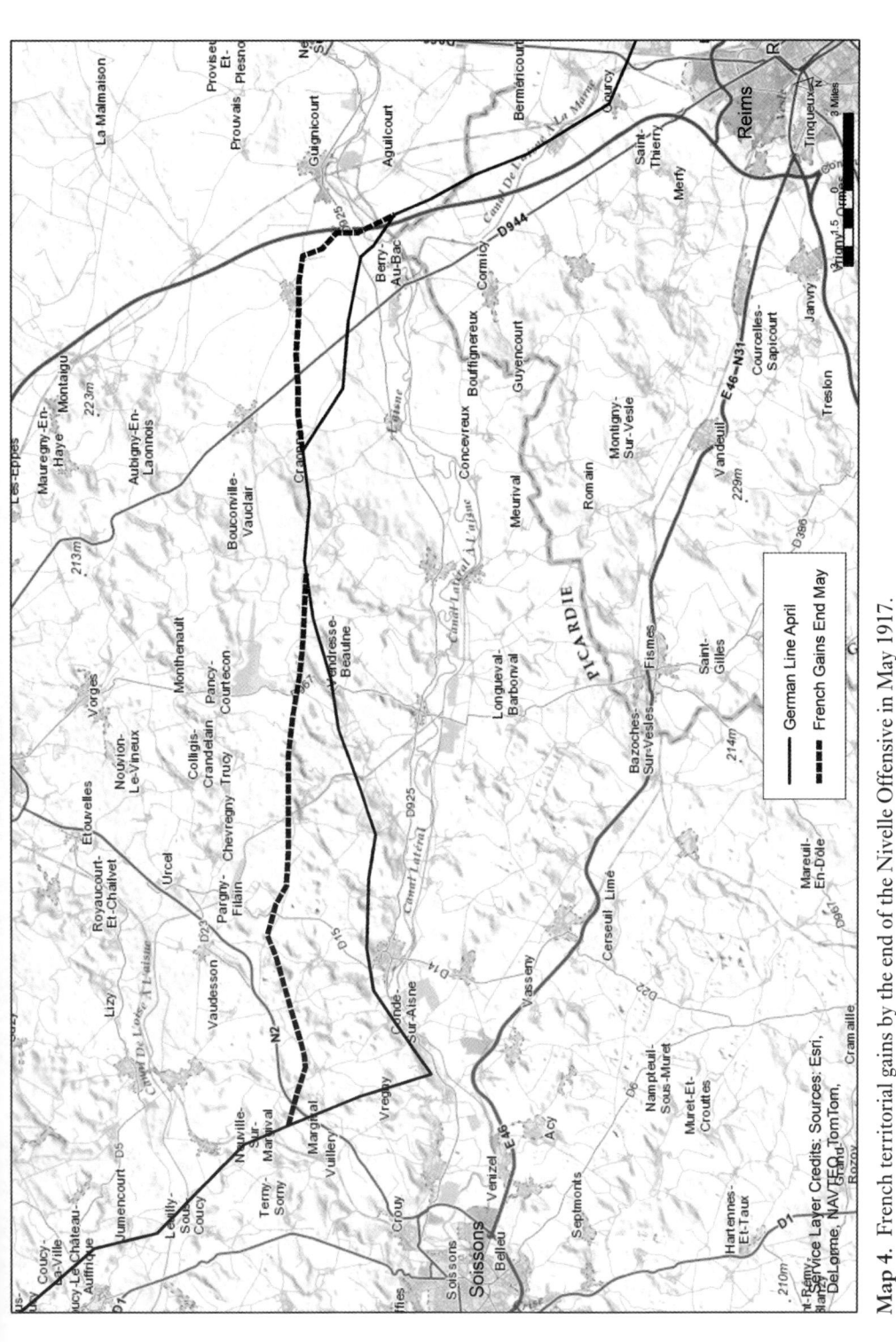

Map 4. French territorial gains by the end of the Nivelle Offensive in May 1917.

Abbreviations

AFGG	*Les armées françaises dans la grande guerre* (11 tomes, Paris, 1922–37)
BEF	British Expeditionary Force
C-in-C	Commander-in-Chief
GAC	Groupe d'armées du centre
GAE	Groupe d'armées de l'est
GAN	Groupe d'armées du nord
GAR	Groupe d'armées de reserve
GQG	Grand Quartier Général
MEBU	Manschafts-Eisen-Beton Unterstand
MG	Machine Gun
SHD	Service Historique de la Défense, Château de Vincennes

Acknowledgements

I am grateful to many people for their help in completing this book. In France, my thanks go to the staff at the Service Historique de la Défense in Vincennes. In particular, I would like to thank Colonel Rémy Porte and Dr Nathalie Genet-Rouffiac. I am extremely grateful to Christian Lapie for allowing me to reproduce a photograph of his sculpture 'Constellation de la Douleur' on the Chemin des Dames. I would also like to thank the staff at the French Embassy in Dublin, including Salendre Maxence and Stephane Aymard.

In Ireland, I would like to thank my colleagues at the Department of History at Maynooth University, in particular Dr Ian Speller and Professor Marian Lyons. The assistance of Catherine Bergin, Peter Twomey and Dr Luke Diver was also much appreciated. The assistance of Dr Ronan Foley of the Department of Geography at Maynooth University in preparing the maps for this volume is gratefully acknowledged. I began this research some time ago while carrying out research in Paris for a project of Professor Ciaran Brady of Trinity College, Dublin, and I am grateful for that opportunity to work in French archives. I am also grateful for the input of Professor John Horne of TCD, Tom Burke of the Royal Dublin Fusiliers Association and Professor Gary Sheffield at the University of Wolverhampton. My thanks go also to Lar Joye of the National Museum of Ireland and Professor Harry Laver of South-Eastern Louisiana University. In the Irish Defence Forces, I would like to acknowledge the assistance and advice of Lt Col. Gareth Prendergast, Capt. Joe Gleeson and Capt. Alan Kearney. At Pen & Sword Publishing, my thanks go to Rupert Harding and Sarah Cook for their efforts in editing and preparing this volume for publication.

The assistance and advice of my sister Sharon was much appreciated. A special 'mention-in-dispatches' to my wife Georgina, for her help and patience during this process.

Introduction

Nivelle had a plan. It was based on the combination of overwhelming artillery support and well-prepared infantry attacks which had served him so well at Verdun. And it would succeed in forty-eight hours, or it could be called off. No more Sommes, no more Verduns.[1]

On 14 July 1919 a grand victory parade took place in Paris. On the first Bastille Day since the end of the war, the people of France lined the Champs d'Elysees and the streets around the Arc de Triomphe. Parisians turned out in force while thousands travelled by train from around France to be present to mark the victory over the Central Powers and also to commemorate France's great sacrifices in the war. Planning for the event was not without its problems. Tragically, the French air ace Jean Navarre was killed on 10 April while practising to fly through the Arc as part of the parade.[2] In the final run-up to the parade, some territorial troops arrived in shabby uniforms and had to be hastily re-equipped at the last minute. During the night of 13/14 July a memorial cenotaph became stuck under the Arc itself and had to be freed by a unit of sweating army engineers. Also, members of the public invaded the seating reserved for dignitaries and had to be dislodged during the night by police, backed up by cavalry.

On 14 July the parade itself went ahead without any major hitch. A three-hour-long procession of troops passed through the Arc de Triomphe. They were led by a group of the war wounded and 'mutilés' in their wheelchairs, followed by Marshals Foch and Joffre, and Pétain leading army units; contingents from the other Allied nations also participated. The celebrations continued for the rest of the day with joyous crowds gathering in the squares and open areas of Paris.

There had also been some political 'unpleasantness' before the event. Field Marshal Haig had to be persuaded to attend, while General Diaz, the senior Italian general, was not present. Question marks hung over some of the French generals and invitations were not certain. Maréchal Joffre, for example, whose star had by now definitely faded, was initially not invited and when he finally was, questions arose as to where he should be in the parade. In general, however, even senior French officers whose wartime record was far from glorious were invited to attend.

One notable exception was General Robert Nivelle, who was commanding French forces in North Africa at the time. Nivelle was specifically excluded and instead supervised a parade in Algeria. For Nivelle, this course of events must have seemed hard to believe. Just a few short years previously, he had been commander-in-chief of the French field armies. During late 1916 and early 1917 he had enjoyed huge public acclaim and had been a darling of the press. For a period of some months he held sway in military matters and associated with the premiers of both France and Britain and senior political figures from both governments. Senior generals within his own army, his former superiors, were his subordinates. And in 1917 he had a plan to win the war. Now, as victory was being celebrated in Paris, he had been relegated to command of a military backwater, removed from the centre of military life and political power. In 1917 Nivelle's career had been soaring like a meteor. Now he had crashed to earth. How had this come to pass?

On taking command of the French field armies in December 1916, General Robert Nivelle exuded total confidence to all who met him. His staff officers, the press, French and British politicians and Allied military commanders all found him energetic and plausible. Having revised French offensive plans for 1917, he pressed home his ideas at planning meetings and promised his listeners a 'splendid harvest of glory for the British and French armies'.[3]

For some, Nivelle was simply too plausible and his promises seemed too good to be true. General Lyautey and Paul Painlevé, who had both served as minister for war during Nivelle's term as the French *generalissimo*, were not convinced. Fellow generals, including Pétain, urged caution and doubted that the battlefield conditions would allow for the results Nivelle expected. Their respective doubts were all shown to be well founded. Rather than a stunning victory, Nivelle's offensive resulted in only modest gains in exchange for significant losses.

Yet the French political-military system served to enable Nivelle and his plans. Having presented him to the French nation as a military genius who would win the war, politicians and fellow generals lacked the resolve to remove Nivelle before the damage was done. Their collective lack of resolve facilitated a military failure at a time when France could not endure yet another reverse on the battlefield. The resulting collapse in army morale led to the 'mutinies of 1917', while public discontent grew. By the summer of 1917 France was in crisis. Dropping out of the war became a distinct possibility. As the American historian James L. Stokesbury put it, Nivelle claimed that he was going to win the war and 'he very nearly did – for Germany'.[4]

Nivelle and his failed offensive are often dealt with only briefly by French and British historians. It is as though the memory is still too painful to discuss. While First World War generals hardly covered themselves in glory, least of all on the Western Front, Nivelle is seen as a particularly poor example of generalship. There is some justification for this. His offensive plans for 1917 were hugely ambitious and made no allowances for the difficult terrain over which he planned to attack. In his planning process, he neglected some of the most basic principles of war, not least in terms of operational security. In some ways, however, it could be argued that Nivelle was no worse than many French generals of the war and, in some cases, he was much better.

Why then did the failure of his plans have such drastic consequences? At a fundamental level, the impact of the failure was due to the timing of the offensive. By the spring of 1917 it was only reasonable for French soldiers, the government and the French public to expect that their generals had learned something since 1914. The failure of Nivelle's offensive was dramatic proof that this was not the case. It seemed that the French army was caught in a cycle of costly offensives that must eventually destroy it. The sheer futility of these offensives drove the French army beyond its breaking point. As Pétain later put it, 'they have ruined the heart of the French soldier'.[5]

If Nivelle's failure highlighted the dysfunctional relationship between the French government, the army and the French people, it also illustrated flaws in the relationship between Britain and France. Nivelle allowed himself to be drawn into an intrigue to limit the power of Field Marshal Haig, the commander of the British Expeditionary Force (BEF). These political manoeuvrings soured the relationship between the British government and the Allied commander and his generals. In the wider strategic context of early 1917, these increased tensions could not have been more poorly timed. Russia was tottering, while the Allies' search for strategic alternatives in other theatres such as Salonika was bringing no real success. All of this came against a backdrop of an increasingly effective campaign by German U-boats. America's entry into the war in April 1917 brought no immediate relief to the Allied armies bogged down on the Western Front and elsewhere.

In every respect, Nivelle had timed his offensive at a time when only the victory that he promised would have been acceptable. His failure merely threw light on the flaws within France and also on the strategic problems faced by the Allies. Elizabeth Greenhalgh, the renowned historian of the French army, has pointed out that Nivelle is the only Allied general to have a Western Front battle named after him.[6] This is an entirely justified distinction. There may be some extenuating factors, and Nivelle was enabled in his behaviour by a whole cast of characters, but the ultimate call to go ahead with the offensive was his. French historians such as Denis Rolland and Nicholas Offenstadt have made considerable efforts to re-examine his actions and psychology, yet Nivelle remains one of the most contentious figures of the First World War, especially within France. It seems unlikely that this will change in the near future.

Chapter 1

The French Army, 1914–17

So it was with the Austrians, the Belgians, the English, the Russians, the Turks and then the Italians. In a single week, twenty million men, busy with their lives and loves, with making money and planning a future, received the order to stop everything to go and kill other men.[1]

By the eve of the Nivelle Offensive the French army had already suffered hugely since the outbreak of war in 1914. From the opening operations of the war, the French army had consistently suffered large numbers of casualties and by late 1916 it had already suffered over a million killed, wounded or missing. Its army commanders seemed rooted in a pre-war doctrine of the offensive and thousands of young lives were squandered in a series of futile assaults throughout 1914, 1915 and 1916. During 1916 the French not only endured the German onslaught during the Battle of Verdun, but also contributed troops to the Somme Offensive. On taking command in December 1916, General Robert Nivelle seemed to promise a fresh approach and the hope of victory. Ultimately, he would push the damaged French army beyond its breaking point.[2]

The seeds of France's military difficulties during the First World War were firmly rooted in the Franco–Prussian War of 1870–1. The French army's performance in that war was little short of a shambles. While there were moments of undoubted heroism, the army emerged with its reputation badly tarnished. In terms of preparation and performance, it was found to be badly wanting at all levels. Its senior commanders performed poorly, while the logistics of the various field forces were a mess. Command and control was shambolic and this resulted in confusion and defeat on the battlefield. An official report on the debacle of 1870–1 later stated, 'We were beaten by the absence of preparation, organisation and direction, and by the small number of our soldiers more than by the arms of our enemies.'[3] The French army had simply proved that it was not fit for purpose. In the decades that followed, successive administrations applied themselves to military reform, while at the same time the French nation engaged in a conversation as to the role of the army in French society and politics.

At the military level, the shortcomings of the army during the war of 1870–1 seemed somewhat obvious. The means by which France's military could be made fit for modern war were less obvious, however. At the most basic level, a debate began as to how the army of the Third Republic should be organised. The debate centred on whether it should be a professional force of long-term, career soldiers or a large conscript army that would reflect the broad character of the French nation, enshrining the political ethos of the Third Republic. This broad debate continued up to 1911, the year of the Moroccan Crisis, without any real resolution. In the immediate aftermath of the Franco-Prussian War, the general consensus was that France's military should be composed of professional soldiers with officers drawn from the aristocracy, gentry and bourgeoisie. This trend was reflected in the government's legislation for the reform of the army that was drawn up between 1871 and 1875, and the military gradually returned to a position of prominence and popularity in French society.

By the late 1880s, however, there were causes for concern. Liberals and members of the extreme left grew increasingly anxious at the growing militarism within French society. Sections of the national press seemed to pander to a military agenda and the dangers of this trend came to the fore during a series of scandals in the late nineteenth and early twentieth centuries.[4]

The Boulanger Affair of the late 1880s confirmed many of the fears of the anti-military faction. General Georges Boulanger was the virtual personification of anti-German aggressiveness, while also possessing huge political ambition. It is testament to his political influence during the 1880s that he was later claimed by members of both the extreme left and the extreme right in French politics. A distinguished veteran of the Franco–Prussian War, Boulanger was appointed as Minister of War in 1886, during the premiership of Charles de Freycinet. He immediately embarked upon a series of army reforms, including the adaptation of the Lebel rifle, the first-ever military service rifle to use smokeless powder. During 1887, however,

Boulanger engaged in a series of provocations against Germany, including building new military emplacements near the border at Belfort and banning the exporting of horses to Germany. The new administration of Maurice Rouvier viewed him as a risk and an embarrassment and Boulanger was sacked in May 1887. This dismissal seemed actually to increase Boulanger's popularity and the cult of 'Boulangisme' was born. By 1889 he enjoyed huge popular support and was elected as deputy for Paris with an enormous majority. Supported by an odd mix of leftists, Republicans, conservatives and (secretly) royalists, he seemed set to become the next prime minister of France, or perhaps its next dictator. Within his own faction, he was urged to seize power but his nerve failed and he fled the country, later being charged with conspiracy and treasonable activity. The publication of his secret correspondence with prominent royalists effectively destroyed his popular support. In 1891 he committed suicide in a Brussels cemetery beside the grave of his former mistress. In the aftermath of the Boulanger Affair, there was a backlash against all things military in France. While Boulanger had brought the country to the verge of dictatorship, politicians also resented the cost of maintaining France's professional army, while the public in turn begrudged the institution responsible for conscripting its young men for long periods.[5]

The infamous Dreyfus Affair, which dragged on for twelve years, was equally divisive within French politics and society, if not more so. Once again, the conduct of senior military officers was brought into the public gaze and they were found wanting. In 1894 Captain Alfred Dreyfus was accused of passing artillery secrets to the German military attaché. Dreyfus was tried in secret and found guilty on the basis of circumstantial and doctored evidence. Dismissed the service, he was sent to the notorious penal settlement on Devil's Island. Soon after, a campaign began to have him exonerated, led by Dreyfus' brother and other prominent figures including Émile Zola. In 1896 new information came to light that implicated another officer, Major Ferdinand Esterhazy, who was acquitted on the second day of his court-martial. Once again, the military establishment was implicated in a scandal that was dividing the country. The Dreyfusard camp was convinced that a vast injustice had taken place, while the anti-Dreyfusards believed that the honour of the army had to be protected at all costs. The case became increasingly bizarre. In 1898 Major H.J. Henry admitted that he had faked some of the original evidence, before committing suicide. Yet in a re-trial in 1899 Dreyfus was again found guilty and sentenced to a further ten years. Amid a public outcry, he was pardoned and released but the original verdict was not reversed until an appeals trial in 1906. He was eventually reinstated in the army and served during the First World War.[6]

In the aftermath of this scandal, it was obvious that senior officers of the general staff had featured among the now-discredited anti-Dreyfusard camp. As Anthony Clayton, the noted historian of the French army, has commented, 'the army became decoupled from the political stage, its leaders widely, if wrongly, suspected of planning a coup d'état. Once again, questions were asked about the nature of the army and the choice of its officers.'[7]

This tendency for senior army officers to become embroiled in political matters continually tarnished the army's reputation and gave various factions within French society cause for concern as to the role of the military within French society. While the army was still dealing with the fallout from the Dreyfus Affair, a further scandal rocked the political establishment and once again a faction within the army played a key role. The 'Affaire des Fiches' of 1904 confirmed the worst fears of those on the right in French politics as to the dangers of 'republicanising' the army. The national elections of 1902 returned a radical legislature, which formed a government in 1903 under Émile Combes, a reforming leftist prime minister who led the 'Bloc des Gauches' faction within parliament. Under this new government, a process was initiated to separate Church and State, the espoused purpose of which was to create a truly republican form of government and thus a truly republican France. The Minister of War, General Louis André, had begun a process of republicanisation within the army as early as 1900 but this accelerated under Combes' new ministry.

Officers with known Leftist or Dreyfusard sympathies were fast-tracked for promotion. All officers were discouraged from going to mass or having other church associations. To the disgust of many officers, the army was used in the forcible expropriation of church property. More insidiously, André encouraged republican officers to spy on their brother officers and a system of files, or 'fiches', was compiled in order to record the activities of officers with church sympathies. André also made use of groups of Freemasons within the army to carry out the necessary surveillance and reporting.[8] Church-going or other outward signs of devoutness were recorded and officers who displayed such tendencies found themselves passed over for promotion. One such was Colonel Ferdinand Foch, who, after a mixed wartime career, would later serve as the supreme Allied commander from 1918. Perhaps unsurprisingly, morale within the officer corps suffered and this had ramifications for the wider effectiveness of the army. When the affair came to light in 1904, the government collapsed and André was forced out of office. Yet again, senior army officers had become embroiled in dubious political activity. For many politicians, pressmen and French citizens, military officers had proved themselves to be a divisive and scheming class, having been implicated in a series of scandals from the 1880s.

Regardless of political affiliations, by 1905 all factions within French society had good reason to distrust and dislike the military. The decision to reduce the length of compulsory service from three years to two in that year reflects a wider disgust with the French army, reinforced by the use of troops to put down industrial unrest in 1906 and 1907. In the Languedoc one regiment mutinied rather than act against striking workers. By 1910 desertions were becoming increasingly common, while large numbers of reservists refused to report for annual training. The French army, in terms of morale and operational efficiency, was at its lowest point since the defeats of 1870–1. Furthermore, the senior officers' unwise practice of dabbling in political matters had alienated potential supporters within government.[9] However, there is nothing quite like a perceived external threat to focus a nation's mind and spirit, and concerns regarding German militarism forced the French people to reconsider the role and place of the army within society. The visit of a German cruiser to Agadir in Morocco in 1911, long regarded by the French as falling within their sphere of interest, galvanised the nation. With a growing German army across its eastern border and German naval power now threatening territories overseas, France decided that perhaps it needed a larger and more efficient army after all. It was also increasingly obvious that German industry was better equipped for war and that, in terms of population, Germany was outstripping France in the manpower contest. Germany was, to put it simply, producing more young men and it also had the systems in place to train and equip them militarily.

During the years immediately preceding the First World War, there was an accelerated series of army reforms in France. These were an attempt to both enlarge the army while also re-equipping it for greater military effectiveness in the field. These reforms were carried out under the supervision of General Joseph Joffre, who had been appointed as chief of the general staff in 1911 in the aftermath of the Morocco Crisis. Under Joffre's command, in 1913 the term of compulsory service was raised once again to three years in order to facilitate specialist and NCO training for the best conscripts. Apart from enabling better training, this move also increased the size of the army by over 200,000 men in 1914. In December 1913 Joffre issued new operational regulations that outlined plans for greater co-operation between the infantry and artillery, while at the same time beginning new production programmes to make up for the disparity in artillery between Germany and France.[10]

With hindsight, one could argue that such reforms came too late. Many years had been wasted with involvement in political scandals and the necessary long-term reforms required after the defeat of 1870–1 were simply not carried out. The French army did have some advantages, however. Many of its officers had seen colonial service, which encouraged initiative and openness to new tactical ideas. Such strengths would be crucial in the upcoming struggle. Also, educational reforms first instigated by Jules Ferry in the 1880s had begun to bear fruit. The standard of education among French conscripts was high, while they had also been immersed in the narrative of the defeat of 1870, the loss of Alsace-Lorraine and the need to defend France and perhaps secure revenge for these humiliations. Following the Moroccan Crisis there was, therefore, increased solidarity between the government, the people and the army.[11]

By 1914 moreover, France did not stand alone. Since the 1890s the French had been engaged in a series of strategic discussions with the Russians, exploring the idea of providing mutual support in the event of a war between Russia and Germany. In late 1892, after a series of discussions, France and Russia entered into a formal convention, agreeing to concentrate their forces against Germany in the event of a war. Regardless of the extreme ideological and political differences between the two countries, France was now firmly allied with Russia. This convention was ratified with an exchange of notes in December 1893 and January 1894, the final agreement stating that French and Russian forces would 'be engaged to the utmost, as quickly as possible, in such a manner that Germany has to fight at the same time in the east and west'.[12] In the early 1900s a series of discussions between French and Russian officers developed the details of these broad plans. During the staff talks of 1911, 1912 and 1913 the principle of defeating Germany first, before turning to deal with its allies, became enshrined in Franco-Russian strategy. Russia also promised to launch an offensive into Germany within a fortnight of mobilising. For this initial attack, Russia planned to mobilise between 700,000 and 800,000 men. French generals, in particular Joffre, found these talks hugely encouraging and were optimistic about Russia's military potential in any upcoming war. The French general staff also promised an early offensive against Germany, using a force of at least 210,000 men, in order to pin German forces in the western theatre of operations. In the event of war it was hoped that, as French and Russian offensives developed in both the west and the east, the Germans would be too over-stretched to fight on two fronts simultaneously.

Forming an alliance with the British was to prove more problematic. France and Britain were age-old enemies and retained a level of animosity in the early years of the 1900s. As late as 1900–4, French military intelligence sent a mission to Ireland to explore the possibility of landing an invading force there.[13] In 1902 the French general staff drew up a secret plan for the invasion of the British Isles with a force of 65,000 men. French concerns about German militarism in Europe and British concerns over German naval expansion made a level of *rapprochement* both possible and necessary. After a series of talks, the Anglo-French Entente was signed in 1904 and further staff talks occurred in subsequent years. The main initial British contribution was to involve the Royal Navy, which was to provide enough force to dominate the North Sea, the Channel and the Atlantic approaches, while the French fleet would concentrate in the western Mediterranean – an arrangement that would also allow France to transfer troops from North Africa. By 1911 the French also envisaged the British army providing over 100,000 men in six divisions and two cavalry brigades for operations in France and Belgium. This force was referred to as 'Army W' in secret French plans but the timing of the arrival of British forces in the event of war, and their disposition, remained uncertain. In broad terms, Joffre hoped that they would be placed on the left of the French line, perhaps for operations in Belgium. Joffre also hoped that, while the British force would be quite small by European standards, it would give him a numerical advantage against the Germans, who would be overstretched by fighting on two fronts.

By 1914 the French army was also very much committed to a single war plan – Plan XVII. In the years preceding the war, two main plans had been developed, focused on the belief that the Germans intended to conduct a rapid campaign to knock France out of any future war. In 1909 General Alfred von Schlieffen had commented on the necessity of winning the opening battles of any future war. Around this, the French general staff (Grand Quartier Général or GQG), and in particular Joffre, formulated the opinion that the Germans intended to commit themselves to an initial all-out attack. The French army began to prepare for such an eventuality. Plan XVI was the brainchild of General Victor Michel, who was designated to become commander-in-chief in 1911. In hindsight, Michel's Plan XVI seems eminently sensible. Reasoning that the Germans would not be able to achieve the battlefield decision that they required by pushing into the Lorraine region or fighting east of the Meuse, Michel was convinced that they would advance via Belgium, using their large reserves. His Plan XVI provided for a pre-emptive entry by the French army into Belgium. He would also reinforce the left flank of the French army, hinging it on the coastline. Furthermore, Michel planned for the immediate use of large formations of reserve troops. Ultimately, however, this plan was rejected by the Minister for War, Adolphe Messimy, and the GQG. The idea of entering neutral Belgian territory was delicate to say the least, while the overall plan was seen to be too defensively minded in its general nature. It was also argued that Michel's plan would take the bulk of the French away from the Lorraine region, the lost territory that France desperately wanted to regain. Michel ceased to be the designate for the commander-in-chief position and his plan was scrapped.[14]

In his stead General Joffre became commander-in-chief. Joffre, who came from a poor family and was a graduate of the École Polytechnique, was seen to embody the true French military spirit. He was certainly not a dazzling character but his service in Indochina, Madagascar and West Africa had shown him to be competent and steady. He also held acceptable military views. For example, he believed that the strength of the French army lay in its offensive spirit and that the recovery of Alsace Lorraine should be factored in to any war plans. Joffre initially tinkered with Plan XVI, even considering a movement of French troops through both Belgium and Luxembourg to counter any German attack. But by 1913 Joffre and the GQG had devised Plan XVII, which would come to dominate both pre-war French planning and the opening French moves in 1914. Plan XVII was, in essence, a plan for the mobilisation and concentration of the French army along the eastern border with Germany. Thereafter it would facilitate operations into Alsace Lorraine or Belgium. The key factor was the speedy mobilisation and movement of French troops to the area where it was thought the Germans would concentrate their forces. As the plan itself stated, 'The intention of the commander-in-chief is to advance with all forces united to the attack on the German armies.' To a large degree Plan XVII was based on the bitter experiences of 1870, when the French armies mobilised inefficiently and then found themselves poorly positioned to face the Prussian onslaught.[15] In retrospect, however, Plan XVII was shockingly vague. It positioned the bulk of the French army along the eastern border with limited and local objectives. If successful, it would force the Germans to fight on ground of French choosing but, if the German army decided not to stick to the French timetable for war and outmanoeuvred them, it did not allow for other contingencies, although it did offer Joffre a level of flexibility once the Schlieffen-Moltke Plan began to develop. At a strategic level, however, Plan XVII did not factor in possible tactical developments. Also, the difficult question regarding the inclusion of reserves in the first phase of the battle was not decided. Joffre felt confident that the Germans would not use their reserves in the initial phase of the war and therefore decided that he could afford not to deploy French reserves. Ultimately, this assumption would prove to be wrong and Joffre's decision would leave the French forces outnumbered once the campaign began.[16]

The great attraction of Plan XVII was that it catered for the French belief in offensive operations. Within the army, it was felt that the great military victories of French history were due to the army's *élan* and its spirit of the offensive. This quality was to be encouraged to the utmost. A defensive plan would, it was argued, only lead to defeat. The great prophet of this philosophy was Colonel Ardant du Picq, who had been killed in action in 1870 but whose writings were published posthumously and acquired a huge following among officers. Du Picq emphasised the importance of moral factors in battle:

> When the confidence one has placed in a superiority of material, incontestable for keeping the enemy at a distance, has been betrayed by the enemy's determination to get to close quarters, braving your superior means of destruction, the enemy's moral effect on you will be increased by all that lost confidence, and his moral activity will overwhelm your own. Hence it follows that the bayonet charge, in other words the forward march under fire, will every day have a correspondingly greater effect.[17]

By the early 1900s Lt-Col. Loyzeau de Grandmaison had developed these theories further in two lectures that had a significant influence on French military thinking. Regardless of the strength of an opposition or defence, Grandmaison argued, the morale qualities of troops who were properly led in an attack would deliver success on the battlefield. Good leadership, rigid obedience to orders, offensive training and small group cohesion would always win on the battlefield. Attacks should be carried through, regardless of casualties. Tactical manuals were published to reflect these concepts. Defensive structures and fortresses were only acceptable to allow troops to be used in attacks elsewhere. The main battlefield tactic would be the infantry assault. Cavalry should not dismount to fight and artillery was to be used to support infantry attacks rather than as preparation. The infantry should be able to cover 50 metres in 20 seconds, and officers and NCOs were encouraged to knock unconscious any soldier showing fear. This philosophy was encapsulated in pre-war French field regulations, which placed a worrying emphasis on bayonet charges.[18]

In 1911 Grandmaison was appointed as chief of the general staff's 3rd Bureau (Operations). By this time he had a following among the French officer corps, often referred to as 'Grandmaisonites'. Among these was Ferdinand Foch, who lectured at the École de Guerre in Paris and developed his lectures in two books, which became required reading on staff courses.[19] In these he developed his theories on what he referred to as 'l'offensive à outrance'. According to Foch, in all circumstances attack was the correct option. The French troops' *cran* (literally 'guts') and *élan* would see the attacks pushed home, regardless of the risks. One of his maxims stated, 'To charge, but to charge in numbers, as one mass: therein lies safety.' On being promoted to brigadier-general in 1907, Foch became commandant at the École de Guerre.[20]

It is often stated that the French army was immersed in this 'cult of the offensive' but certain officers did express doubts. Colonel Philippe Pétain was among their number. Pétain realised the potential of both machine guns and the new quick-firing artillery and could foresee the probable results of large-scale infantry attacks against such weapons. Equally, he argued for a more prominent role for artillery in preparing for infantry attacks; in effect, using artillery to 'soften up' the enemy. Pétain was dismissed as a crank, as was General Charles Lanrezac, who recognised that this emphasis on the offensive could result in chaos at the tactical level, with junior commanders initiating local attacks without reference to wider strategic objectives. Equally, within the GQG itself, some officers admitted the possibility that the war would not be decided in a few weeks and might indeed drag on. In general, however, there was a confidence that the coming war would be swift and decisive. The October 1913 Field Service Regulations stated:

> The nature of war, the size of forces involved, the difficulties of resupplying them, the interruption of the social and economic life of the country, all encourage the search for a decision in the shortest possible time in order to terminate the fighting quickly.[21]

Even advocates of the offensive expressed caution. Du Picq, in his writings, had stated, 'Do not neglect destructive action before using moral action: so employ fire up to the last possible moment; otherwise, given existing rates of fire, no attack will reach its objective.'[22] Foch, who is often condemned as a commander who mindlessly followed the cult of the offensive, also emphasised the need for proper supporting fire:

> They will encounter great difficulties, and suffer heavy casualties, whenever their partial offensive has not been prepared by heavy fire.

They will be thrown back on their starting point, with still heavier losses. The superiority of fire becomes the most important element of an infantry's fighting value.[23]

Recent wars had, to a large extent, only increased the level of theorising. During the 2nd Anglo-Boer War (1899–1902) the British army had suffered at the hands of Boer marksmen. For many British and European observers, the huge casualties inflicted on British massed formations at battles such as Colenso in 1899 marked a significant shift in the nature of warfare. Modern rifle technology allowed the Mauser-equipped Boers to decimate British formations at long range. Essentially, the British formations were stopped by marksmen that the soldiers on the ground could not see, let alone engage, due to the advent of smokeless rifle cartridges. Field artillery and cavalry suffered a similar fate if deployed within range of Boer troops. As one British commentator remarked: 'cavalry, armed and equipped as the cavalry of the continent, is as obsolete as the Crusaders'.[24]

The 2nd Anglo-Boer War led to reforms within the British army and across Europe. Tactically, the emphasis switched to small units and dispersed formations, preferably amply supported by field artillery. The war sparked reforms in France and in many ways the doctrinal shift ran counter to the prevailing cult of the offensive. The new infantry regulations of 1904 abandoned the concept of advancing in large formations. Instead, the infantry would advance in small groups and open order, supported by artillery fire. This was a doctrine of fire and manoeuvre, with initiative devolved down to junior officer and NCO level. But while this may have been the official doctrine, various factors ensured that these tactics were not adopted in practice. For a start, due to the limited time and space available for training, it proved difficult to introduce junior officers, NCOs and troops to these methods. The French army's reliance on reserves exacerbated this problem – how could training cadres adequately instruct reserve troops who only had a limited period in uniform each year? Moreover, within the senior staff there was a marked reluctance to accept this new doctrine. Officers such as General Hippolyte Langlois argued against what they perceived to be a marked timidity based on the supposed lessons of the 2nd Anglo-Boer War. Langlois referred to this as 'acute transvaalitis' and even founded a new journal, *Revue militaire generale*, to counter these 'un-French' military ideas.

The Russo-Japanese War of 1904–5 also seemed to provide evidence of the importance of the moral factor in war and the validity of the massed military assault. The Russians had heavily fortified their positions at Port Arthur and Mukden but were ejected from both by massed Japanese attacks. The cost for the Japanese had been huge; during the various assaults at Port Arthur they suffered over 50,000 casualties, while during the ten-day battle for Mukden they lost more than 70,000 killed or wounded. For adherents of the offensive strategy, this merely proved that determined infantry assaults could work. Of course, the Russo-Japanese War also highlighted the need for proper artillery preparation and demonstrated the effectiveness of heavy artillery, especially when used in the indirect fire role. But these lessons seem to have been given less importance.[25]

Despite the predictions of commentators such as Ivan S. Bloch, within the French army the emphasis remained fixed on the doctrine of the offensive. As Joffre later commented on the reaction within the military to wars in South Africa and Manchuria:

> A whole series of false doctrines began to undermine even such feeble offensive sentiment as has made appearance in our war doctrines, to the detriment of the army's offensive spirit, its confidence in its chiefs and in its regulations. An incomplete study of the events of a single war had led the intellectual élite of our army to believe that the improvement in firearms and the power of fire action had so increased the strength of the defensive that an offensive opposed to it had lost all value.[26]

Joffre went on to comment that the success of the Japanese assaults in Manchuria had resulted in a return to 'a more healthy conception of the general conditions prevailing in a war'.

It is perhaps too easy to criticise the French senior command for its adherence to offensive ideals on the outbreak of war. Ultimately, all of the major belligerent powers would adopt offensive strategies. In their initial moves, the Russians, Austrians and Germans all adopted an offensive posture. There were differences of approach, however. The Germans' Schlieffen-

Moltke Plan was essentially a plan for offensive envelopment; the German attacking formations hoped to avoid major French formations until they had outflanked and enveloped them. Then the campaign would be decided in a major action. The French Plan XVII facilitated offensive action and contact with the enemy was a priority in the hope of achieving a battlefield decision.

In modern popular thinking a central idea has achieved prominence in the public consciousness of the campaigns of 1914; i.e., that the generals planned for a short war and at little human cost. This is a misconception. While all generals on both sides hoped for a swift victory, few believed that it could be won without significant loss of life. Recent campaigns in South Africa, Manchuria and the Balkans suggested as much. Indeed, it has been argued that the willingness to endure high numbers of casualties in a land campaign was one of the indicators of 'world power' status. As Schlieffen himself had remarked, 'those troops will prove superior who can bear the greater losses and advance more vigorously than the others'.[27]

The opening phases of the war in 1914 would show how redundant all of this pre-war military theorising was. In August 1914 more than 1.5 million French troops were mobilised for the war. Within six weeks over 385,000 of them had become casualties. Of these, 110,000 had been killed in action, the majority in the large encounter battles that occurred during the first months of the war. And while there had been a huge number of casualties, this had not been translated into decisive victory in the field. In the months that followed, the French army would be forced to face up to the possibility – indeed, the probability – of a long and costly war. The army's operational methods would continue to change between 1915 and 1917 but it could be argued that, until the failure of the Nivelle Offensive, the French staff clung desperately to the idea that offensive action would achieve decision on the battlefield. This would be at the cost of hundreds of thousands of French lives.[28]

The written histories of the French army during the opening months of the First World War often focused on the battle of the Marne in September 1914, a battle that it was crucial for the Allied armies to win. In contrast, the opening phase of the fighting along the French frontier with Germany has received remarkably little attention. In accordance with Plan XVII, the majority of the French troops were sent eastwards to deploy opposite the frontier with Germany, the direction from which the German army's main thrust was expected. Following the Franco-Prussian war of 1870, the French had built fortresses along their eastern frontier. It was expected that the Germans would attempt to avoid these and attack from the Metz area of Lorraine, and Plan XVII allowed the French army to deploy and react to any German incursions.

Of course, the Germans had opted instead for a strategy of envelopment; the much-discussed Schlieffen-Moltke Plan allowed for the German army to send a large force, in fact the main effort of this attack, in a wide sweeping manoeuvre through Belgium. This group of armies would, it was hoped, sweep past Paris and into the rear of the main French armies. The French, sandwiched between two German army groups, would be destroyed in a decisive battle. This short campaign would then allow the Germans to turn eastwards to deal with the Russian army, which, it was thought, would be mobilising much more slowly. With the benefit of hindsight, the numerous flaws in the German plan seem obvious but it should be borne in mind that similar plans for large-scale enveloping manoeuvres were to prove successful on the Eastern Front, in particular at Tannenberg in August 1914.[29]

Joffre was not unaware of the possibility of a German attack through Belgium but he refused to believe that this would be the main German effort and as a result sent just a single army to cover his left flank to the north. This was the French Fifth Army under General Charles Lanrezac. Joffre would cling stubbornly to this belief as the early battles developed, refusing to believe the reports from commanders on the spot that they were facing the bulk of the German army in its advance through Belgium.[30]

Joffre also planned for a series of vast spoiling offensives that would shut down any German plan. The first of these would be launched into Alsace, the Saar and Lorraine. The line of eastern fortifications would force the Germans to attack through the Trouée des Charmes (the Charmes Gap), an unfortified area between Toul and Epinal, and this would allow Joffre to concentrate his forces to respond. A second wave of French offensives would be launched towards Metz and, if the Germans came through Belgium, he would attack through the Ardennes and detach the German right wing from the rest of the army. France was, after all, numerically weaker in the field and these plans allowed for the possibility of gaining local numerical superiority.

Joffre was confident that his plans would be successful and this would allow the five French armies to contain and isolate the German forces in Belgium while also engaging their central group of armies along the eastern frontier. Within the French strategy there was, however, a dangerous tendency towards 'mirror imaging' when predicting German moves. Perhaps the single biggest flaw in Joffre's plans was his assumption that the Germans would conform to his ideas as to how they should deploy. The result was to be a near disaster.[31]

Mobilisation began in France on 1 August 1914 and deployment followed the minutely detailed timetables of Plan XVII. France called up twenty-seven year classes for service, while also deploying its standing conscript army and available colonial troops. Over 4,000 trains carried these men across France to their designated railheads and from there they covered up to 30km per day in route marches to their deployment areas. At this early phase of the war French troops were still dressed in what can only be described as nineteenth-century military splendour. The infantry wore red trousers and their uniforms were topped with a red kepi. In the weeks that followed, officers would lead attacks wearing white gloves and waving swords. The French cavalry similarly wore red breeches but topped their uniforms with a polished brass helmet, complete with plume. Cuirassier regiments wore polished breastplates. The opening battles would show how unwise it was to advance on the enemy wearing such distinctive and visible uniforms.[32]

The initial French attack took place on the extreme right flank of the French army when VII Corps of the First Army, supported by a cavalry division, was sent to occupy Mulhouse. This would gain a foothold on the Rhine and allow for later operations. On 7 August VII Corps duly crossed the frontier but its commander, General Bonneau, was far from audacious as local intelligence reports alarmed him with accounts of an Austrian outflanking move through Switzerland. Nevertheless, his troops advanced with determination and after a six-hour battle overcame German resistance at Altkirch with a bayonet charge, as per regulations – but at the cost of over a hundred men killed. Bonneau sent a telegram directly to the Minister of War, Adolphe Messimy, in Paris, trumpeting a great victory while also by-passing the chain of command. The next day Bonneau took Mulhouse without further fighting but on 9 August his position began to unravel. He was ejected from Mulhouse by a series of counterattacks by the German Seventh Army (von Heeringen) and was beaten back to the vicinity of the fortress at Belfort. Soon after, Bonneau was removed from command. This initial phase of attacks had opened promisingly, only to quickly disintegrate into a veritable rout. The organisation and firepower of the German forces had overwhelmed the French formations. The French artillery had proved ineffective while the standard infantry weapon, the much-lauded Lebel rifle was found to be outdated. The Lebel proved to be overlong and poorly balanced, while its tubular magazine made reloading much slower. These problems were exacerbated by battlefield conditions.[33] The French senior commanders had been shown to be wanting, while at regimental level officers found that there were too few maps and communications were poor. The tendency for infantry and cavalry to put in spirited attacks, while awfully gallant, also resulted in significant casualties.

In the immediate opening phases of the war there was little time to process such lessons. The early battles of August 1914 – referred to collectively as the 'Battles of the Frontiers' – comprised four simultaneous battles in Lorraine, the Ardennes forests, Charleroi and Mons. The fighting developed as the French army conformed to Plan XVII and the Belgian and British armies also deployed in an effort to counter the unfolding German plan. French offensives into Lorraine and the Ardennes followed a pattern that mirrored General Bonneau's experiences and they were repulsed by tactically superior German forces.[34] In front of Nancy, the French prepared to contest the German advance, only to find that their southern flank in the Ardennes was exposed. Full-scale retreat followed on 23 August. As the northern wing of the French army at Charleroi also retreated, alarming gaps began to appear in the Allied line. When the BEF retreated from Mons, a gap opened on its right between it and its nearest French support. By 24 August all of the Allied armies were being pushed back from the German advance, despite desperate rearguard actions such as at Le Cateau on 26 August.

In Paris these developments were met with considerable alarm. On 27 August the *Union Sacrée* coalition government was formed under Premier René Viviani but any public confidence in this act of political unity soon disappeared as the government was evacuated from Paris on 2 September and sent to Bordeaux to escape the worsening situation. It is estimated that as many as 500,000 Parisians followed the example of their political masters and left the city.

The First Battle of the Marne, fought between 5 and 12 September, ultimately stabilised the Allied situation. It was, in fact, a series of battles fought out along a 150km front that stretched from Compiègne to Verdun, while at the same time other actions were developing on the eastern front in Lorraine. These desperate days saw convoys of taxis used to ferry over 6,000 reservists to the front. The key moment came on 4–5 September, during the prelude to the main battle, when General Gallieni realised that General von Kluck's First Army was swinging away from Paris and exposing its left flank. This provided an opportunity for a French counter-stroke. Thereafter, now also hampered by poor communications, the German commander Helmuth von Moltke found his plan falling apart. The French armies and the BEF stubbornly held their ground south of the Marne river, and when Colonel Hentsch, a German staff officer, ordered a general retreat of the German First and Second Armies on 9 September, the battle was as good as lost. The German armies re-established themselves over 60km away along a line on the Aisne river, which would be the scene of another battle (the First Battle of the Aisne) later in September.[35]

While this battlefield success was hailed as the 'Miracle of the Marne', it was obvious to both sides that the inconclusive end to these opening phases meant that the war would not be a short affair. Both the Schlieffen-Moltke Plan and Plan XVII had failed to bring a decisive victory. In a similar vein, the commanders and armies of both sides had exhibited problems in terms of battlefield command, communications, training and equipment. Joffre, who was lauded as the 'hero of the Marne', had shown great calm in the face of the rapidly deteriorating situation, yet he had also displayed a certain slowness and lack of imagination. In the months that followed, a series of battles was fought in northern France and Flanders as the Germans and Allies sought to outflank each other in the phase of fighting that came to be known as the 'Race to the Sea'. By the end of 1914 the front was static, with trench lines running from the Belgian coast to the Swiss border. A large tract of France was occupied by German forces, which over time developed more elaborate defences and trench systems. For the next four years French commanders would try to figure out how to eject these German forces from

French soil. It was a problem that confounded many a high-ranking French general, and in the immediate sense Joffre showed himself unequal to the new battlefield conditions.

It was during the early battles of 1914 that Robert Nivelle first came to popular notice. At the outbreak of the war Nivelle was an obscure colonel, commanding a regiment of artillery. Born in Tulle in 1856, he was the son of a French officer; his English mother was the daughter of one of the Duke of Wellington's officers.[36] Following training at the École Polytechnique, Nivelle was commissioned into the artillery in 1878 and later attended the cavalry school at Saumer (1881). His early service was in the artillery and he served in Tunisia and also in the Boxer Rebellion in China. In 1908, with the rank of lieutenant-colonel, he was posted to Algeria. In 1912 he was promoted to full colonel and commanded both the Fourth and Fifth Artillery Regiments in the years before the war.

During the Alsace Offensive in 1914 Nivelle displayed great skill in the deployment and use of his guns, and during the Battle of the Marne (5–12 September 1914) he displayed great bravery and coolness under fire. During this battle Nivelle realised that the infantry brigade to his front was beginning to disintegrate and as the terrified infantrymen began to stream to the rear, he limbered up his guns and drove them forwards through the retreating troops. Technically speaking, it was exactly the opposite of what he should have done at that moment. But instead of ordering his unit to safety in the rear he deployed his regiment of 75mm guns and engaged the advancing Germans over open sights. At point-blank range he coordinated an intense fire on the German troops, halting their advance and stabilising his section of the line. It was a courageous act; indeed, Nivelle never lacked personal courage. In the First Battle of the Aisne (12–15 September 1914) he again laid down a devastatingly effective fire on German formations.[37] In reality, what we refer to as the Battles of the Marne and the First Aisne consisted of a series of dispersed and confusing actions but Nivelle performed well throughout this period, especially at the engagements at Crouy and Quennevières.

Nivelle's actions brought him to the attention of Joffre, who was impressed by his initiative and offensive spirit. In November 1914 Nivelle was promoted to command of a brigade, and in February 1915 was promoted again, to command of a division. Thereafter, his rise was nothing less than meteoric, and in December 1915 he was appointed to command III Corps of Pétain's Second Army. By 1916 Nivelle had established a reputation that made him a contender for the commander-in-chief's position. He would be the prime architect of the disastrous events of 1917. Nivelle was highly intelligent and an excellent artillery officer. He was extremely effective in coordinating artillery at regimental, brigade and divisional level. But it could be argued that his later promotions took him beyond his abilities and out of his 'comfort zone' as an artillerist.

For Joffre, the immediate problem was how to break the German lines and restore a war of movement. From late 1914, and throughout 1915, he followed a programme for offensive action. These offensives came to be characterised by the increased use of artillery, successive attacks by the infantry and high casualty figures. In late 1914 Joffre initiated his First Champagne Offensive, which ran from 10 December to 17 March 1915. This intense phase of fighting saw separate battles developing along a wide front, including three battles for the town of Perthes alone, with further fighting around Noyon and Givenchy. Supplementary attacks took place at Verdun, Artois and Woëvre. By the end of the campaign the French had advanced to a maximum depth of 2km into the German lines. French casualties stood at more than 90,000 killed, wounded or missing.

Unperturbed, Joffre turned his attention to the Artois sector. He was convinced that the Germans were sending forces to the east to counter the Russians and felt sure that he could break the line there. His Artois Offensive was launched on 9 May and ran until 19 June, and incorporated the British First Army under Haig. There were some significant successes. The French preceded the attack with a five-day preliminary bombardment and Pétain's corps covered more than 5km in 90 minutes in one assault towards Vimy. The British attack at Neuve Chapelle on 9 May was preceded by minimal artillery preparation, however, and resulted in 11,000 casualties. Later French and British attacks made minimal gains. When the offensive was finally shut down, the French had lost more than 100,000 casualties.

Despite shell shortages and the difficulties of coordinating such large-scale attacks, Joffre persisted –with similar results. The Artois–Loos Offensive and the Second Champagne Offensive, which ran simultaneously from 25 September to 6 November, resulted in 48,000 and 145,000 French casualties respectively. By the time these two offensives had been called off in early November, the French army and the BEF had suffered over 320,000 casualties collectively.

In light of such enormous losses, it became increasingly obvious to political leaders that they needed to exert greater control over the military commanders, in particular Joffre. While the military complained about the difficulties on the Western Front, German success in the Baltic during their Vilnius Offensive in September 1915 spurred the Viviani administration to try to gain control of the war. Yet the politicians would be thwarted in these efforts. Since early 1915 Viviani had been pressuring Joffre to allow deputies to visit the front on tours of inspection but permission was not forthcoming. The government also wished to free up French forces for a campaign in Serbia but Joffre would not release them. The final straw was Bulgaria's entry into the war on the side of the Central Powers in October. This occurred despite the best efforts of the French foreign minister, Théophile Delcassé, to keep Bulgaria on the Allied side. Exasperated and looking increasingly ineffectual, Viviani resigned in October 1915. He was succeeded by Aristide Briand, who would fare no better.

In the aftermath of such huge casualties the French army hoped for a period of rest and recuperation during the winter months of 1915/16 but on 21 February 1916 the Germans took the battlefield initiative to launch a massive offensive against Verdun. This bloody battle would run in several phases and last until December. As a result, it became the longest battle in human history. Both sides allowed themselves to be drawn into a contest over objectives of questionable strategic value. For France, the battle would later define the struggle against Germany. In the decades after the war the '300 Jours de Verdun' would be depicted as an existential battle and an iconic period in French history. French efforts on the Somme in the summer of 1916 were largely successful, indicating that the army was developing tactically but the Verdun battle overshadowed all other efforts. This is unsurprising. When the battle finally wound down in the winter of 1916, the French had suffered more than 550,000 casualties. To a modern reader, such casualty rates are simply beyond comprehension. Yet in his plans for 1917, Joffre was intending to unleash a further series of offensives.

Nivelle was also to play a significant role in the French army's struggle to maintain its grip on Verdun. At the outbreak of the battle he was still in command of III Corps in Pétain's Second Army. In April 1916 he mounted a series of attacks with III Corps on the right bank of the Verdun sector and achieved some success. But it was not without cost. Once again Nivelle's offensive spirit came to the attention of Joffre, who was impressed with Nivelle's confidence and 'can do' attitude, which was in striking contrast to the pessimism of Pétain. Joffre saw an opportunity and promoted Pétain to command the Groupe d'Armées du Centre (Central Army Group or GAC) and on 27 April 1916 Nivelle was promoted and appointed to command the Second Army. In less than two years Nivelle had been promoted from colonel to lieutenant-general.[38]

At a time when the French people needed positive news from the Verdun front, the choice of Nivelle to command the Second Army seemed a wise one. Apart from his capabilities as a soldier, Nivelle knew how to handle visiting pressmen and politicians and had a flair for providing well-timed quotes for the press – what we would refer to today as 'sound-bites'. After the German capture of Fleury on 23 June 1916, and at a particularly desperate time for the French, Nivelle concluded his order of the day with the inspiring line 'Ils ne passeront pas!' ('They shall not pass!'). This was trumpeted from the headlines of newspapers and later became a national slogan that would be used on recruiting posters and in army bulletins. Nivelle was not without his critics, however, and some criticised him for the casualties incurred in his counter-offensives.[39]

It is worth taking a moment to discuss some of the other personalities associated with Nivelle at this time. One of his divisional commanders was General Charles Mangin, who commanded the Fifth Infantry Division, made up largely of colonial troops. Mangin was an extremely tough and competent soldier, who had seen much campaigning in the colonies before the war. He had been wounded three times in various campaigns and had served in Mali, Senegal, Tonkin and in the Fashoda expedition of 1898. In the immediate pre-war years Mangin had pushed strongly for the establishment of a 'Force Noire', effectively an army of black troops made up with regiments from France's colonies in Africa. In 1910 he published a work on the subject. Within Mangin's central idea lurked his belief that African and Arab troops were less imaginative and less sensitive to pain and suffering. It now seems evident that he apparently also viewed them as expendable, or perhaps just more expendable than metropolitan troops. To modern sensibilities, Mangin's views can only be seen as intrinsically racist and insensitive but at the time he was considered to be a successful commander and was valued by Nivelle within the Second Army.[40] During the summer of 1916 Mangin had pushed some reserve units to their breaking point and there were calls for him to be removed, but Nivelle intervened on his behalf and he remained in command. Among the common soldiers Mangin was known as 'the Butcher' and his callous tendencies would become apparent once again during the 1917 offensive.

An equally dark and somewhat mysterious figure was Lieutenant-Colonel Audemard d'Alançon (often referred to as d'Alenson in English sources). D'Alançon occupied the role of *chef de cabinet* for Nivelle. This was a uniquely French appointment, combining the roles of military secretary and chief of staff. The two men had first met in Algeria before the war and it is now recognised that d'Alançon had a major influence on Nivelle in the planning of operations. D'Alançon was suffering from a terminal disease – tuberculosis according to contemporary accounts – and as a result he was driven by an overwhelming desire to see the war concluded with a French victory in the limited span still allotted to him. He was also a firm believer in the potential of offensive action and he supported Nivelle's offensive actions at Verdun. He would later be a prime mover in the 1917 offensive, pushing Nivelle's agenda despite the doubts that were mounting on all sides. Edward Spears wrote that he was 'far more acute and intelligent than would have been gathered from his appearance and he was no mean judge of men'. At a more negative level, Spears noted that he:

> Urged constantly, such was the frenzy of his haste, that the tempo of the attack and the speed of the preparations should be increased, until the impression one gained ceased to be that of high authority prescribing dispatch but rather of an uncontrolled force like a swollen torrent rushing madly onward.[41]

His French counterparts expressed similar concerns. They found that d'Alançon pushed for offensive action while also acting as a shield for Nivelle against the doubts expressed by senior officers. General Micheler referred to his 'keen intelligence and character' but also was concerned about his influence over Nivelle, stating that d'Alançon seemed often divorced from reality, showing a marked tendency to twist facts to fit his desired reality.[42] Jean de Pierrefeu, who served on Nivelle's staff in 1917, was equally critical of d'Alançon and later wrote that:

> Colonel d'Alançon had the true gambler's temperament, as was proved by his reply to Colonel Fetizon, deputy-chief of the Third Bureau, a calm methodical man of considerable common sense, who had asked, 'And if we fail? What then?' D'Alançon replied, 'Well, if we fail, we will throw our hands in.' We certainly lived in a gambling atmosphere.[43]

These tendencies would reappear during preparations for Nivelle's offensive in 1917. The Nivelle–Mangin–d'Alançon partnership resulted in further offensives during the later phases of the Verdun battle. Having organised the counterattacks on the right bank of the Verdun sector in April 1916, Nivelle now focused his attention on Fort Douaumont, which had been lost to the Germans in February. Quite apart from its symbolic value to the French, the fort stood on a height at 1,200ft and dominated the surrounding area. Despite this dominant position and its comprehensive defences, the fort had fallen to the Germans quite easily. To add further insult, the Germans also captured Fort Vaux in July and Nivelle's attempt to recapture this fort was beaten off with such high casualties that Pétain forbade any further attempts to recapture the forts. However, during July Nivelle continued to mount counterattacks against the German assaults. Mangin mounted a particularly effective counterattack before being stopped in his tracks, with heavy casualties, on 11 July.

While it is easy to criticise such offensives, the alternative was to allow the Germans to break through and exploit. Nivelle also persuaded Pétain to allow him to engage in further efforts to retake the forts but accepted the caveat that he had to engage in very thorough preparations. In the weeks that followed, Nivelle engaged in massive artillery preparations, gathering more than 500 additional guns, including two 400mm railway guns, in his planned attack zone. These were to support the Second Army's existing artillery.

Ultimately there would be one artillery piece for every 15 yards of front, with over 15,000 tons of shells stockpiled. The assault troops rehearsed over ground prepared to resemble the approaches to Fort Douaumont and their advance would be preceded by a creeping barrage once the attack began. On 19 October a three-day preparatory bombardment began, which targeted not only Douaumont but also other known German positions and lines of communication in that zone. This bombardment proved accurate and devastating, while the use of gas shells proved extremely effective.[44]

By the time the infantry assault began on 24 October 1916 the fort had been rendered virtually untenable due to the intensity of the barrage and had already been partially evacuated. A thick mist aided the attacking troops while the creeping barrage moved ahead of their advance. The light artillery fired 70 yards ahead of the advancing French infantry, while the heavy artillery fired 150 yards ahead. The whole movement was coordinated using field telephone communications and the barrage lifted in stages to allow the troops to advance. The troops crossed the devastated landscape at a rate of about 25 yards per minute and on reaching the fort Mangin's divisions (made up of Moroccan and Senegalese troops and units of *Coloniale* infantry) cleared the defences using flamethrowers. Nivelle repeated this success at Fort Vaux on 2 November and in a subsequent eight-division attack on 15 December he pushed the Germans back a further 3 miles and captured more than 9,000 prisoners. The key to Nivelle's success seemed deceptively simple: methodical preparation followed by massive and focused artillery bombardment. But unlike in previous offensives, this artillery fire was concentrated along narrow corridors to create lanes for the attacking infantry.

In the context of this vast attritional battle that had ground down the French army and nation throughout much of the preceding year, these successes seemed little short of miraculous. Criticism over continuing these attacks as winter drew on, and the casualties incurred, was lost amidst the general public rejoicing. Nivelle became a national hero and received much attention in the French press. The Briand government, which was looking increasingly threatened, also made much of this new public hero.

It has been repeatedly suggested that Nivelle's fellow generals, and in particular his immediate commander, Pétain, disapproved of his methods.

Yet at this time Nivelle was keeping step with Pétain's own philosophy of thorough preparation followed by a focused attack for a specific and limited objective. In this context, Nivelle's methods had potential for success. Problems would occur in 1917, however, when he tried to develop attacks based on these principles but on a vast scale. His success in 1916 imbued Nivelle with the vast confidence that would later prove so damaging. To his staff officers he announced 'We now have the formula', while in his parting address to the Second Army he announced 'The experience is conclusive, our method has proved itself.' Nivelle would later refer to these tactics as the 'Verdun Method', while in the press it was referred to as 'Nivelling'.[45]

By late 1916 new armaments programmes were supplying better equipment to the French army. There was more and better artillery, while at battalion level there were increased numbers of weapons such as trench mortars, light machine guns and flamethrowers. New infantry doctrine was drawn up to reflect this and lessons were incorporated based on German infiltration tactics. On the surface at least there was much to be confident about.

The French army was still wedded to the idea of the offensive and this would have dangerous consequences in 1917. Also, it became increasingly obvious to any observant staff officer that the troops were exhausted. Morale in the winter of 1916/17 was at an all-time low. This was against a backdrop of discontent on the home front and political uncertainty. All the indicators should have urged for caution but instead Nivelle precipitated perhaps the biggest gamble undertaken by the French army during the war.

Chapter 2

The Rise of General Robert Nivelle

He was, I thought, a most straightforward and soldierly man. As regards operations, Nivelle stated that he is unable to accept the plans which had been worked out for the French armies under Joffre's directions. He is confident of breaking the enemy's front now that the enemy morale is weakened, but the blow must be struck by surprise and go through in 24 hours.
(Field Marshal Haig on General Nivelle, 20 December 1916)[1]

General Nivelle rose to command the French armies during a particularly chaotic period in the war. In France the relationship between the government and the army was becoming increasingly strained, while at the same time there was growing discontent on the home front. The relationships between the various Allied nations were also difficult and the gruelling and costly battles of the Somme and Verdun had only recently ended when Nivelle was appointed to command. He inherited a French army that was badly damaged and with its morale at a particularly low ebb. The British army had also suffered huge casualties on the Somme and it was unlikely that it would be able to contribute to major operations until at least the late spring of 1917.

The process that brought Nivelle to the role of commander-in-chief of the French armies had actually begun in October 1916 and grew out of an increasing sense of disillusionment with Joffre. There were various factors at play. The government under Briand realised that Joffre intended to return to the offensive once the German assault on Verdun had been finally contained. Between October and December they sought a means to remove him from the commander-in-chief's position without creating a public outcry. As the year was drawing to a close, it was natural that representatives of the Allied nations should meet to discuss possible ways of ending the war in 1917. Within the French government and the GQG it was felt that major changes were required to facilitate operations in 1917. The French wanted victory and wresting control from Joffre seemed necessary for this to happen. Also, the relationship between the British government and the commander of the BEF, Field Marshal Sir Douglas Haig, was becoming equally strained. These factors would later contribute to Nivelle's rise to command. As the battles of the Somme and Verdun waned in the closing months of 1916, a new campaign was under way within the French government and the GQG to replace Joffre. On being appointed to command, Nivelle would be used by Lloyd George, the British Secretary of State for War, in early 1917 in an effort to gain more political control over Haig.

In mid-October the French government invited its Allies to gather for a conference on 15–16 November to discuss war plans for 1917. Joffre outlined the French position, stating that the Allied goal should be to 'prepare for coordinated offensives in spring 1917 similar to those undertaken in 1916 but which will be more powerful and more fruitful'.[2] Within the Briand government, this statement caused considerable alarm. While a multi-front strategy was implicit in Joffre's statement, the conditions on the Western Front had not changed in any significant way. It seemed that 1917 would see further attempts to break the German line relying on the flesh, blood and fighting spirit of the French and British armies. These plans also caused concern within the British government and through the War Committee it was suggested that the meeting should be delayed in order to allow the Allied leaders to reflect on recent operations and develop new strategies. Lloyd George suggested that French, British and Italian representatives should travel to Russia in order to discuss the wider strategy. Yet despite these misgivings and delaying tactics, the conference went ahead in Paris on 15 November. Or rather it would be more correct to say 'conferences', as the military commanders met to discuss their plans while the political leaders met separately.

The military conference opened with the reading of a memorandum by Joffre's staff, which summarised the current situation and also his plans for 1917. It stated that the offensives of 1916, in particular the Somme Offensive and the Brusilov Offensive on the Eastern Front, had 'shaken' the armies of the Central Powers. Both the Germans and the Austrians had suffered serious casualties, while the Austrians in particular had been 'demoralised by recent bloody defeats'.[3] There was some discussion of Romania's late entry into the war. It was suggested that in the spring of 1917 the Allies should begin a large-scale offensive on the Western Front while at the same time engaging in operations against Bulgaria. The Bulgarian factor occupied some of Joffre's staff's attention and it was suggested that knocking Bulgaria out of the war would isolate Turkey from the other Central Powers. It was also recommended that further efforts be made to provide weapons, munitions and equipment to the Russian army. When Joffre himself spoke, he called for a series of offensives by all the Allied powers and on all fronts: the Western Front, the Eastern Front, Italy and Salonika. These should take place, he suggested, as early as possible in the spring of 1917.

In some respects Joffre's strategy was ultimately sound; large-scale offensives on various fronts could only put the Central Powers under pressure. Equally, he urged the Allies to act immediately in order to avoid a repeat of the situation in 1916 where the Germans took the initiative early in the year with their Verdun offensive. His proposals, however, made no allowances for the huge attrition that all the Allied armies had suffered in 1916. Also, he did not seem to acknowledge the considerable difficulties that trying to coordinate such a multi-front strategy posed. Communications with the Russian high command in particular presented serious practical difficulties. At this point in the war Joffre's plans simply did not constitute a realistic strategy.

Following these presentations by Joffre and his staff, the other Allied representatives responded. Haig, who perhaps had a better appreciation of the state of his own army, pointed out that the BEF would not be in a position to mount a major operation until May. The Russian and Italian representatives stated that this was their position also. Despite these objections, the military conference ended with an agreement that 'to keep the enemy from gaining the initiative in operations, the armies of the coalition will be ready to undertake combined offensives in the first half of February 1917 with all the means at their disposal'.[4]

The political conference was equally vague and aspirational. In recent months Lloyd George had been increasingly vocal on the conduct of the war. He felt that the military leaders of all the Allied armies had been allowed too much autonomy, while the national governments, which bore the ultimate responsibility for the conduct of the war, had abdicated too much control. Lloyd George had drawn up a memorandum on this subject but Herbert H. Asquith, the British prime minister, felt that this would deeply offend the military commanders of all the Allied armies. Now, at their meeting with the French prime minister, Briand, at the Quai d'Orsay, a heavily edited version of the memorandum was presented. Ironically, Lloyd George's opinions were actually quite close to those of Briand at this time. Briand came to the meeting directly from a session in the Chamber of Deputies, in which he had been grilled on the conduct of the war. In Joffre, he was dealing with a military commander who seemed blissfully unaware of the political reaction to his wasteful offensives and who seemed determined to return to the same strategy in 1917. It is perhaps unsurprising that he appeared distracted throughout the meeting with Asquith and Lloyd George, but he did ask for a copy of the memorandum. The conference that afternoon involving the political representatives of the Allied powers seems to have been reasonably general in its discussions. Briand recommended a more strenuous Balkan strategy to take Bulgaria out of the war, mirroring the proposals of the military conference. Both Briand and Asquith called for greater help for Russia and Romania. More significantly, Briand suggested that the Allied governments should 'take the initiative in regard to operations'.[5] It would appear that by this time he had already determined to replace Joffre and his move would be facilitated by this wider discussion within the British and French governments on how to regain control of the conduct of the war.

At the end of both sessions, the military and political leaders met to discuss their findings. Opinions on the outcome of these meetings were varied. Lloyd George dismissed them as 'little better than a complete farce' and was depressed that the 'bloody stupidities of 1915 and 1916' were about to be repeated.[6] Joffre, on the other hand, saw the outcome totally differently. He wrote in his memoirs that 'the fruits that we had let ripen in 1916, we would gather in 1917'. He felt the conference had given him sanction for a series of offensives in 1917 that would see coordinated attacks by the BEF and the French Northern and Central Army Groups, while offensives by the Russians, Romanians, Italians and the Allied force at Salonika would relieve pressure on the Western Front. As early as 1 November, Joffre had written to his army group commanders and also to divisional and corps commanders outlining his plans for attacks in the Somme and the Chemin des Dames sectors. In terms of tactical advice, Joffre's memorandum spoke the language of the cult of the offensive. He would see none of these plans to come to fruition, yet his November memorandum sounded alarmingly similar to the rhetoric of 1914:

> Attacks prepared and conducted in this manner will always succeed if those making the attacks have confidence in their success. Results will be obtained if the troops are trained and disciplined; if leaders at all echelons are actively involved in the preparation and carefully pay attention to every detail; if, finally, these same leaders, ardently convinced of success, seize every opportunity to convey the faith that motivates them to the hearts of their subordinates.[7]

By the time Joffre wrote this memorandum in November 1916 the French army had lost more than a million men killed or missing in action, not including the wounded. Yet his vision for massed offensives in 1917 had not changed and mirrored his costly strategy for 1915. Seemingly unaware of the political storm that was gathering around him, Joffre continued with his plans for offensive actions that would take place on the Somme and Verdun fronts during the winter of 1916/17. This would, he argued, not only prevent the Germans from taking the initiative but also prevent them from sending troops to the Eastern Front. Then, in early February 1917, Joffre planned to launch a series of decisive major offensives.

There were numerous factors that should have given him pause. It is interesting to note that although Joffre expected these attacks to fundamentally undermine the German army, he seems to have made no allowances for the attritional damage that would be inflicted on his own army. At the same time the winter of 1916/17 was one of the worst ever recorded and morale among the troops plummeted, with postal censors recording evidence of serious discontent among the soldiers concerning the conduct of the war and the conditions at the front. On a more positive level, Joffre did initiate a series of reforms and also demanded increased weapons production, but he would not survive in office to see these reforms carried out.

The processes were by now well under way that would see him removed from his role as French commander-in-chief. Almost immediately the strategic situation worsened dramatically. Within a week of the end of the Allied conference, the Germans and Austrians had pushed deep into Romania and on 6 December they took Bucharest. While Romania would not agree an armistice with the Central Powers until December 1917, it had effectively been knocked out of the war. This possible platform for operations against Bulgaria, and a central feature of recent Allied strategising, would soon become an irrelevance. At the same time unrest in Russia foretold the greater upheavals that were to come in 1917, while concerns increased of a German attack through Switzerland that winter.

The Salonika front continued to be problematic and General Pierre Roques, the Minister for War, was sent on a tour of inspection. It is now clear that he had been encouraged by Briand to recommend the removal of General Serrail, the French commander of the Allied force in Salonika. Ultimately Roques would disappoint both Briand and Joffre with his report and would discredit them politically. He pointed out that Serrail was performing well in a difficult situation and recommended that responsibility for the Salonika front should be taken from Joffre and Serrail given total autonomy on that front. With this suggestion Roques was implying that the decree of 2 December 1915, which had placed Serrail's army under Joffre's ultimate control, should be modified. Furthermore, Roques recommended that Joffre should be reduced from commander-in-chief to commander of the armies in the north-east. In an effort to extend his own remit, Roques further suggested that the Minister for War should be given authority to approve plans and allocate resources – a move that would effectively have subordinated all theatre commanders to him.

On 27 November the Chamber of Deputies met to discuss Roques' proposals; in the heated debate that followed, Briand realised that he had been damaged by the affair. Having pulled the pin on a political hand-grenade that he hoped would finally scupper Joffre, Briand found himself caught in the blast and now scrambled to limit the political fallout. Roques was persuaded to withdraw his report and would eventually be dismissed as Minister for War and sent to command the Fourth Army. Between 28 November and 7 December the Chamber of Deputies met in closed session to discuss the conduct of the war in general and the higher command in particular. Fighting for his political life, Briand promised to separate the command of the home front from the Salonika front. Furthermore he promised that the government would regain control over the conduct of the war. He announced that a general would be appointed as 'technical adviser' to the government; trying to be as unspecific as possible, he suggested that this general would merely advise and coordinate, while ultimate strategic control would rest with the government.

On 3 December Briand met with Joffre to offer him the appointment as the 'technical adviser' to the government. Joffre later recorded that he was promised promotion to the rank of 'marshal of France' and responsibility for the overall direction of the war. It would now seem clear that Briand was being less than truthful with him as he sought to juggle the commander-in-chief and also the members of the Chamber of Deputies. On 4 December Briand outlined the new arrangement in the chamber and survived a vote of no confidence (344 to 160 votes).

Briand's work was not yet over. He secured General Hubert Lyautey's agreement to act as the new Minister for War but again it seems that Briand was reasonably vague as to the specific powers that the new minister would enjoy. A new war committee was established, consisting of just five members, including Lyautey, which would control all aspects of the direction of the war. On 13 December Briand formed a new government but all the indications suggested that this new government would not be long-lived; on the day it was formed it survived a vote of no confidence by only thirty votes.

On 13 December a presidential decree confirmed Joffre's appointment as 'general-in-chief of the French armies, technical military adviser to the government, consultative member of the war committee'.[8] Joffre immediately recognised the distinct difference between 'commander-in-chief' and his new role as 'general-in-chief'. In the weeks that followed, he realised that his powers had been greatly reduced and that he had been shunted sideways. His new role was effectively meaningless and without power. On 26 December he was elevated to the rank of marshal of France; on the same day he asked to be relieved of his responsibilities. The 'hero of the Marne' had finally been edged out of the supreme command. Briand had shown a level of political subtlety that few thought he possessed. An alternative view would be that he had merely prolonged his premiership by engaging in some *ad hoc* political manoeuvring.[9]

It was against this backdrop of near political implosion that Nivelle was appointed as 'commander of the armies of the north and the northeast' on 13 December 1916. This appointment made him the senior field commander in the French army. He was not an immediate first choice and to many his appointment came as a considerable surprise. Nivelle had only limited experience as an army commander, having commanded Second Army since May 1916.[10] To an objective eye, there were other more senior general officers who were potential choices. The chief of staff at the GQG, General Castelnau, seemed to many to be an obvious choice to succeed Joffre but his long association with Joffre meant politicians doubted his ability. He was also a devout Catholic, which increased doubts among the more radical factions within government. There were also three army group commanders (Foch, Pétain and Franchet d'Espèrey) who were all senior to Nivelle, but were passed over. Foch was also a devout Catholic and furthermore had recently been injured in a car accident, raising doubts as to the state of his health. Pétain was also a Catholic, albeit not a very observant one, but he was also known for his brusque manner with politicians and his forthright realistic attitude to tactical difficulties had led to him being branded a pessimist. Franchet d'Espèrey was a *confidant* of Briand but his performance as an army group commander had been lacklustre so he was discounted as a possible commander-in-chief. Seven other army commanders were also passed over for the senior command for a variety of similar reasons.[11]

Thus for the Briand government Nivelle, a relatively junior army commander, emerged as the best option. He had much to recommend him and was, in reality, the only French general with sufficient political and public credibility to be a realistic candidate at that particular time. In his dealings with visiting politicians, Nivelle had always been welcoming and open, clearly explaining the operational situation within the Second Army's sector. His directness and courtesy had gradually created a base of political support for him within the Chamber of Deputies. He had the approval of several prominent deputies, including André Maginot, himself a veteran of Verdun, who recommended Nivelle to President Poincaré as an excellent candidate for the commander-in-chief's appointment. Nivelle also had other qualities to recommend him. He was a Protestant and this made him acceptable to anti-clerical factions within the government. Politicians were also aware that Nivelle enjoyed huge public support. He had emerged from the Verdun battle as a national hero for his actions in retaking the forts of Vaux and Douaumont, and the government was keen to be seen to be associated with his earlier success. Nivelle also had the sanction of Joffre, who had always been impressed with Nivelle's confident manner. Nivelle was, after all, a believer in the primacy of offensive action and this appealed to Joffre.[12]

Before the formal announcement of his new appointment, Nivelle dined with Joffre and thanked him for his support in the process that was then still unfolding. Around the same time he also wrote a note to the acting minister for war recommending that Joffre should have no further direct link to any of the army group commanders or, for that matter, with Field Marshal Haig under the terms of his new appointment. This showed a certain level of duplicity. In the months that followed, Nivelle would engage in further political manoeuvring. Ultimately, however, political support and the legacy of Nivelle's success at Verdun led Briand to summon him to Paris on the evening of 12 December. The following day he was confirmed in his new appointment.

Even for those who had supported this move there were notes of concern. The offensives that Nivelle had instigated in conjunction with Mangin at Verdun had indeed been successful but they had also resulted in casualties. How casualty-sensitive would Nivelle be in his future operations? Also, while he had relatively little experience as an army commander, he had none whatsoever as an army group commander. He now commanded three army groups on the Western Front, the bulk of the French army, but had no experience of such senior command, nor indeed any experience of operating as a strategic level commander. There was nothing to indicate how he would work with subordinate commanders, let alone how he would interact with the Allied commanders, in particular Field Marshal Haig.[13]

In the initial phases of his new role these doubts evaporated in light of the huge energy and optimism that he brought to his new command. To officers on his staff and any visiting politicians or newspapermen, he repeatedly insisted that 'We now have the formula.' At the end of December he issued new instructions on offensive methods to the army. While still wedded to the offensive, Nivelle's vision was dramatically different from the doctrine that had proved so costly to the French army since 1914. He abandoned the idea of an offensive across a broad front, composed of a series of slow and ultimately costly attacks. Successive attacks in such methodical battles had proved ineffective as it allowed the enemy time to regroup and counterattack and also to gather artillery to counter further Allied attacks.

Instead, Nivelle wished to expand the methods that he had perfected at Verdun. He would mass artillery in order to devastate the enemy's defences in focused, narrow zones rather than over a wide area. Within specific zones, the artillery would fire throughout the depth of the enemy defences up to a distance of 8km. Within the artillery plan, there would be provision for a creeping barrage to protect the infantry. In essence, Nivelle wished to use his artillery to blast a narrow corridor through the German lines. The infantry would then attack along this corridor in a continuous thrust rather than in successive waves. They would then engage in lateral exploitation, destroying enemy artillery, reserves and lines of communication. It was nothing short of audacious. Nivelle summarised his approach to Lyautey, stating: 'Objective: total destruction of active enemy forces by manoeuvre and battle.'[14]

Nivelle had abandoned the idea of trying to create a breakthrough over a wide front. Instead, he sought to break the enemy line at a specific point, rapidly penetrate the defences and then break through. While Joffre had tried to steamroller through the German lines on a wide front, Nivelle wanted to cut through as though using a sharp sword. In terms of timing, he was confident that he could achieve all of this in 24 to 48 hours. In its simplicity his plan seemed brilliant and Nivelle was never less than convincing during his initial weeks in command. (*See* Map 1.)

This then was Nivelle's doctrine and the development of these concepts will be outlined in Chapter 3. On taking command, Nivelle set about revising the existing plans to conform to his own intentions. He cancelled preparations for the offensive plans initiated by his predecessor and provided his *chef de cabinet*, Lt-Col. d'Alançon, with an outline of his own plans.

Due to rumours that the GQG at Chantilly was something of a pleasure palace for young officers, Nivelle was asked to move his HQ to Beauvais, where it was installed in the austere surroundings of the *Institut Agronomique*.

It would move again in April 1917 to Compiègne to be closer to the front in the run-up to the offensive. Both of these moves were major operations requiring more than 400 officers and 800 clerical staff to be relocated, along with all their files and equipment. Nivelle's wisdom in relocating the GQG for the second time has been questioned due to the resulting upheaval and disorganisation immediately prior to a major operation. Nevertheless, it appears that his relationship with his staff was good, at least initially. One officer later wrote about how Nivelle interacted with his staff:

> The General betrayed great friendliness towards everybody and was rewarded with a lively sympathy. For my part, I was rarely greeted with so cordial a welcome as during his reign and encouragement was never grudged me. My humble duties received his personal attention, and he never failed to notice my efforts with a friendly word denoting his appreciation.[15]

As Nivelle's officers gathered at the new GQG in Beauvais in the weeks after his appointment, they were briefed on their commander's methods as preparations continued for the major offensive planned for 1917. On 19 November Nivelle sent a more developed outline of his plans to Field Marshal Haig. Broadly, he wanted to fix the enemy's forces with a combined British and French attack in the Noyon sector, with attacks to the north and south of the Somme. The Germans occupied a salient in this sector, which bulged into the British and French lines. Nivelle's basic idea had some merit. By attacking on both sides of the salient, the Allies could pinch off this German section of the front, creating a breach up to 70km wide. Nivelle's own main effort would then come in the Aisne sector and, having broken through the German lines using his methods, he would push further forces through the breach – the 'manoeuvre force' as he termed it. These formations would exploit laterally, destroying the main German defences. Nivelle wrote 'the success of our operations will thus depend essentially on the manoeuvre force'. This was an interesting concept. He had identified the German forces as the 'centre of gravity' for this operation. He was not planning to seize territory but rather, to put it bluntly, to kill or capture Germans.[16]

A major element of Nivelle's plan was the participation of the BEF under Haig. On taking command, he lost no time in making personal contact with Haig; their initial meeting was cordial, and Nivelle was extremely forthright when discussing his subordinate commanders. Apart from being totally indiscreet, this revealed a lack of tact that would dog his later dealings with fellow French commanders and also with Haig. Haig recorded their initial meeting and his account gives an interesting insight into Nivelle and also the wider discord within the French army at this time:

> Wednesday, December 20. I reached Cassel at 4.30p.m. and soon after General Nivelle, the new C-in-C of the French armies in place of General Joffre, arrived to see me. We had a good talk for nearly two hours. He was, I thought, a most straightforward and soldierly man. He remained for dinner (7p.m.) and left by train at 9p.m. to return to Chantilly. He is to be solely responsible for the operations of the French armies. Gen. Joffre will gradually disappear. Many other changes in the High Commands are also to be made. Foch, Castelnau, Franchet d'Espèrey are to go. He is to appoint his own men as army commanders. Of these, there will be two, Mangin and probably Pétain. A terrible scene occurred at the War Committee meeting in Paris yesterday. Joffre had written certain statements regarding some of the above-named officers, but when confronted by them was afraid to tell them to their faces what opinion he had written in his report. I am sorry to say that I personally have also noticed that Joffre had been weak and not really straight. As regards operations, Nivelle stated that he is unable to accept the plans which had been worked out for the French armies under Joffre's directions. He is confident of breaking through the enemy's front now that the enemy's morale is weakened, but the blow must be struck by surprise and go through in 24 hours.[17]

Despite the seemingly positive nature of this initial meeting, the relationship between the two commanders rapidly deteriorated. Unity of command is a fundamental principle of war and, while an eminently sensible concept, it has always proved difficult to achieve. Quite simply, senior generals tend to be quite forceful characters and many army group or force commanders in history have resisted moves to subordinate them to another commander. This was especially evident during the First World War when unity of command eluded the Allies until April 1918, when Maréchal Foch was appointed as supreme commander. Even at that point Allied force commanders such as Haig and Pershing still retained a level of autonomy. Similar tensions would arise again during the Second World War. What is evident is that, even at this early stage in his command, Nivelle saw himself as the senior commander on the Western Front. He saw no reason why the BEF should not be subordinated to his command and in the weeks that followed he allowed himself to be drawn into a web of intrigue with this purpose in mind.

He was aided in these efforts by Lloyd George, who had risen to the premiership in Britain on 5 December 1916, following the collapse of the Asquith government. Lloyd George had previously criticised Haig for his conduct of the war and had sought ways to limit his power and return control of the war to the government. Nivelle's appointment as commander-in-chief was timely and his ambitions to exercise control over the BEF suited Lloyd George's own plans.

In early January 1917 Lloyd George attended the Allied conference in Rome, where he suggested an Allied offensive in Italy. Briand opposed this plan, stating that all troops were necessary on the Western Front in order to carry out Nivelle's plans for a war-winning offensive. Although thwarted in his design for a new effort in Italy, Lloyd George met Nivelle at a railway station near Paris during his return journey. He found him extremely persuasive and invited him to London to meet the War Cabinet. Nivelle was equally persuasive in a meeting with the French War Committee on 15 January. Citing his successes at Verdun in October and December 1916, he argued for the concentration of forces on the Western Front in order to destroy 'the principal mass of the enemy's forces'.[18] As an operating principle, this was in fact a sensible suggestion but despite Nivelle's confidence it was unclear if the assembled Allied armies had the capacity to achieve this aim. Events would ultimately prove otherwise and in the final analysis this seemingly simple plan would evolve into an overly elaborate scheme, which also proved to be obvious and predictable to the Germans.

On 15–16 January Nivelle and Haig travelled to London for a meeting with the British War Cabinet. At the meeting Nivelle outlined his plans for the upcoming offensive, explaining how he would use his artillery to create corridors in the enemy's defences to a considerable depth in order to allow his troops to advance. Again he cited his recent successes and pointed out that his December attack at Verdun had lost only 1,550 soldiers. For his offensive to succeed he needed the BEF not only to engage in offensive action but also to take over a section of the front from the French in order to release troops for the offensive. Haig countered with reservations about the early date set for the attack (early February), the need for additional British divisions and concerns about the state of the Russian and Italian armies. It is apparent that Nivelle emerged as the more convincing. Haig was notoriously inarticulate at such meetings. Edward Spears, the British liaison officer to the French GQG, later wrote that Nivelle 'expressed himself with the greatest lucidity, and I thought that, even for a Frenchman, he was a fluent talker'.[19] But although Nivelle had gained broad support for his plans, the date was pushed back to the first half of April as it was impossible for the BEF to be ready to cooperate in such a large operation in February.

Of course, these plans ran counter to Haig's aspirations for an offensive in Flanders. Haig wished to organise an offensive to clear the Germans from the Belgian coast in order to hamper U-boat operations; this was an operational concept that Nivelle described as an *idée fixe*.[20] Haig was also concerned about the duration of the offensive: how could any commander gauge success within 24–48 hours? Also, how long was he expected to support Nivelle's efforts if they proved unsuccessful? Certainly he got little support from Lloyd George, who had privately thrown in his lot with Nivelle. As he later wrote, 'Nivelle has proved himself to be a Man at Verdun and when you get a Man against one who has not proved himself, then you back the Man.'[21] To Haig himself, Lloyd George stated that the French army was 'better all round' and able to succeed with less loss of life.[22] Haig responded hotly, referring to the lack of 'discipline and thoroughness' within the French army. Over the weeks that followed, the tensions between Haig and Nivelle, and Haig and his own government worsened. Haig complained about the lack of rail transport, stating that this would delay him further. The Chief of the Imperial General Staff, General Sir William Robertson, was pressured at a War Cabinet meeting to ensure that British preparations did not delay the offensive.

On 27 February 1917 the political and military leaders met for a conference at Calais. On the agenda, alongside practical issues such as rail transport and force deployment, was the question of unity of command. On the French side, Briand, Lyautey and Nivelle attended, while Lloyd George, Robertson and Haig represented British interests. During this meeting the French delegation gave Lloyd George a note that asked him to subordinate Haig and the BEF to French command, a move that would effectively reduce Haig to the role of an army group commander. The French added a comprehensive list of demands in this note, requesting power for 'the planning and execution of offensive and defensive actions, [and] the dispositions of the forces by the armies and groups of armies'. They also requested that a BEF chief-of-staff be placed at the GQG. Some confusion remains about the exact sequence of events. Some sources state that Briand passed this written request to Lloyd George, while others state that it was Nivelle himself.

Whatever the truth of the matter, British feathers were now severely ruffled. Robertson met with Nivelle and complained to him about putting this proposal directly to the political leaders without prior consultation. Nivelle defended himself, saying that the idea had originated not with him but with the two governments. He had only been asked to figure out the details and was, he claimed, working on the assumption that it had been agreed by Lloyd George beforehand. Nivelle concluded to Robertson that 'naturally, therefore, I assumed that you knew as much about it as I did'.[23]

Lyautey also scrambled to disassociate himself from this manoeuvre, denying having played any part in the formulation of the document. The proposal had originated, he claimed, in a conversation in London between Lloyd George and the French military attaché to London. Lloyd George, the French claimed, had seen it as absolutely necessary that Nivelle should have total control of all the troops on the Western Front, including the BEF. This message had been sent to Briand and the French government and resulted in Nivelle's proposal. In essence, Lyautey followed Nivelle's line: they were operating on the assumption that this was cleared in London through the Chief of the Imperial General Staff – i.e. Robertson.

Unsurprisingly, there was further reaction to the French request. That evening both Haig and Robertson confronted Lloyd George in his room. Faced with the anger of the military men, it seems that the prime minister's nerve failed and he made an effort to pass responsibility to the War Cabinet. Haig and Robertson then met with Colonel Maurice Hankey, the secretary of the War Cabinet, who assured them that Lloyd George had not received full authority from the cabinet for this proposal. Later Haig, his chief-of-staff Sir Lancelot Kiggell and Robertson discussed the matter further and considered resigning, or even facing court-martial, instead of submitting to such an arrangement. The next day Haig discussed the matter directly with Nivelle and Lyautey, both of whom, Haig wrote, were appalled at 'the insult offered to me and the British army by the paper which Briand had produced. They assured me that they had not seen the document until quite recently.'[24]

It appears that Lloyd George had overplayed his hand. Nivelle's protestations must be viewed with some doubt, as he had already displayed a capacity for duplicity in his dealings with Joffre. In the event, Haig focused everyone's minds by setting out the possible outcomes quite clearly in a memo to Robertson:

In my opinion there are only two alternatives, viz.,

1. To leave matters as they are now.

Or

2. To place the British army in France entirely under the French Commander-in-Chief.

The decision to adopt the second of these proposals must involve the disappearance of the British Commander-in-Chief and GHQ. What further changes would be necessary must depend on the French Commander-in-Chief and the French Government under whom he acts. So drastic a change in our system at a moment when active operations on a large scale have already commenced seems to me to be fraught with the gravest danger.[25]

Apart from the operational dangers of such a move, Haig pointed out the obvious to Lloyd George – any government that put the BEF under French command would not remain long in office due to the resulting political fallout and public outcry.

Haig's reaction to this rather clumsy political ambush led to a compromise solution being reached. The general direction of the forthcoming offensive would be in Nivelle's hands and Haig would conform to his plans, with the caveat that he could act independently if he felt that the safety of the BEF, or the success of British operations, was threatened. Haig retained the freedom to use his own methods and deploy his troops as he saw fit in order to achieve his set objectives. Finally, this arrangement would be in force for the duration of the offensive only. This was far from what Nivelle and Lloyd George had been hoping for and the fallout from the Calais conference was to create long-lasting ill-feeling between Haig and Lloyd George and also between Haig and Nivelle. Lloyd George would later complain that Haig and Robertson had effectively scuppered any possibility of unity of command and an early offensive. To some degree, Nivelle's desire for unity of command, embodied in his own person, was sensible but the whole matter was handled poorly by all concerned, not least by Nivelle, resulting in simmering resentment between the two military staffs at a crucial time. Matters were not improved by Nivelle insisting that General Henry Wilson be assigned as chief liaison officer at GQG – yet another move calculated to undermine Haig. Nivelle also demanded that he be informed of all directives that Haig issued to the BEF. This level of oversight, had it been fully complied with, would have reduced Haig to the subordinate role that Nivelle sought for him. The push for unity of command had, instead, created a sense of disunity. Edward Spears later described a liaison meeting with Nivelle that ended with an outburst from the French commander:

> General Nivelle burst out. Under the influence of anger he revealed the resentment I was alarmed to see he felt against the British commander-in-chief. He could not but notice, he said, that Sir Douglas attached undue importance to matters of prestige and was lacking in that spirit of cooperation without which work between allies was so difficult; he did not visualise the front as a whole and in fact was always trying to draw all the blanket to himself.[26]

In the weeks that followed, Nivelle showed extreme tactlessness in his dealings with Haig, essentially adopting a tone with him that suggested that the British commander was his subordinate. Haig complained to Robertson about Nivelle's tone in his communications and the matter would later resurface at meetings of the British War Cabinet. The Nivelle–Haig correspondence survives and it offers a fascinating insight into the relationship between the two senior commanders. Haig was always courteous but in his letters to Nivelle he underlined the disparity in their ranks and emphasised the fact that he held an independent army command. His letters were always addressed to the 'Commander-in-Chief, French armies of the North and North-East', and Haig described himself as 'Commander-in-Chief, the British armies in France'. Haig often began his letters with 'My Dear General' but signed himself as 'D. Haig, Field Marshal'. In turn, Nivelle's letters to Haig often seem peremptory in the extreme.[27]

One might argue that this was due to the language barrier but Nivelle spoke perfect English. Many of the surviving letters were written by Nivelle's staff officers, reinforcing the fact that he viewed Haig as a subordinate. Also, while Haig's letters were businesslike, they were also personal, whereas Nivelle's communications were often bluntly instructional in tone. Jean de Pierrefeu, an officer on Nivelle's staff at this time, has also suggested that in fact these communications were penned by Lt-Col. d'Alançon, which accounted for the brusque tone used towards Haig. In his memoir, *French Headquarters, 1915-18,* Pierrefeu stated that 'to him [d'Alançon] was attributed the quarrel which had early arisen between Field Marshal Haig and General Nivelle, and the imperative letters addressed to Generals Pétain and Anthoine'.[28]

Valuable time was lost in this needless bickering and sparring between the two commanders and their respective staffs in the early weeks of 1917. It was also somewhat ironic that, as the Allied commanders and politicians were wrangling at Calais and as tensions between the two commanders simmered, the Germans were preparing to seize the operational initiative once again. On 4 February the Germans began preparations to 'straighten their line' along a large section of the front. They had spent the previous months preparing new defensive positions in their rear areas. These defences-in-depth were known by the Germans as the 'Siegfried Stellung' and subsequently by the Allies as the Hindenburg Line. In the weeks that followed, the pace of the

German preparations increased and in late February they began to move. Their planned and carefully coordinated withdrawals allowed them to shorten their line and thus reduce the number of men needed to hold the front-line positions. The move reduced their front by 40km and freed up thirteen or fourteen divisions from front-line service. These units could then be deployed elsewhere, or be held as reserve divisions for counterattacks. They also abandoned their positions in some exposed salients. In short, this prudent move allowed the Germans to defend their front more effectively, using fewer troops, by utilising the carefully positioned defences of the Hindenburg Line.[29]

The Germans codenamed the withdrawal 'Operation Alberich', after the spiteful dwarf in the Nibelung saga. Over the course of a few weeks the Germans drew back from all their front-line positions from the Arras sector in the northern British zone to east of Soissons in the southern French zone. In essence, they left the Noyon salient to take up new prepared positions around 10km east of their original line. They began by leaving the small salient between Arras and Bapaume that had been created during the Somme offensive in 1916. They left this salient on 24 February and began their larger withdrawal from the Noyon salient on 16 March.

The German commanders, Hindenburg and Ludendorff, were aware of the vulnerability of the Noyon salient to attacks from both north and south. This was the very factor that had been recognised by Nivelle and it was this vulnerability that he had hoped to exploit with combined Allied attacks on the salient. The exposed nature of the Noyon salient was the key feature of his plan, and the German withdrawal effectively negated his offensive intentions as the Noyon salient had ceased to exist. Yet in the weeks that followed, Nivelle refused to change his plans. Rather than pinching off the Noyon salient to create a breach, he would now refocus on the Chemin des Dames, despite the fact that the Germans were now in well-prepared positions along this dominant ridgeline.

Alongside the operational ramifications for Nivelle's plans, the German withdrawal also served to increase tensions between the French and the British. The Germans had spent months preparing their new positions and there had been much activity behind their lines. In one of the most crucial intelligence lapses of the war, neither the French nor the British had picked up on this for some weeks. German control of the air over the front also prevented adequate aerial reconnaissance. By early January 1917 the British had been alerted to the activity to their front; increasing their aerial reconnaissance efforts, they urged the French to follow suit. In late February a large collection of aerial photographs had been assembled and it was possible to get a greater understanding of the German preparations. The line of the new defences was evident, as were several interim lines that the Germans intended to use as phase lines as they drew back. Within the Allied staffs, the general consensus was that the Germans were constructing a 'defence in depth'.

After the Germans began pulling out of the small Bapaume–Arras salient on 24 February, however, the photographic intelligence suggested another interpretation – that the Germans were planning to shorten their front considerably. Nivelle was sceptical. He did not believe that the Germans would give up so much territory, least of all positions so close to Paris. Haig saw that these withdrawals impacted on his own role in the upcoming offensive. He suggested that he should attack only at Vimy and Arras with his First and Third Armies. This would allow him to shift forces towards Ypres in the event of a German attack. Furthermore, Haig felt that the new situation endangered his position and thus gave him the freedom to disregard Nivelle's directives. He was effectively freeing himself from the provisions of the Calais conference, which had only been agreed a week previously. Apart from the very practical consequences of the German withdrawal for his own offensive, Nivelle realised that he was on the verge of losing his political backing. He responded to Haig's waywardness by sending him yet more 'directives' in an effort to preserve his offensive plans. He conceded that the Bapaume supporting attack should be called off, but insisted that the Arras and Vimy attacks go ahead.

The evidence of a German withdrawal was amply supported by reports provided by French military intelligence, the Deuxième Bureau. As early as 23 February the bureau had forwarded reports that the Germans were preparing to withdraw and shorten their line on the Aisne. They were evacuating French civilians, destroying houses and any shelter and also laying booby-traps and poisoning wells. By March the officers of the Deuxième Bureau could report that they were tracking the rearward movement of

German radio posts, which suggested the withdrawal of German HQ and command units. These reports went unheeded by Nivelle.[30]

Primed by Nivelle, Briand complained to London about Haig's attitude and yet another conference was called in London for 12–13 March. It was an opportunity for both sides to air their grievances. Lloyd George, himself primed by Robertson and Haig, and obviously feeling that he had to amend for past transgressions, complained about the tone of Nivelle's communications to Haig. The meeting resulted in a new agreement that confirmed Haig's position as an army commander in his own right. The BEF would 'remain in all circumstances under the orders of their chain of command and of the British commander in chief'.[31] The chief British liaison officer would report directly to Haig and would keep both commanders informed on relevant matters connected to both armies. This new agreement effectively ended Nivelle's attempts to deal directly with Haig's army commanders and to treat him as a subordinate force commander. Satisfying as this must have been for Haig, the weeks of contention between the commanders had destroyed all hope of mounting the new offensive in the first half of February, which had been Joffre's and then Nivelle's intention. This had allowed the initiative to pass to the Germans.

The lack of operational preparation that was the result of these weeks of wrangling also made it glaringly obvious that the Allied armies were not in a position to use the German withdrawal to their advantage. The German operation was still developing and this could have offered an opportunity to go on the offensive and perhaps catch German forces off-balance as their retrograde move developed. The delay in preparing for offensive action made a large-scale offensive impossible.

Also, and perhaps uncharacteristically, Nivelle dithered. In early March General Franchet d'Espèrey, who had taken over command of the Northern Army Group (GAN), noticed the German preparations to withdraw. He recommended abandoning the wider plan and springing a surprise attack. D'Espèrey proposed an intense two-day barrage and, on the second day of the barrage, a large-scale attack by his army group. Furthermore, he suggested that tanks be used *en masse* to support this attack. As the French had yet to use tanks, these would further catch the Germans by surprise. All of this should be launched within ten days, d'Espèrey suggested, in order to achieve maximum impact on the withdrawing German troops. Nivelle, however, remained unconvinced that the Germans were withdrawing on a large scale, despite mounting evidence to support this conclusion.[32] While he ordered his staff to begin contingency planning for a German withdrawal, he remained blind to the opportunity that had been presented. It was a classic example of strategic 'tunnel vision'. Having formed a plan, Nivelle seemed unable to deviate from it, despite the operational advantages of doing so in this case. It was a problem that would resurface later.

When the German withdrawal finally became obvious, Nivelle still hesitated. The shortening of the front line also allowed him to redeploy troops, and he duly reorganised his army groups; sixteen divisions, plus their divisional artillery, now became available for redeployment and Nivelle used them to strengthen Pétain's Central Army Group (GAC) while he also tweaked plans for his offensive. As the German operation developed, he still seems to have considered it only in the light of the ramifications it had for his plans, rather than as an opportunity that was being presented to him. D'Espèrey was encouraged to keep up an 'energetic and continuous' pressure on the enemy as they fell back to the Hindenburg Line but there were no wider instructions issued for a more general pursuit. Ultimately, the Germans would withdraw to their new prepared positions while the French army advanced and maintained contact. The Germans moved back in carefully planned phases, each successive withdrawal covered by machine gun companies that laid down a continuous fire.

It is easy to criticise Nivelle for this missed opportunity but, in his defence, the French army found itself on the horns of a strategic dilemma. If contact with the Germans was not maintained, then the enemy would be allowed time and space to manoeuvre. The idea of leaving the evacuated zone vacant, as some vast extension of no-man's-land, was simply not an option. Nivelle had to pursue but the advancing French troops found themselves in a devastated zone. Alongside the damage caused by years of war, the Germans had destroyed everything as they withdrew. Farms and villages were flattened to deny the French any shelter. Livestock had been slaughtered, crops destroyed and wells poisoned. Roads had been demolished and the Germans had left behind numerous mines and other booby-traps.

By this stage of the war the Germans had developed new types of fuses for use with booby-traps. These included delay fuses and also instantaneous fuses. These were attached to artillery shells concealed on the battlefield. Larger mines were constructed and these utilised a mix of delay and instantaneous fuses. Grenade devices were also used, with instantaneous detonators. These could be deployed in trip wire booby-traps and in some cases boxes of grenades were left behind with instantaneous detonators fitted. These would subsequently kill or maim any French soldier who tried to use them. Shells and mines were also concealed under duckboards in trenches with pressure-pad initiators. At the non-explosive end of the spectrum, the Germans laid metal man-traps, left pits lined with steel spikes and also left spiked 'bear traps'.[33]

The advancing French troops found that even the trees had been cut down in order to deny them shelter and building materials. Such wanton destruction horrified the French, many of whom came from rural backgrounds. One soldier wrote, 'those bastards cut down all the trees as they cleared off. We've got to get our own back.' Another wrote: 'What really makes us mad is seeing all these trees – fruit trees and others – hacked down to the base. Only cold fury and a desire to destroy for its own sake can have inspired such a decision by the German high command, and the troops carried out their orders to perfection.'[34] Scorched earth policies had been carried out in warfare before. French soldiers and politicians were aware that such destruction had taken place during the Russian withdrawal from Napoleon's army in 1812, for example, and during the American Civil War. It came as a considerable shock, however, to see that such a comprehensive strategy had been applied on French soil and this destruction caused a sensation in the press and a resulting public outcry.

From a purely military perspective, it was not a battlezone that encouraged hasty pursuit and French troops followed cautiously. Film footage survives of Nivelle visiting the zone evacuated by the Germans. A somewhat forlorn-looking figure, he was filmed inspecting this scarred and devastated landscape.

The German withdrawal coincided with yet another political upheaval within the French government. Briand's tottering *Union Sacrée*, which had been engaged in desperate damage limitation for months, finally fell. General

Lyautey, the Minister of War, had refused to share secret information on French military aviation during a closed session of the Chamber of Deputies. In recent weeks Lyautey had looked increasingly uneasy as minister and had also criticised the total lack of security within government. Too much of the government's military business was becoming widespread knowledge among journalists and even the general public. Lyautey's main point was quite barbed: even if the matter were discussed in a closed session, information would leak out. Therefore, the nation's politicians were not to be trusted. In the political outcry that followed, Lyautey resigned. Briand found himself unable to find another candidate who would agree to be Minister of War and his government fell. It was the final chapter in the history of an administration that had ultimately proved that the *Union Sacrée* did not work. Riven with internal discontent, Briand's government had become increasingly dysfunctional and lurched from crisis to crisis. Lyautey's resignation had proved to be the final episode in this troubled administration's history.

A new government was formed on 20 March 1917 under the elderly Alexandre Ribot, now in his eighties. Ribot was a Socialist and a renowned economist who had served as Minister for Finance for two previous wartime administrations. As his new Minister of War he chose Paul Painlevé, who had actually served in the Briand administration. Painlevé, a mathematician by profession and a former lecturer at the Sorbonne, was an able politician and had previously served as Minister for Inventions. In this capacity he had been involved in some of the early discussions on the development of the tank within the French army. He was an advocate of total war and firmly believed that harnessing the potential of both science and industry would assist in achieving a final French victory. As Minister for Inventions he had also developed a network of contacts within the senior French command. In December 1916, however, Painlevé had refused office in Briand's new administration because of objections over the continued role of Joffre in war planning and the appointment of Nivelle. Painlevé was an advocate of Pétain's cautious command style and the use of limited offensives to pursue war aims. Painlevé had visited Pétain at Verdun several times and they had discussed the future conduct of the war. They found that they were of the same mind on the nature of future actions and these contrasted starkly with

Nivelle's vision. This opposition to Nivelle delayed his appointment as minister and it was only after Ribot had obtained an assurance from Painlevé that he would work with Nivelle that he was appointed.[35]

On 22 March Painlevé met with Nivelle and urged him to reconsider his plans in light of the German withdrawal, the situation in Russia and also the expectation of America's entry into the war. In a neat summation of the new strategic situation, Painlevé noted that the original focus of the attack – the Noyon salient – no longer existed. Also, the Russian collapse (the Tsar had abdicated on 15 March) would surely result in a Russo-German peace treaty, thus freeing up further German divisions to resist Allied attacks on the Western Front. Furthermore, Painlevé pointed out that he had heard details of Nivelle's plans before taking office and he had not supported his idea for a grand offensive. Finally, he pointed out that he knew the planned date for this offensive (then set for 8 April) and, as this was common knowledge, operational secrecy had been compromised. The offensive, Painlevé assumed, would be called off.

This was an ideal opportunity for Painlevé to assert his authority while also averting the looming military disaster. Yet it would seem that Nivelle was at his most persuasive. He pointed out that the German withdrawal also freed up French divisions and that decisive action at that time would yield results. He no longer intended to pinch off a salient but rather he now planned to crack the German line. He anticipated an advance of up to 30km over three days. Nivelle dismissed any German build-up, stating, 'I do not fear numbers. The greater the numbers, the greater the victory.'[36] Unsure of himself and seemingly unable to persuade Nivelle to rethink his plans, Painlevé capitulated.[37]

In the weeks that followed, complaints poured in to Painlevé's office from politicians, Ministry of War officials, the army group commanders and also officers within Nivelle's own staff. Virtually all the assessments of Nivelle's plan were negative. Colonel Georges Renouard, the chief of operations on Nivelle's staff, had even written up a damning assessment but this was suppressed by d'Alançon.[38] Painlevé was informed that General Micheler was a major critic of the plan, despite the fact that he commanded the Group d'Armées de Reserve (GAR) – the army group responsible for the main French effort. On 22 March Micheler wrote to Painlevé stating that he saw little chance in obtaining a breakthrough. On 25 March Charles de Freycinet, an elderly and much-respected politician, brought Painlevé a memorandum written by a staff officer on the GAR that described the upcoming offensive in the darkest terms. The Germans, the report stated, were aware of the offensive and were preparing to meet it. Its failure would damage some of the best formations in the French army.

Seeking a way to end the crisis, Painlevé decided to discuss Nivelle's plans with his army group commanders in the hope of gaining their support for a heave against Nivelle. On 28 March he met with Micheler, who expressed his doubts on the potential for success but became evasive when asked directly if the attack should be cancelled. Painlevé discussed the possibility of the Germans taking the initiative or the fact that they would be freed up to decisively defeat the Italians or the Russians. Painlevé's meeting with Pétain on 1 April at GAC headquarters was more frank. Pétain dismissed all possibility of a breakthrough and proposed instead a limited offensive that would maximise damage to the Germans while minimising French casualties. The following evening Painlevé dined with Pétain and Franchet d'Espèrey. Pétain again criticised the Nivelle plan, while D'Espèrey was more reserved. Nevertheless he stated that he thought the German defences were strong and that they were expecting the French attack.

Yet despite the fact that he had largely negative reports from three army group commanders, Painlevé still failed to replace Nivelle. This was potentially a decisive moment but Painlevé simply did not feel empowered to act. Political support for him sacking Nivelle was not forthcoming, while the army group commanders simply did not deliver the momentum he needed to replace him. In hindsight, the fall of Briand's government would now seem to have been an obvious opportunity to replace Nivelle. Instead, Painlevé found himself caught between two dangerous options. If he forced Nivelle to resign or sacked him, there would be yet another political crisis and the new Ribot government would fall. This was simply not an option. Apart from wanting to save his own political career, Painlevé was conscious of the growing public discontent at the conduct of the war. Would the collapse of another administration precipitate unrest similar to that emerging in Russia? The second option was to allow Nivelle to forge ahead with his plans. This, Painlevé realised, might result in a military disaster, which might also result in political collapse. But this scenario would not occur for some weeks, by which time other factors, such as the American entry into the war, might be in play. In any event, Painlevé adopted a 'Mr Micawber' approach – 'Something would turn up' to save the situation. He did not feel politically secure enough to act on his doubts, so Nivelle would be allowed to see his plans through, at least for now. Painlevé resolved to bide his time and return to the issue in early April.

Painlevé was also not helped by the support Nivelle enjoyed in the press. Nivelle knew how to court pressmen, and his enthusiasm and energy were infectious. Building on the reputation he had established at Verdun, by March 1917 Nivelle had become that most dangerous of creatures within French politics and society: a Messiah figure. While the press and public might be disillusioned with French politicians and the government in general, they were confident in Nivelle. He was about to win the war, rapidly and at little cost. The bursting of the bubble of these expectations would plunge France to its lowest point since the start of the war.

Chapter 3

General Nivelle and his Plan

I don't know what they have in store for us, but the preparations are huge. Troops and ammunition keep pouring in. If they could at least wait until I have returned from leave.
(French soldier's letter of March 1917).[1]

Most English-language histories of the Western Front dismiss the Nivelle Offensive in just a few lines. It is often portrayed as a failure that was bound to happen. The actual truth is more complex and it is worthwhile examining Nivelle's plan in some detail. In his operational orders Nivelle was in the habit of describing his intentions in the broadest and most ambitious terms. In one communication he stated:

> I insist on the violence, brutality and swiftness of our offensive and most particularly on its first stage, breaking up the front, with the immediate targets of capturing the enemy positions and the whole area of its artillery.[2]

Nivelle's plan was founded on a number of very simplistic assumptions. Firstly, his methods had worked at Verdun. Therefore, if suitably resourced, they could be applied on a vastly larger scale; in this case a front ten times larger than the front he had assaulted at Verdun. To counter any difficulties, Nivelle simply increased the scale of his effort and assembled over a million men in four army groups, complemented with appropriate tank, artillery, supply and air assets. Secondly, any operational difficulties presented by the German defences could be overcome with surprise, speed and brute force. Finally, the choice of terrain was inconsequential, if his methods were employed properly.

The choice of location for the focus of his attacks was based on the fact that the new German line near Soissons (*see* Map 1) presented a unique operational opportunity, with a pronounced bend or 'elbow' to the southeast of the town. If he could break the line to the north and south of this bend in the line, his armies could exploit laterally and destroy the German artillery and reserves in an open battle. Nivelle's plan was not about seizing territory or terrain features but rather destroying German forces and, in that aim, it was not unintelligent.

The problem was that the area chosen for the main French effort contained terrain features that would affect the planned attacks. In this, Nivelle was guilty of some very poor terrain analysis. The Chemin des Dames ridgeline was to be a main focus of his attack. This impressive ridgeline, more than 40km long, acquired its name as it was a favourite ride of the daughters of Louis XV. Even without the defences added by the Germans, this ridgeline presented any attacking troops with some difficult problems. Below the ridgeline itself, the Aisne river and an associated canal network presented awkward water obstacles. Opposite the Chemin des Dames the French held a 20km long bridgehead on the right bank of the river but in other locations the Germans held the right bank and in some areas both banks of the river. The ridge itself was over 180m high, with several prominent points that dominated the surrounding landscape. Indeed, during the nineteenth century it was such an obvious defensive feature that the French had built several forts on the Chemin des Dames. Two of these, Fort de Malmaison and Fort Brimont, were now held by the Germans. In short, the Chemin des Dames was a difficult objective for infantry and it was virtually impossible to cross with artillery. Despite the fact that a rapid follow-up by the artillery was a crucial part of Nivelle's plan, he did not realistically assess the difficulties that would be presented by the Chemin des Dames.[3]

A further factor that should have suggested caution was Nivelle's almost complete lack of intelligence as to what would face his troops once the attack began. While the French commanders knew that they faced the army group of Crown Prince Wilhelm, the full extent of the German defences was not clear. It was difficult to obtain aerial photographs of the new defences because of German air superiority, so the French had very little idea of what defences the Germans had built on the far side of the Chemin des Dames ridgeline.

In fact, the Hindenburg Line made the best use of any significant terrain features, while also incorporating a network of machine-gun positions, pillboxes, underground bunkers and integrated artillery fire. The German front line was only lightly held, and attackers passing through it would find themselves facing fortified MG positions and concrete pillboxes. The Germans referred to these pillbox systems as 'MEBU' ('Manschafts-Eisen-Beton Unterstand', roughly translated as 'iron/concrete man shelter').[4] The German artillery had the coordinates of possible lines of attack within their defensive zones and artillery spotters could call in accurate supporting fire once any attack began. Counterattack formations were protected within deep concrete bunkers and could issue forth to oppose the French as they struggled through the lines of defence. MEBU were positioned on the reverse slopes of the Chemin des Dames ridge and also in disused quarries and in some caves. This defence-in-depth network extended for up to 8–10km.[5] The attacking French armies would have to successfully pass through all of these defences before they even encountered the main German reserve armies and artillery positions, the supposed objective of the whole operation. Following the battle, a French officer described the extent of the defences they had faced:

> Three positions, sometimes four, with at least two lines [of trenches] each, spread a deep network over the terrain. The older trenches, around the Chemin des Dames, had been reorganised with support positions flanked by 'blockhaus' placed at intervals covering every inch of the ground with their machine guns. On the plain east of the bluff, as well as on top of the bluff itself and its slope, the Germans had dug out spacious galleries, which backed up and served the whole system.[6]

To carry out his plan, Nivelle would use four army groups: essentially the entire French army. These were the Groupe d'Armées du Nord (GAN) under General Franchet D'Espèrey, the Groupe d'Armées de Reserve (GAR) under General Micheler, the Groupe d'Armées du Centre (GAC) under Pétain, and the Groupe d'Armées de l'est under General Castelnau, which was tasked with supplementary operations. Micheler's Group d'Armées des Reserve (Nivelle preferred 'de Rupture') would carry out the main effort

General Nivelle and his Plan   57

on the Chemin des Dames, while all the other army groups would carry out subsidiary and diversionary attacks along the front.

If the lack of intelligence on the German defences and also the terrain issues were ignored, there seemed to be much to actually commend this plan, especially as the BEF would carry out a series of associated attacks in Flanders. Nivelle's logic was simple – if the Germans were attacked across the totality of the Western Front, they would be unable to send adequate reserves to counter any breach in their line. His whole plan was predicated on the belief that the Germans would be too thinly spread to allow them to counter his main effort on the Chemin des Dames. Unfortunately, he did not factor in the effectiveness of the new German defence-in-depth, which would allow them to move reserves with considerable freedom. This was yet another, significant, oversight as the Germans had made increasing use of multiple lines of defence since 1915. But a 'best case scenario' attitude was adopted by Nivelle and many officers within the GQG.

As previously stated, the main effort of Nivelle's attack would be carried out by Micheler's GAR, which comprised the Sixth Army (Mangin), the Tenth Army (Duchêne) and the Fifth Army (Mazel). Mangin's Sixth Army was composed of seventeen divisions in five corps, plus a cavalry division and a territorial division. His focus was to be the elbow in the German line to the east of Soissons. To his right, Mazel's Fifth Army was composed of sixteen divisions and a Russian brigade, grouped into five corps. These would carry out his main attack towards Craonne; in reserve Mazel had a further three divisions and a second Russian brigade. Mazel also had eight battalions of the new Schneider tanks (128 tanks) to aid his attack. Positioned behind these two armies was Duchêne's Tenth Army, which was tasked with passing through the breach created by Mangin's and Mazel's armies. Duchêne had thirteen divisions in five corps, including a cavalry corps. It was envisaged that Duchêne's army would pass between the Sixth and Fifth Armies and exploit the breach that they had made. Finally, behind the Tenth Army was positioned the First Army under Nivelle's own command. He intended to use this to further exploit following the initial breakthrough.[7] (*See* Map 2.)

This then was the Nivelle plan in its broad strokes. There would be a build-up in pressure along the whole front to force the Germans to dissipate their force, followed by a focused and massive attack on a particular section of the line. Taking a 'Principles of War' metric to examine Nivelle's plan, it could be argued that he was conforming well with some of the most important of these principles. The principle of 'Mass', for example, would dictate that he assemble and concentrate his forces at a particular point for an attack at a specific time. In his plan, Nivelle had allowed for precisely this, with the positioning of a strong army group on the Chemin des Dames to carry out his main effort.

In other respects, Nivelle neglected some of the basic principles of war. Not least of these was operational security and in his neglect of this principle, he forfeited another – that of surprise. In his efforts to convince fellow generals and also French politicians of the soundness of his plan, Nivelle was in the habit of freely sharing details with others – much too freely. Visiting politicians and pressmen were briefed on the plan and were even shown maps! Aspects of the plan were debated in the Chamber of Deputies and in the French press. On one occasion in early 1917 the Prince of Wales (the future Edward VIII) visited Nivelle's HQ at Beauvais and was briefed on the plan. Security was so poor that by February 1917 it was said that every waiter in Paris had an understanding of the outline of Nivelle's plan. During his visits to London Nivelle horrified his hosts by discussing aspects of his plan at dinner, in the presence of civilian guests who were not security cleared. A French staff officer remembered that 'No one had bothered to keep the date of the offensive secret. It was an open subject. I am still wondering why, in the circumstances, everyone was so talkative.'[8] These breaches of security made a joke of the instructions issued to the troops. General Mazel had told his men that 'Surprise, born of secrecy and speed' was a key element, while a GQG order exhorted every soldier to 'Stay quiet! Stay alert! Stay hidden!'[9] Sadly, a collection of staff officers, politicians and pressmen did not seem to think that such instructions applied to them.

Due to the lack of adherence to the most basic 'need to know' principles of operational security, German military intelligence began to build up a picture of Allied plans during the spring of 1917. To compound matters, Nivelle circulated orders to units too far in advance of the attack and some of these orders fell into German hands. The first occasion when the Germans obtained hard intelligence came as early as January 1917. During a raid at Main de Massiges the Germans captured some orders sent to the French

2nd Division, which gave details of the planned attack on the Aisne. In his memoirs General Ludendorff commented that this was a 'capital piece of information'. In the middle of February the Germans captured more French plans during another raid and these also outlined an attack on the Aisne scheduled for April. On 3 March 1917 a further German raid captured what Crown Price Wilhelm later described as:

> The French regulation document known as 'Instructions concerning the aim and conditions of a general offensive'. This had been implemented by General Nivelle on 16 December 1916. It contained highly valuable information. It made clear that this time it would not be an attack on a specific target but a sweeping breakthrough offensive.[10]

Later in March a French lieutenant went missing while on a reconnaissance mission; he too was carrying plans for the upcoming operation. Finally, during the night of 4/5 April a French NCO disappeared during a German attack between Loivre and Berry-du-Bac. Realising that there were sensitive plans in the battalion HQ, an officer had sent the hapless sergeant to the rear in order to save them from falling into German hands. Why they had not simply been burned remains a mystery. It was somewhat ironic that the sergeant was then taken prisoner by the Germans, who found themselves with the orders outlining the roles of the 3rd Zouaves, the 37th Infantry Division and also VII, XXXII and XXXVIII Corps in the upcoming offensive.[11] On being informed of the loss of these orders, just over a week before the attack, Nivelle refused to change any part of his plan.

From the German perspective, it was initially thought that such material had been planted to deceive them. It was simply inconceivable that the French would allow so many lapses in basic operational security. But by February they were convinced that a French attack was imminent. They increased their forces in the Reims–Aisne sector and also transferred in more pioneer units in order to speed up the construction of defences in that sector. In the weeks that followed, their photographic reconnaissance aircraft recorded signs of the huge French build-up, which confirmed the validity of the other intelligence they had gathered.

Throughout this period French military intelligence struggled to get an appreciation of what was happening on the other side of the German lines. Since 1916 they had made huge advances in direction finding and analysis. They began to publish lists of German radio posts and linked these to command posts. They updated these lists every ten days. By monitoring German radio communications, they could observe the movement of HQ groups into the Aisne sector and argued that the Germans were building up troop numbers. French intelligence had also had considerable success in breaking German codes and on occasion they could 'read' German communications. As a result, French intelligence identified a German build-up opposite Micheler's army group. Between mid-February and 14 April it was reported that the Germans had brought in new divisions opposite the Sixth Army. In January there had only been four German divisions opposite the Sixth Army, but by April there were seven or eight, in response to the captured French plans. In the Fifth Army area the five German divisions had been increased to nine or ten by April. The report also pointed out that a further five to seven divisions were immediately available to the Germans as a reserve in that sector, while another six divisions were within reach. Some estimates put the German reserve capability as high as fifteen divisions. Alarmingly, the Deuxième Bureau also reported that captured German soldiers knew the actual date for the planned French attack. None of this information seems to have given Nivelle pause.[12]

This intelligence situation was the exact opposite from that of the Germans. The German senior commanders, Hindenburg and Ludendorff, and the local commanders, Crown Prince Wilhelm and General von Boehn of the Seventh Army, all had a growing appreciation of French intentions on the Chemin des Dames sector. This was due to captured intelligence, information gleaned from captured French soldiers and also the reports of spies that were forwarded through Switzerland. Moreover, the obvious signs of a French build-up could point to only one conclusion.

The evidence provided by the Deuxième Bureau was supplemented by front-line observers and also by the work of French photographic reconnaissance aircraft, which struggled to carry out their missions in skies dominated by the Germans. A build-up of artillery emplacements was becoming noticeable in the Chemin des Dames sector. The number in front of the Sixth Army had increased from 39 to as many as 200.[13] In front of the Fifth Army they had increased from 53 to around 320! In the Aisne sector, therefore, the Germans now had forty-one divisions, with another fourteen divisions east of Reims. On the Aisne front the French had forty-nine infantry divisions and five cavalry divisions, which was not inconsiderable but local superiority had been lost due to the security lapses. The modern guideline requires that an attacking force should outnumber the defending force by a ratio of 3:1; using this as a guide, it is evident that the French formations were no longer adequate. But, despite the overwhelming evidence of a German build-up opposite the intended point of attack, Nivelle refused to be dissuaded from his plan. This would merely allow the French to capture more Germans, he claimed.

Nivelle never lacked in confidence and, while he disregarded various causes for concern, his positive attitude was no doubt buoyed up by the huge force now at his disposal. In terms of manpower, Nivelle had more than 1.2 million men available. Of these, more than 500,000 would take part in the main effort on the Chemin des Dames/Aisne sector. Nivelle was also an artillerist, and firepower had played a significant role in his success at Verdun in 1916. As he now intended to repeat these methods on a larger scale, he accumulated the greatest concentration of firepower that had ever been put at the disposal of a French commander. By the opening of the attack in mid-April 1917 he had assembled an artillery force that included 2,900 field guns, 1,650 heavy guns, 160 long-range heavy guns and 1,550 mortars. In addition, he had also borrowed twenty-four 150mm howitzers from the British. This gave a total of more than 5,300 artillery pieces within the Sixth and Fifth Army sectors. There was one heavy gun for every 20 metres of frontage and one field gun or trench mortar every 21 metres. A stockpile of over 11 million artillery rounds would supply the preparatory barrage and the creeping barrage that would precede the advancing infantry.[14]

To help coordinate the artillery operation, Nivelle had also requested a huge effort from the French air force – the *Service Aeronautique*. More than 500 reconnaissance and artillery cooperation aircraft in forty-seven squadrons were available on the Chemin des Dames front. In their operations they would be supported by thirteen squadrons of fighters, which would prove to be far too few once operations began. Nivelle was also acutely aware that the artillery needed to follow-up any infantry success and made provision for the rapid transportation and repositioning of batteries. These provisions included motor and tracked artillery tractors and also the assistance of specially assigned pioneer units. In the weeks that preceded the offensive, roads in the rear areas were widened, supply dumps established, gun emplacements built and new telephone lines laid down.[15]

The infantry units scheduled to attack were put through a rigorous programme of instruction in the weeks before the offensive. In training camps in the rear they were versed in the 'Verdun Method'. Nivelle had not neglected the infantry part of his plan. He had increased the numbers of light Chauchat machine guns (in fact automatic rifles) within the infantry units in order to provide the troops with increased mobile firepower. The Chauchat had a mixed performance and the infantry complained that it was sensitive to mud and dirt and prone to jamming. But it was capable of being carried by one man and thus increased the firepower potential of infantry units. In a similar vein, Nivelle had increased the numbers of the 37mm portable cannon in infantry units. These small field pieces were capable of being carried by just two men and could be brought forward to deal with German machine-gun positions. Despite the fact that there was no evidence that the Germans were developing tanks, Nivelle also planned to use these portable cannon as an integral part of an anti-tank defence if such a threat should develop. Based on new tactical instructional manuals, Nivelle also refocused on training the infantry in open warfare tactics – tactics that had not been on the training programme since 1914. While this would prove to be wildly optimistic, it does give an indication of how Nivelle saw the infantry battle evolving once a breakthrough was achieved.

Within the infantry formations, especially in the Sixth Army, there were battalions of colonial troops. These included Senegalese from the French colonies in West Africa, who had a fearsome reputation as stormtroops. There were also Algerian and Moroccan tirailleurs, who were equally renowned. These colonials seemed to be possessed of limitless courage and in previous actions had followed their French officers with devotion. There were some doubts as to their ability to adopt complicated tactics and in bad weather they suffered considerably. Yet they were placed in the first waves of the planned attack due to their effectiveness in assaults. They were to prove to be victims of their own fighting reputation and would suffer large numbers of casualties.[16]

Much attention was given to infantry–artillery cooperation. A key element of Nivelle's Verdun Method was the use of a creeping barrage to shield the advancing infantry. Large training grounds were built to aid in the rehearsals for these advances. A key question was the speed of the infantry advance and, in keeping with the unthinking optimism that prevailed at that time, commanders seemed to compete in guessing how fast their troops could move forwards. Perhaps unsurprisingly, it was Mangin who came up with the most optimistic estimate, suggesting that his troops could advance at a rate of 100m per minute. This was absurd, considering that peacetime regulations stipulated a rate of 240m per 3 minutes on open roads.[17] In what was a sadly common feature during First World War operations, the generals did not factor in the effects of not only enemy opposition but also the difficulties posed in crossing a battle zone that had been cratered by artillery. Exploitation by cavalry was also part of the plan and Mangin confidently predicted that 'by dawn of the second day the cavalry should ride onto the plain of Laon'.[18]

During the weeks before the attack, morale among the French troops rose. It was impossible for the men not to consider themselves part of an unstoppable force as they witnessed the massive preparations under way. Never before had such a gigantic force been assembled and it seemed to the average *poilu* that this time the infantry was properly supported by artillery, air power, cavalry and even tanks. Postal censors reported a surge in troop morale. One infantryman wrote: 'The great victory will come soon. The Boches are on their last legs, they're starving. Believe me, you'll hear of great things before long.' Others were more pessimistic. Another infantryman wrote: 'Christ, what a job it is to be in the infantry! I am not sure that the enemy will give up the terrain we are considering taking from them. If not, we're going to have a hell of a time.'[19] In general, however, the tone of the soldiers' letters was markedly enthusiastic. Troops marching towards the front were reported to be in high spirits and sang the *Marseillaise*, in scenes that were reminiscent of the opening weeks of August 1914. Hopes for victory were huge; inevitably this would create a vast sense of disappointment as the offensive unfolded and ultimately failed.

While the French army made its preparations and the BEF under Haig got ready to support the assault, the political wrangling continued. The offensive had originally been scheduled for 8 April but was postponed to 16 April owing to bad weather. The supporting operations of the BEF were scheduled to begin on 9 April. So, as the final preparations were under way, and as the artillery programme began on 2 April, there was a last round of meetings in the hope of postponing or cancelling the offensive. On 3 April Painlevé invited Nivelle to dinner at the War Ministry in what can only be described as an attempt to ambush him. Among the other guests were Premier Ribot and the ministers for the navy, armaments and the colonies, the latter being the influential André Maginot. After dinner, Painlevé began discussing the upcoming offensive and again rehearsed the ramifications of the German withdrawal, the Russian collapse and the entry of America into the war. Did not these factors, he argued, make a reappraisal of the situation necessary? He then outlined his own doubts as to the chances of success overall.

Nivelle was not about to be cowed and, indeed, it is likely that he was expecting this ambush and had prepared his arguments. He countered by pointing out that he and his staff had planned for all eventualities. They were military experts, rather than anxious politicians, and they were aware of the changing situation at the front. Once again he pointed out the need to take the initiative to relieve pressure on both the Russians and the Italians. Furthermore, the German defences were not as strong as was being suggested and he was confident that his forces would break through the German third and fourth lines. He asserted confidently that Micheler's and d'Espèrey's army groups would meet north of Laon within 72 hours. His argument gained momentum when he discussed the arrangements made with the British, which provided for some unity of command and also a concentration of effort that could prove decisive. A delay or a postponement would result in this partnership coming to naught.

It was a bravura performance. Towards the end of the meeting Nivelle went to a wall map to indicate, with wide sweeps of his hand, the territory that would be recaptured during the initial few hours of the offensive. Painlevé, momentarily convinced, also went to the map to view the area indicated and stated that if the 'offensive resulted only in giving us back this vast territory and all it contains, the government and the nation would consider it a great victory and owe you an immense debt of gratitude'.[20] Nivelle demurred and summed up his own vision for the attack:

> That would be nothing. A poor tactical victory. It is not for so meagre a result that I have accumulated on the Aisne one million, two hundred thousand soldiers, five thousand guns and five hundred thousand horses. The game would not be worth the candle.[21]

So yet another meeting ended. Significantly, Nivelle promised to call off the offensive if it did not succeed within 24 to 48 hours. He would not, he assured Painlevé and the assembled ministers, be dragged into another battle like the Somme and feel obliged to mount further, successive, attacks.

The dynamics of these meetings remain a source of historical fascination. If Painlevé's purpose was to unseat Nivelle, why did he not ensure that he had the support to carry this through? Or was it that, in the full glare of Nivelle's confidence, his nerve simply failed? Or perhaps in those moments when Nivelle was at his most persuasive, Painlevé allowed himself to believe that this huge gamble could bring victory.

Whatever the case, and despite Nivelle's confidence that he had finally convinced the Minister of War and Premier Ribot that his scheme would work, further controversy followed. A number of factors drove Painlevé to confront Nivelle for a final time. The presidents of both the Senate and the Chamber of Deputies visited Micheler's army group and were greeted with pessimistic reports from several of Micheler's subordinate generals. At the same time General Messimy, a former Minister of War, wrote directly to Premier Ribot, predicting failure and heavy losses. Messimy concluded his letter with the remark, 'I summarize here the opinions of the most highly regarded leaders of our army and most notably the leader himself who will direct the approaching offensive, General Micheler.'[22] Any confidence that Nivelle had created during his performance on 3 April soon evaporated and, in a panic, Painlevé asked Pétain for his appreciation of the situation. Once again, Pétain predicted failure and 'useless casualties'. Ribot and Painlevé called for another meeting with Nivelle, this time with his army commanders, on 6 April.

The meeting between the political leaders and Nivelle and his subordinate generals on 6 April 1917 remains one of the most controversial of the war. No minutes were taken in order to encourage a frank exchange of views but several accounts survive of the meeting. It is unclear what Painlevé hoped to achieve. Meetings such as these were not uncommon but it appears that this time Painlevé hoped to bring the debate on the wisdom of Nivelle's offensive to a decisive end. However, if that were the case, then Premier Ribot was, to use a modern term, wildly 'off-message'. Equally, if Painlevé hoped that the army group commanders would force a decision, he was to be disappointed. In the end it seemed as if his nerve failed yet again.

The meeting took place in a railway carriage at Compiègne and was attended by President Poincaré and Premier Ribot representing the government. Nivelle attended as commander-in-chief and was accompanied by his army group commanders, Castelnau, d'Espèrey, Micheler and Pétain. Painlevé opened the meeting, expressing the government's concerns once again about the upcoming offensive. It seems that he tried to be as diplomatic as possible, acknowledging that the conduct of operations fell within Nivelle's remit but pointing out that the government was responsible for the conduct of the war. They needed to review all factors before the offensive was launched, as failure might jeopardise the safety of the nation. Here Painlevé was obviously referring to the situation in Russia, suggesting that defeat might lead to revolution in France. Painlevé discussed the unfavourable strategic situation further, making reference to Italy and Russia and also the hope of American help. (Ironically, the meeting took place on the same day that America declared its entry into the war.) Finally, he pointed out that France was down to her last reserves of manpower, and the losses that would inevitably be incurred might outweigh any strategic gains. Surely, Painlevé argued, to defer the offensive was only wise?

Nivelle's response was measured. It seems certain that he had been expecting this line of inquiry and had prepared himself accordingly. The Russian and Italian situation he acknowledged, but delaying the offensive for America's entry into the war was unwise. In any event, Nivelle pointed out, unrestricted submarine warfare was taking its toll on shipping crossing the Atlantic. To delay now would end all hopes of finishing the war in 1917 and this was, he reminded the assembled parties, the avowed aim of recent Allied conferences. He had never been ordered to go into a defensive posture and abandoning the offensive would allow the Germans, with over forty divisions now available to them, to launch their own attack. The risks associated with delaying were great. An immediate offensive was necessary. Nivelle concluded: 'The offensive alone can give victory; the defensive brings only defeat and shame.' At this point it seems that Premier Ribot became a tad over-excited and started banging his fist on the table and, echoing Nivelle, exclaimed 'The offensive! The offensive! The defensive always leads to defeat!'[23] It was hardly the input that Painlevé was hoping for.

Thus encouraged, Nivelle expanded on his idea, objecting to both a delay or the mounting of a partial, limited offensive:

> The objective of the battle is not to conquer this or that fortified position, to gain a geographic advantage, but to beat and, if possible, destroy the enemy army. There is no such thing as a half battle, neither in time nor in space. If one is considering a deliberate halt in the middle of the effort, on routes already opened through bloody sacrifice, it is better to cancel the offensive at the beginning.[24]

But he reiterated his previous promise to call off the attack within 48 hours if it proved unsuccessful. Satisfied that he had made his point, Nivelle sat back, having delivered this thinly veiled ultimatum. The army commanders spoke next; if Painlevé hoped that they would urge caution and postponement, he was to be largely disappointed. General d'Espèrey pointed out the difficulties of cancelling the attack so close to zero hour. Micheler and Pétain, while they expressed doubts about the possibility of a successful breakthrough, also advised against cancellation. Micheler further pointed out that he thought he could take the first two German lines, but exploitation into the third and fourth lines was not feasible. Pétain now warmed to the subject and stated that he thought the offensive would not achieve any strategic success, and urged for a limited offensive that would focus on the first two German lines. On Nivelle's plan, he stated: 'We have not the means to carry it out. Even if we were to succeed, we could not exploit it. Have we five hundred thousand fresh troops to make such an advance? No. Then it is impossible.'[25]

It was Castelnau, however, who dropped the real bombshell. Having just returned from a fact-finding tour in Russia, Castelnau was very cautious but summed up by stating that, if the government did not believe in Nivelle, they should dismiss him. Sensing the general lack of confidence in him and his plan, Nivelle followed this up by offering his resignation: 'Since I am in agreement neither with the government nor with my own subordinates, the only course open for me is to resign.'[26]

If the politicians were indeed trying to achieve this result, in the minutes that followed they botched the attempt entirely – or perhaps they backed down, realising the political chaos that would follow such a high-profile resignation at this critical juncture. If their aim was to force a postponement, they had also failed miserably in this. It seems that the atmosphere became extremely heated, with both the politicians and the generals urging Nivelle to stay. Pétain, perhaps the sternest critic of the offensive, declared to Nivelle that 'you cannot submit your resignation at this moment. That would have a very bad effect on the army and the country.'[27]

In an effort at damage limitation, Painlevé wrapped up the meeting, summarising that they had agreed to 'an offensive battle followed by the prudent engagement of the reserves if a rupture of the enemy front is obtained, or the halting of the battle if a wide breach is not made in the enemy front in the first efforts'. Echoing Nivelle's previous promises, Ribot announced that 'we will not stubbornly continue the battle indefinitely as we did on the Somme'.[28] This was the last real chance to halt the upcoming offensive. As Winston Churchill later wrote:

> So Nivelle and Painlevé found themselves in the most unhappy positions which mortals can occupy: the Commander having to dare the utmost risks with an entirely sceptical chief behind him; the Minister having to become responsible for a frightful slaughter at the bidding of a General in whose capacity he did not believe, and upon a military policy of the folly of which he was justly convinced. Such is the pomp of power.[29]

Nivelle was now tied to his previous promises to halt the offensive if it was not successful within 24 to 48 hours. He was undertaking a huge gamble. In military parlance, a gamble is an undertaking that you cannot recover from in the event of failure, but Nivelle was committed to the offensive through his previous assurances that his methods would achieve victory. Given his undoubted intelligence, it is difficult to understand just where his unswerving vision came from. It has been suggested that Nivelle was now dangerously under the influence of d'Alançon, who was pushing for offensive action. Pierrefeu later described the atmosphere at GQG at this time and referred to d'Alançon's influence, stating that Nivelle was 'carried away by him'. Pierrefeu later wrote:

> It was plain that Colonel d'Alançon's credit and authority were growing, that he entrusted to no one the care of preparing this great event, and that he found opposition around him of which, in his determined resolve, he took no heed. This silent and frigid giant, formerly indifferent to everything outside his duties, stood revealed as an autocrat of the most pronounced type, convinced of the important part he played, and confident to the extent of rashness in his own star.[30]

In any event, Nivelle seems to have likewise closed his ears and ears to the naysayers and also to solid indications that his plans would encounter grave obstacles. Referring to modern military decision- making metrics, it is obvious that he had made huge errors by April 1917. Nivelle's terrain analysis was poor, as was his intelligence analysis. Indeed, it could be argued that he ignored intelligence totally. He did not plan or wargame for contingencies, and he discouraged debate and dissent within his own staff. Nivelle's response to dissent was to engage in increasingly irritable, over-controlled and paranoid behaviour, mirroring that of his *chef de cabinet*, d'Alançon.

Some of the classic and negative traits that we associate with First World War commanders are sadly visible in Nivelle. He held tenaciously to a belief in the offensive despite ample proof of the costliness of these methods. While he was open to the possibility of new technology and had also tried to introduce methods to increase the effectiveness of artillery, he was also guilty of ignoring evidence that did not fit in with his operational assumptions. Finally, it can only be said that the behaviour of his subordinate generals and the fluctuating attitudes of politicians only facilitated this behaviour. It was perhaps Lloyd George who best summed up Nivelle's transformation: 'General Nivelle in December was a cool and competent planner. By April he had become a crazy plunger.'[31]

Dissent and dispute continued after the Compiègne meeting of 6 April. Pétain continued to argue that the offensive was a 'huge mistake'. Micheler continued to voice his dissent but found that his subordinate, General Mangin, who was a supporter of Nivelle's plans, was bypassing him during the final build-up and was communicating directly with Nivelle. But the die was cast. The BEF supporting operations would begin on 9 April. The Nivelle Offensive itself would begin on 16 April.

Of course, the hundreds of thousands of *poilus* marching to their assembly areas knew none of this. Nivelle had modified Pétain's war cry of the previous year, 'On les aura!' ('We will get them!') to 'On les a!' ('We've got them!'). Confident in victory, they repeated this phrase often as they marched. Army postal censors noted the surge in morale in letters home. One soldier of the 57th Infantry wrote home describing the mood in his assembly area at Fismes:

> Big groups of zouaves and colonial troops were strolling around. The whole French army appeared to have gathered there for the victory push. We were in the grip of a tremendous fever. Officers and men refused to go on leave to make sure they didn't miss the great offensive.[32]

Jules Ninet of the 89th Infantry wrote:

> 'For several days now the amount of noise from the front line has been steadily increasing. The roads are full of soldiers in blue and yellow [colonial troops in khaki], all marching off in the same direction, along with whole columns of artillery, and lorries filled with ammunition and stores. We watch these huge convoys pass by, shake our heads and think, 'Those Boches are going to cop it.'[33]

Unaware of the doubts of their political leaders and Nivelle's fellow generals, the troops jostled and waited for zero hour. For some, the presence of large numbers of tanks in the Fifth Army area reinforced their confidence and seemed to ensure victory. After almost three years of unremitting warfare, the French army gathered itself for victory. Few could have foreseen the extent of the disaster that was about to unfold. General Nivelle's order for 16 April concluded with his characteristic confidence: 'The hour has come! Courage and confidence! Long live France!'[34] There were some ominous notes in soldiers' letters, however. One more pessimistic *poilu* wrote: 'The end will not come in two months as some imagine. I think that if we are still alive one year from now, we won't have got any further than today. If the offensive is launched, that's 500,000 dead men.'[35]

Chapter 4

The French Tank Programme

Can anyone stand up to these machines? No, it's absolutely impossible. So victory is certain! The end of the war! With tanks, why not? Can you stop a tank or kill it?

(Jules Ninet, 89th Infantry)[1]

The timing of the Nivelle Offensive coincided with the first French tanks becoming available to commanders in the field. The French tank programme had been initiated under Joffre but had developed at a slower pace than its British counterpart. On taking command, it became increasingly obvious to Nivelle that by the spring of 1917 a potentially large number of tanks would be available to him. During the weeks that followed, he developed plans to factor the tanks into his attack plan. Unlike the British, Nivelle eventually planned to deploy as many tanks as he could. This would result in the largest tank attack of the war so far. Ultimately, the limitations of the French tanks meant that they did not materialise as the decisive weapon that was hoped for.

By 1915 warfare on the Western Front had ground to a standstill. For the remainder of the war commanders on both sides sought desperately to solve the deadlock. While it is easy to criticise First World War generals for their lack of success in these efforts, and the huge cost in lives, it is also true that they faced a tactical problem never before encountered on such a scale. As lines of trenches snaked from the Belgian coast to the Swiss border, there was no possibility of carrying out a flanking manoeuvre. Frontal assault seemed to be the only option. Over the next few years, commanders sought ways to gain an advantage that might finally allow one of these assaults to succeed.

Various attempts were made to try to break the deadlock. Initially, commanders sought to break their enemy's lines by amassing larger and larger numbers of troops, often without adequate supporting firepower;

such assaults were usually costly failures. The battles of 1915 are striking examples of this failure in tactics, especially in the case of Loos, the Second Battle of Ypres and the Champagne sector offensives of that year. Both sides also sought to deploy more artillery in the belief that devastating artillery barrages would destroy enemy defences and enable their own troops to advance. The vast artillery barrages of the battle of Verdun in 1916 – the initial German barrage expended over a million shells – also proved to be disappointingly indecisive and only chewed up the landscape, making an advance more difficult.[2]

Technology was also deployed and by 1915 both sides had used chemical weapons. For the remainder of the war, various technologies and methods were used in the hope of breaking enemy lines – everything from flamethrowers to underground tunnelling operations.

Distilled down to its essence, the problem was deceptively simple. The initiative in warfare had shifted to the defensive. As defences and trench systems became more elaborate, a tactical stalemate ensued. Barbed wire, sophisticated trenches and an increase in defensive firepower effectively shut down major attacks. Attacking infantry had to cross no-man's-land in the face of devastating rifle, machine-gun and artillery fire. Those who reached the enemy's barbed fire then had to find a way to get through it; if successful in that enterprise, they then had to fight through the enemy trench systems in the hope of achieving a breakout.

It was in this context of tactical stalemate that the French tank programme was born. Indeed, in pre-war France artists and writers had speculated on the nature of the battlefield of the future and also on the use of armoured vehicles. The realities of trench warfare on the Western Front led some French officers and engineers to begin experiments in the development of armoured fighting vehicles. Both France and Britain began developing tanks in 1915 but France did not introduce them into battle until several months after the first British deployment of tanks on the Somme in September 1916. As France's tank programme (or rather programmes) progressed, it was generally agreed that they would not be deployed until they could be amassed in large numbers. Their eventual debut was to come during the Nivelle Offensive in 1917, when more than 120 tanks were deployed in the first-ever mass tank attack. The French tank programmes evolved from a series of diverse influences, which eventually resulted in two major tank designs: the Schneider and the St Chamond.

The French army had been interested in armoured cars since the first one was displayed at the Salon de l'Automobile in Paris in 1902. By the outbreak of war in August 1914 the Ministry of War had already ordered an initial consignment of 136 armoured cars and by September these had been attached to French cavalry formations. These cars were largely confined to the roads and had no cross-country capability. As a result, the stalemate conditions that developed as 1914 progressed ended their usefulness on the battlefield. The armoured cars had, however, shown that they could withstand rifle and machine-gun fire and also shell splinters. The emphasis then turned to exploring the possibility of developing a tracked (rather than wheeled) armoured fighting vehicle.[3]

In 1915 early experiments began in developing such a tracked armoured vehicle. Some of these experiments proved to be less than promising. The French army's *Section Technique du Genie* (STG) built ten armoured tractors based on the Filtz agricultural tractor system. It was hoped that these could cut through barbed wire while also serving as mobile machine-gun platforms. Combat trials in the Verdun sector in late 1915 proved to be disappointing. Further efforts were made to develop an armoured wheeled tractor based on the Archer system, and also a wheeled, wire-cutting tractor known as the Breton-Prétot machine. In 1915 there were also trials of an armoured steamroller. All these designs were limited by the lack of performance and unsuitability of the civilian tractor designs upon which they were based; agricultural and construction tractor designs were difficult to reconfigure for military use. This problem would in fact hamper the future projects of both French and British designers.

The French also experimented with remote-control tracked vehicles. These were the Aubriot-Gabet and Schneider-Crocodile land torpedoes or *chariots lance-bombes* ('bomb-throwing vehicles'). These small vehicles used electric engines and it was intended that they would be driven into the enemy wire carrying explosive charges that would then be detonated to create a breach. Neither proved effective. Similarly the two devices designed by Louis Boirault to breach enemy wire – the *Diplodocus militaris* ('Military

Dinosaur') and the *Appareil Boirault No. 2* – both proved over-elaborate and vulnerable in trials.

The development of the first remotely practical French armoured fighting vehicle took place at the armaments firm of M.M. Schneider & Cie. The chief engineer at Schneider's Creusot plant, Eugène Brillié, visited England in January 1915 with another Schneider engineer to view trials of tracked vehicles. As a result of this visit, the Schneider company bought two Holt caterpillar tractors with the aim of developing them as artillery tractors. These tractors were tested at the Creusot works in May 1915 and the idea developed of using the lighter of the tractors, the 45hp Baby Holt, as the basis for an armoured fighting vehicle. Brillié proposed adding an armoured superstructure with machine-gun positions in order to create a tracked vehicle for the cavalry that was capable of operating off-road. By July the design process was well advanced and by August the Creusot engineers had developed a set of plans that basically envisioned a lengthening and widening of the Baby Holt chassis in order to allow for the development of a more practical fighting vehicle.

At this point the project stalled, due to the opposition and interference of Jules-Louis Breton, a government official who served as undersecretary of state for inventions. Breton's opposition was not entirely objective. Apart from his official role in the Ministry for Inventions, he was an engineer and inventor himself and had developed the Breton-Prétot wire-cutting tractor mentioned earlier. Breton's design incorporated a mechanical wire-cutter mounted on an agricultural tractor, and trials in August had been well received. The basis for Breton's design was, however, the Bajac wheeled tractor, which proved inadequate for the task. Through his position within the Ministry for Inventions, Breton convinced officials at the Ministry of War to place an order at the Schneider plant for ten of his devices using the available Holt caterpillar tractor units. This design would ultimately prove unsuccessful but trials were undertaken between December 1915 and February 1916. The time and effort spent trying to develop mobile wire-cutters was shown to be utterly futile but it was found that the tracked tractor units were capable of crashing through barbed wire entanglements on their own.[4]

At this point the development of France's first tank design gained momentum, largely due to the timely intervention of Colonel Jean-Baptiste Eugène Estienne. An artillery officer in General Pétain's Sixth Division, Estienne had already established a reputation as a military innovator. Born in 1860, he was commissioned into the French army in 1883 as a second lieutenant in the artillery. He was one of a new generation of inquiring, scientific officers and in 1880 he presented a treatise on ballistics to the French Académie des Sciences. This ground-breaking work served to stimulate further debate on the development of indirect fire methods. Estienne rose quickly and by 1907 he had been appointed as commandant at the artillery school in Grenoble. He was an advocate of early telephone systems, realising that these would allow artillery batteries to coordinate with forward observers. This would facilitate changing targets and could also make indirect fire and creeping barrages more effective. In 1909, with promotion to lieutenant-colonel, he was appointed to command the Fifth Aviation Group at Lyon. Military aviation was at this time still in its infancy but one of its primary roles was seen as artillery-spotting and Estienne, as a progressive artillery officer, was seen as a logical choice for command of this new unit.[5]

At the outbreak of war he was appointed to command the 22nd Artillery Regiment, which formed part of Pétain's division. At the Battle of Charleroi on 21 August 1914 Estienne's artillery took a heavy toll of the advancing German formations. While the battle resulted in a German victory, Estienne laid down a devastating artillery fire, coordinating his guns with spotter planes. The impact of rifle and machine-gun fire on the infantry made a huge impression on him and he was one of the advocates of providing attacking infantry with some form of protective armoured shield. Some trials of primitive wheeled armoured devices were later carried out by the French army.

Estienne was alive to the possibilities of technology. In a prophetic remark, he stated to his officers, 'Gentlemen, the victory in this war will belong to which of the two belligerents which will be the first to place a gun of 75mm on a vehicle able to be driven on all terrain.' He is considered by many historians of the French army to be the *Père des Chars* (Father of the Tank).

During the summer of 1915 Estienne heard of the experiments being carried out by the Schneider company under Brillié and he sent a series of letters to General Joffre, who was then still commander-in-chief. Despite Estienne's reputation, these letters initially did not get beyond Joffre's staff officers. In their defence, they were deluged with letters from officers, politicians and the general public suggesting ideas, many of them of a crackpot nature, on how the deadlock on the Western Front could be broken. Estienne's idea was for the conversion of tracked tractors to produce 'land battleships' for tackling German machine-gun nests. Armed with 37mm guns and two machine guns, these vehicles would be capable of clearing barbed-wire entanglements, crossing trenches and also towing an armoured trailer holding twenty infantrymen. On 1 December 1915 Estienne wrote directly to Joffre and was subsequently granted an interview with General Maurice Janin, who was responsible for equipment on Joffre's staff.

In the meantime, Estienne had attended the prototype trials at Souain on 9 December. Souain was a former battlefield and had surviving defences and trench systems. Here, a prototype tank design, based on the Baby Holt tractor and following the 'armoured wire-cutter' concept, was put through its paces. The vehicle performed reasonably well and was found to be able to clear shell holes and cross trenches of up to a metre wide. However, water obstacles and trenches wider than this proved to be beyond the vehicle's capacity. The official report stated that 'the machine can only cross through a cut-up terrain if some basic trench sustainment is prepared'.[6] The relatively small size of the prototype meant that in any potential battlefield situation, it would have to be accompanied by infantry or engineers tasked with filling in sections of trench in order to allow the vehicle to cross. In essence, this negated the potential of the vehicle as a 'breakthrough' weapon.

Despite these limitations, Estienne was convinced that the prototype could be developed and following his meeting with Janin on 12 December 1915 he was granted permission to approach several arms manufacturers to discuss the possibility of taking the project further. On 20 December he met Louis Renault at his factory in Paris. Renault was simply overwhelmed with various war projects at this time and simply could not commit to another development idea. Later the same day Estienne met Eugène Brillié at the Schneider plant; almost immediately, he signed up to the idea of producing an armoured fighting vehicle. Brillié had, after all, been involved in Schneider's earlier tests with the Baby Holt tractor. It proved to be a fortuitous partnership. Estienne had combat experience and knowledge of the challenges posed by the new battlefield. Brillié had the technical knowledge to design the new vehicle and also a connection to a major armaments firm.

Thereafter the programme gathered momentum. Brillié discussed the project with senior company officials at Schneider and was given the go-ahead to advance the project. On 27 December, a week after his initial meeting with Estienne, Brillié completed a preliminary design. The following day Estienne presented this design to Janin and also outlined plans for the construction of 300–400 machines. On 31 January 1916 Joffre sanctioned the plan and wrote to the undersecretary of state for war, requesting that 400 vehicles be built following the design developed by Estienne and Brillié.

The supply of these new vehicles rested with the Army Technical Services, but they did not look on this scheme with favour as it had not been initiated by them. However, on 26 February 1916 the Ministry of War confirmed an order with the Schneider company for the supply of 400 machines. Production was to take place at Schneider's SOMUA facility (Société d'outillage méchanique et d'usinage artillerie) at St-Ouen on the outskirts of Paris.

While most people referred to such vehicles using the generic term 'tank', following the British example, in France these vehicles were initially given the cover name of 'Tracteurs Estienne'. Estienne himself preferred the title 'chars d'assaut' – assault vehicles. They were also referred to as 'chars Schneider' or 'Chars CA' in official correspondence of the time. It is interesting to note that the French order for the Schneider was placed only two weeks later than the British government's first order for tanks and involved four times as many tanks. Yet the production process in France was to prove to be very slow and the first tank was completed later than its British counterpart.

The basic design was not far removed from Estienne's own early ideas. The main differences were that it was to have a shortened version of the 75mm gun rather than the 37mm gun originally envisaged by Estienne, and a crew of six, rather than the four-man crew that was initially planned. The 75mm gun was mounted in the front right of the tank in a mount that allowed

Contemporary portrait of General Robert Nivelle from *L'Illustration*. On being appointed, Nivelle became the focus of a publicity campaign and was lauded by both French and British politicians. (*Author's Collection*)

General Charles Mangin. Tough and ruthless, Mangin had served with Nivelle at Verdun. He would play a major role in Nivelle's plans for 1917. (*Author's Collection*)

General Joseph Joffre. Hailed as a national hero in 1914, Joffre had long outlived his usefulness by 1916. His fall from grace would facilitate the rise of Nivelle. (*Library of Congress*)

Paul Painlevé, Minister for War in the Ribot government. Popular and highly intelligent, he ultimately failed to halt Nivelle's plans. (*Library of Congress*)

General Nivelle at his HQ, 1917. This is one of a series of publicity photographs taken of Nivelle in 1916 and 1917. This copy was signed by Nivelle during his 1920 tour of the USA. (*Author's Collection*)

French troops in 1914. This publicity photograph shows troops preparing to engage in a campaign of open warfare. By late 1914 all such misconceptions had been dispelled. (*SHD*)

NCO and warrant officers on a machine-gun course. During the course of the war the French army endeavoured to increase the firepower available to infantry units. (*Author's Collection*)

A French *Poilu* of 1917. A far cry from the dashing troops of 1914, this infantryman's uniform and equipment reflect the realities of trench warfare by 1917. (*SHD*).

Fort Brimont. This fortification was taken by German troops early in the war. The remains of the fort would prove to be a considerable obstacle for attacking troops in 1917. (*Author's Collection*)

Cartoon depicting Nivelle from La Rire. This cartoon makes a play on the French word for 'to level' – *niveleur*. Hence, 'Nivelle the leveller'. (*Author's Collection*)

Cheerful French troops on their way to the offensive, 1917. Observers reported the high morale of the troops before the offensive began. (*Author's Collection*)

Poster depicting colonial troops of the French army. Troops from North Africa and Senegal were to play a major role, and suffer huge casualties, in the opening attacks in April 1917. (*Author's Collection*)

French aerodrome, 1917, with an early version of the SPAD. Despite their best efforts the French *Service Aeronautique* lost control of the skies over the Chemin des Dames at an early stage. (*Library of Congress*)

Hurtebise Farm before the war. (*Author's Collection*)

The remains of Hurtebise Farm in 1917. German troops had dug-in in the remains and cellars of the former farm. The fighting to clear this position was intense. (*Author's Collection*)

Destroyed French Schneider tanks. The slow-moving Schneiders proved to be highly vulnerable to German artillery. French troops have stripped out some spares from these destroyed tanks. (*Author's Collection*)

Contemporary illustration of a St Chamond tank. This second French tank version saw its combat debut in the later attacks in May. The over-long superstructure is obvious here. This often resulted in St Chamonds becoming trapped nose-down in German trenches. (*Author's Collection*)

French troops examine German defences. Such pillboxes were invisible to air reconnaissance and caught attacking troops by surprise. (*Author's Collection*)

US troops inspecting a German pillbox in 1918. The Germans continued to employ networks of these simple but effective field fortifications until the end of the war. (*Author's Collection*)

The Chemin des Dames battlefield. Human remains are clearly visible in this devastated landscape. (*Author's Collection*)

General Pétain and King George V. In the months following the offensive Pétain not only had to suppress a series of army mutinies, but also needed to rebuild the army. (*Author's Collection*)

Renault FT17 tank. While early French tank projects had been disappointing, the FT17 was a more successful design and was the first tank to have a turret capable of rotating through 360 degrees. (*Library of Congress*)

The theme of the 'Grand Guerre' inspired generations of French artists. This is Jean Droit's 'Les Boues de la Somme' (1916), which captures the grim realities of the existence of so many poilus. (*Author's Collection*)

General Nivelle during a visit to the USA in 1920, contributing to a Christmas Fund for wounded and sick soldiers. Despite the disastrous effects of his failed offensive, by 1920 he had returned to public favour and he was warmly received in the USA. (*Author's Collection*)

Since the end of the war various monuments have been erected on the Chemin des Dames battlefield. This is Christian Lapie's ensemble of sculptures entitled *Constellation de la Douleur*. Unveiled in 2007, it is a powerful and moving monument to those who died. (*Courtesy of Christian Lapie*)

it to be swivelled through an arc of 20 degrees. The Schneider also mounted two Hotchkiss machine guns in ball mounts on either side. It carried 90 rounds for the 75mm gun and more than 3,800 machine-gun rounds. In its basic design, the Schneider consisted of an armoured box hull mounted on a modified Baby Holt tracked chassis. The chassis had been lengthened to aid trench crossing and tails were fitted to the rear to further facilitate this. A wire-cutting device was also mounted on the tank's ship-like bow. The tank's armour was to be 11.5mm thick. Fully loaded, the Schneider weighed more than 13 tons and its four-cylinder Schneider engine only generated 70hp. This gave the tank a top speed of 6km/h (3.7mph).

The first prototype was completed in March 1916. The Schneider may appear primitive to modern eyes, but its development presented numerous challenges to the engineers and workers at the SOMUA plant. This was particularly true of the process for making the armoured plate. Completing the initial order for 400 vehicles posed a series of problems for the Schneider company and the first production model was not delivered until September 1916. By the end of November only eight vehicles had been delivered, of which five were training versions without hardened steel plate. Early trials of the prototype also emphasised the slowness of the vehicle and its difficulty in crossing trenches. This would factor into a debate among officers of the fledgling tank service and also officers at divisional and army command level. While the programme had been intended to develop a breakthrough weapon, in reality the new tanks did not have the performance to make this concept a reality.[7]

The limitations of the new tanks did convince the GQG that, when they were finally deployed, they would have to be deployed in sufficient numbers to maximize the surprise effect on the Germans. These plans were compromised, however, by the British decision to deploy a relatively small number of tanks on the Somme in September 1916. Field Marshal Haig had originally intended to incorporate tanks into the battle plan for the first day of the Somme offensive in July but they had not been delivered in time. By September, when planning was under way for the Flers-Courcelette offensive, the tanks were available; Haig had requested a hundred tanks, but only forty-nine were ready. The Flers-Courcelette offensive was a classic breakthrough attempt, where it was hoped that massed artillery and infantry would break the German lines and allow for exploitation by the cavalry. The use of tanks in such small numbers was, and has remained, a controversial decision. Ernest Swinton, a former member of the Landships Committee, and a major protagonist in the development of the British programme, warned against the premature use of the tank.

As Flers-Courcelette also included French army participation, the French GQG got wind of Haig's plans and protested. Both Estienne and Jean-Louis Breton were sent to London in the hope of convincing the government to overrule Haig. These efforts were in vain and the available tanks were deployed in battle on 15 September.[8]

This first-ever use of tanks in battle was far from decisive. Of the forty-nine available, only thirty-two had reached their start lines by zero hour. Of these, seven broke down, leaving just twenty-five to carry out the attack. Only nine of them would reach and pass through the German lines. Quite apart from mechanical issues, the tanks found it difficult to cross the broken ground at anything more than walking pace. They did, however, prove to be a huge psychological asset for the attacking troops and had a corresponding negative effect on the Germans. The attack took the hamlets of Martinpuich, Flers and Courcelette, and also the much-fought-over 'High Wood'. It was reported that the tanks performed particularly well at Flers. Debate on Haig's decision to deploy this small tank force still continues but it seems probable that he viewed this action as a combat test for the tanks. He immediately requested more and suggested that their design should be improved. Those who had been involved in the long and difficult development process were far from happy, however. Winston Churchill, the former chairman of the Landships Committee, commented 'My poor "land battleships" have been let off prematurely on a petty scale', while in his *War Memoirs*, Lloyd George, the British Minister for Munitions in 1916, later wrote:

> The decision of the army chiefs to launch the first handful of [tanks] on a comparatively local operation has always appeared to me to have been a foolish blunder. I saw the Prime Minister and begged him to intervene authoritatively. [The answer was:] 'Haig wants them.' So the great secret was sold for the battered ruin of a little hamlet on the Somme, which was not worth capturing.[9]

The French were understandably furious. Estienne correctly concluded that, now that the Germans knew this technology was available to the Allies, they would take countermeasures to limit their potential in future attacks. Estienne suspected that the Germans would plant mines, widen their trenches and also bring larger numbers of light artillery pieces up to their front lines. He was to be proved largely correct. Estienne was also acutely aware that the trench-crossing ability of the French Schneider was actually worse than that of the British tanks. The British Mark Is deployed at Flers were of a rhomboidal shape, and this allowed for overhead tracks. Despite this, the British Mark Is had crossed obstacles and trenches only with difficulty. How would the Schneiders fare with their shorter tracks? The inadequate nature of the Schneider's armour also became apparent and the struggling construction programme had to factor in an up-armouring process. Extra 8mm plates were to be added and these modifications were facilitated with the dispatch of 'surblindé' kits to up-armour the Schneiders that had already been completed.

Estienne was also forced to revise his tactical ideas. He had originally planned for the French tanks to attack in large formations ahead of the infantry. On crossing the first line of German trenches, one half would remain as infantry support to contain the German defenders until the infantry arrived to secure the enemy trenches. Any level of surprise was no longer possible and Estienne realised that it was likely that the tanks would have to fulfil a more diminished role – that of reducing machine-gun positions and strongpoints in the enemy lines and effectively acting as infantry support. Some hopes of using tanks as breakthrough weapons still remained and tank commanders were instructed that they could move ahead of the infantry if the opportunity presented itself.

Numbers remained a problem. By 25 November 1916 all 400 Schneider tanks should have been delivered but only eight had actually been supplied to units. By January 1917 there were still only thirty-two training tanks. The delays were due not only to the manufacturing problems at the SOMUA plant but also to the fact that a second tank design was now in production. This was the St Chamond, which had been developed by the Army Technical Services. Both programmes had to compete for available resources. At 23 tons, the St Chamond was considerably larger than the Schneider at 13.5

tons. It also had an enormous superstructure in relation to its track length, and in trials performed very poorly across country. Nevertheless, as the design project had been initiated from within the army itself, it was factored into the overall programme and further delayed delivery of the Schneider tanks.[10]

The final delaying factor was General Nivelle himself. On taking command in December 1916, Nivelle began redirecting resources in keeping with his vision for his planned offensive. He was an artillery officer and wished to find ways make the artillery more effective. Based on his experiences in the battle of Verdun, he realised that mobility was key so he requested that priority be given to the production of tractor units for the towing of artillery.[11]

As increasing numbers of Schneider tanks became available in early 1917, they were organised into units. There were tank depots and training centres at Marly near Paris and Cercottes near Orléans, with a tank camp at Champieu behind the front lines. The first French tank units were formed within the artillery branch and classed as *Artillerie Speciale* (AS) and as a result the units were organised along artillery lines. Each *groupe* consisted of four batteries of four tanks each. There were also associated supply, recovery and workshop units. By March 1917 there were also two groups of St Chamond tanks. In all, seventeen Schneider groups were formed, numbered AS1 to AS 17. Eight of these groups were committed to the initial phase of the Nivelle offensive (AS 2, 3, 4, 5, 6, 7, 8 and 9), while some St Chamonds would take part in the last phases of the battle in May.

The officers and crews for this new tank force came from a number of sources. Most were from artillery and cavalry units but there were also some officers and men from the navy. Many lacked technical and mechanical skills. Also, considering that some of the Schneider groups were formed as late as March 1917, just a month before the offensive, it is certain that some of these crews were relatively inexperienced.

On the eve of the offensive, it could be argued that the fledgling French tank force had made great progress. Estienne had achieved a huge success in initially gaining sanction for the programme but thereafter the story of the French tank force had been dogged with technical, political and administrative delays. Also, while the French were undoubtedly correct in husbanding their tanks until they were ready to deploy them *en masse*, the

Schneiders were vehicles of limited potential while their crews were vastly inexperienced. In total, 132 tanks (128 Schneiders and 4 St Chamonds) would be deployed during the Nivelle Offensive, carrying out the first mass tank attack in military history.

Chapter 5

The Offensive

This offensive? It's got to be our final effort, the end of all our suffering; it's got to bring a quick victory and put the enemy to rout. Everyone's talking about it and we're all confident. Everything's been carefully planned and any problems anticipated. High command has even had the forethought to tell us where, when and for how long we must pause before going forward. That might perhaps be taking it a bit too far.

(Georges Bonnamy, 131st Infantry)[1]

The opening phase of the Nivelle Offensive was preceded by a series of British attacks in the Arras sector. As part of the agreement with the British, the BEF under Field Marshal Haig was to begin offensive operations in advance of the French main effort (*see* Map 3.) It was hoped that the British offensive, and also other smaller French offensives, would keep the Germans off-balance and draw in their reserves. It was also hoped that if the main effort on the Chemin des Dames was successful, further pressure by the BEF would break the line elsewhere and precipitate a catastrophic collapse of the German army. The main focus of the British operation was the Arras sector, where they hoped to break through to the north and south of the town and then wrest control of the high ground to the east that dominated the plain of Douai. Having achieved this breakthrough, and if Nivelle was successful in his own offensive, then a war of movement would follow.

The British line extended from Vimy in the north to Bullecourt in the south-east (*see* Map 3). The main French effort on the Chemin des Dames would take place about 80km to the south. The BEF faced considerable difficulties on the ground. Haig's plan had also been affected by the German withdrawal to the Hindenburg Line and he had to adapt his plans to a rapidly unfolding situation. The attack, or more accurately series of attacks, took place along a 20km section of the front line, where the terrain had some problematic features and obstacles such as the Scarpe river. Also, the Germans had fortified the ruined towns and villages in the area, not to mention the ridgeline at Vimy, which dominated the surrounding area.[2] The attacking British forces also encountered the German defence-in-depth system and progress proved difficult once the attack had begun.

Haig had three armies concentrated in the Arras sector: First Army (Horne), Third Army (Allenby) and Fifth Army (Gough). These armies were composed of not only British troops but also Australians, New Zealanders and Canadians. Fourteen British divisions took part in the assault on the first day, with a further nine in reserve. They were opposed by the German Sixth Army (von Falkenhausen) and Second Army (von der Marwitz). In keeping with the new German defensive philosophy, the German forces were organised in three groups (Gruppes Souchez, Vimy and Arras), with nine divisions in the front line and a further eight in reserve. It was hoped that this concentration of the BEF would give the British armies local superiority at their point of attack. The German Sixth Army, for example, held its section of the front with six divisions but it would be attacked by fourteen British divisions. This facilitated an initial British advance but the German commanders' disposition of their troops allowed them to react to the British attack and to send counterattack divisions to plug the line.

The weeks that preceded the British attack saw massive preparations. Since October 1916 tunnelling companies had been burrowing into the chalky soil of the sector to create an elaborate series of deep underground bunkers. By April 1917 they had built enough underground bunkers to conceal more than 20,000 men. This would allow the British to move forward assault forces by night and then conceal them from observation. Furthermore, the tunnelling companies excavated assault tunnels towards the German lines. These would be blown at zero hour and would allow the attacking troops to emerge close to the German line. Conventional mines were also buried under the front line to be blown at zero hour. The Germans ran countermining operations and a grim subterranean war developed that claimed the lives of many BEF tunnellers.

A similar amount of energy was put into building new roads and supply depots, and an extremely elaborate artillery plan was developed. The Royal

Flying Corps made a huge effort to obtain local superiority over Arras in order to conduct reconnaissance operations. This resulted in significant RFC losses as they struggled to compete with squadrons of the German Air Service (the *Luftstreitkräfte*), which had better planes and more experienced pilots. In March and April RFC losses mounted. April, known as 'Bloody April' within the RFC, was the worst month, with 245 aircraft shot down, resulting in 211 aircrew killed or missing and a further 108 being taken prisoner. Manfred von Richthofen's Jasta 11 alone shot down eighty-nine British aircraft. Apart from the fact that the German aircraft were superior, they were also operating mostly over their own territory. To counter the mounting casualties, many new RFC pilots were rushed to the front before their training was complete. The results were shocking, with many of these inexperienced young men lasting only a day or two before being shot down. It was an extremely high price to pay for 'eyes on' the German defences but this costly effort would aid the artillery greatly in the preliminary and assault barrages.

During the final stages of Haig's preparations he also found himself being drawn into the political debate on Nivelle's fitness to command. After an extremely fractious beginning, the relationship between Nivelle and Haig had improved greatly. It seems that Nivelle gradually became more courteous in his dealings with his British counterpart, and Haig shared his desire for a decisive battle that would end the war in 1917. Following a meeting on 23 March Haig wrote: 'He is in complete agreement with me regarding the general plan, namely to launch our attacks as arranged and, if the enemy does not await our attack, to follow him up and, at the same time, to organise attacks elsewhere.' Haig continued: 'Nivelle was most pleasant and, I think, is a straightforward man. On the whole, I like Nivelle, but he seems rather under the influence of Colonel d'Alançon, who dislikes the British.'[3]

The following day, Haig was visited by Painlevé, who tried to sound him out regarding Nivelle's plans. Showing considerable loyalty and consideration to Nivelle, Haig recorded that:

> I was careful to say that he struck me as a capable general and that I was, of course, ready to cooperate with whoever was chosen by the French government to be their commander-in-chief. I said that my

relations with Nivelle are, and have always been, excellent. The Calais conference was a mistake, but it was not Nivelle's fault.[4]

It was somewhat ironic that Haig defended Nivelle, who had previously tried to undermine him, while his thinly veiled barbed comment towards politicians cannot have gone unnoticed by Painlevé.

The British attack was preceded by a five-day preliminary bombardment by more than 2,800 guns. This was an intensive and sophisticated barrage that would expend more than 2.6 million shells, including thousands of gas shells. This was more than a million more shells than had been used on the Somme the previous year. New fuse heads were used, notably the No. 106, which detonated on hitting barbed wire; this was a development resulting from the poor wire-cutting capabilities demonstrated by the British artillery during the Somme offensive. The RFC had done considerable work in 'flash-spotting' to identify the German artillery and sound-ranging methods would also be used. On the first day of the offensive, therefore, the artillery would neutralise many of the German guns, some sources claiming that as many as 80 per cent of the German artillery units had difficulty in bringing their guns into action. Finally, once the attack was under way, a creeping barrage would move across no-man's-land and shield the advancing troops. This would deny the Germans the time to man their trenches and bring their machine guns into action. Machine guns were also factored into the artillery plan to avoid long-range interdicting fire. Of course, the intensity of the preliminary barrage telegraphed the British intentions to the enemy and any hope of achieving surprise was lost.[5]

The BEF's attack opened at dawn (5.30am) on 9 April 1917, Easter Monday. The dreadful winter weather had continued into an unseasonably cold spring and the attack started in conditions of driving rain and sleet. After a final, brief, hurricane bombardment, the troops left the trenches. The offensive met with initial success, and Allenby's Third Army advanced 3km on the first day. This first phase (9–14 April) included what came to be known as the Battle of the Scarpe, where the attacking troops confounded German plans to use their 'elastic defence' methods. The German commander, von Falkenhausen, was later severely criticised for not bringing his counterattack divisions into action more quickly. The Canadian Corps was also successful at Vimy Ridge, passing through the German defences to capture this key terrain feature by 1pm on Day 1, despite suffering heavy casualties (more than 14,000 killed, wounded or missing). In some places the Canadians penetrated the German defences to a depth of almost 4km. The fighting around the village of Bullecourt on 10–11 April proved less successful, however, as the German reaction became more organised. The eleven tanks supporting the BEF suffered mechanical problems and this caused delays. Advancing British and Australian troops found wire uncut, while erroneous reports about their success resulted in their artillery support being called off. Following a bitter contest in the German lines, the attackers were driven back and two of the tanks were captured by the Germans. For the Australians 11 April saw their worst day's losses on the Western Front.

On 14 April Haig halted operations in order to await news of Nivelle's attack on the Chemin des Dames. There followed an operational hiatus as artillery was repositioned and supplies brought up before a second phase of operations ran from 15 April to 17 May. These were run in conjunction with the French main effort, which kicked off on 16 April. The attacking BEF forces were met by German reinforcements that looked increasingly effective and organised. The results of this month of phased BEF attacks were mixed. At Lagnicourt the Australians fought off heavy German counterattacks and, although their lines were breached and they even lost some artillery, they finally restored their own line. Two further assaults were carried out in the Scarpe sector, both being called off after only limited gains. The Canadian and British troops were more successful at Arleux in an operation to secure the south-eastern flank of Vimy ridge. Yet, despite achieving their objectives and beating off German counterattacks, they too suffered heavy casualties. Another phase of operations at Bullecourt (3–17 May) succeeded in securing that village and making some other limited gains before being called off in the face of mounting casualties.

In the final analysis the Battle of Arras had been a very uneven experience for Haig and the BEF. The first few days had seen a surprising level of success and territorial gains – modest from a modern viewpoint but quite spectacular by First World War Western Front standards. Thereafter the fighting followed a grimly familiar pattern as the Germans reacted. There were difficulties in coordinating infantry, artillery, tanks and aircraft.

Continued attacks brought few gains but huge casualties. By the end of the offensive the British had suffered more than 150,000 casualties. German losses were around 100,000.[6]

The German commander Erich von Ludendorff later commented that 'no doubt exceedingly important strategic objects lay behind the British attack, but I have never been able to discover what they were'.[7] Despite his comments, and the fact that the defenders had inflicted such heavy casualties on the BEF, Ludendorff was not happy with how the 'elastic defence' method had been used. Von Falkenhausen was removed from command, as were several other senior German commanders, and the Germans began a major reappraisal of their operational methods.

In Britain the government tried to present the battle as a success. It was a hard sell. There was serious criticism of the conduct of the battle in the press, and Allenby, who had played a significant role in formulating the BEF's operational plan, was removed and sent to the Middle East, where he later enjoyed great success. Criticism of Haig's persistence in maintaining the offensive continues to this day. As the German defence solidified, it was argued that he should have shut down the offensive after the initial phase. While there is some truth in this, Haig was tied by the agreement with the French and felt duty-bound to continue with the offensive, especially when the extent of French difficulties became apparent later in April.

Apart from the operations carried out by the BEF in support of Nivelle's main effort, the French and Belgian armies also engaged in further supplementary attacks. The largest of these was carried out by General Franchet d'Espèrey's GAN, which was initially tasked with maintaining pressure on the Hindenburg Line through artillery bombardments and limited ground attacks. D'Espèrey realized, however, that the Germans had artillery observation posts in the high ground in his zone. These, he argued, could be used to call in artillery support for the German defenders further south once Nivelle began his attack. On 29 March he secured permission from Nivelle to use his Third Army to attack the German positions near St Quentin in order to deny them these artillery observation posts. Once Micheler's GAR began its attack, he would increase the intensity of his own operations in order to threaten the German artillery positions opposite his Third Army. It could be argued that this was engaging in a level of 'mission creep' quite late in the planning process. Yet D'Espèrey's plan had considerable merit as artillery fire from flanking German positions had effectively closed down many previous attacks. Other late additions to Nivelle's plan included a limited attack by the Belgian army and also an artillery demonstration by the French Seventh Army in the Vosges.[8]

Despite these sideshows, the weight of the artillery bombardment in the Chemin des Dames sector clearly telegraphed where the main blow would fall. On 2 April the French artillery units began registering their guns and also engaging in counter-battery fire. On 5 April the bombardment increased in its intensity and switched from known German battery positions to defensive positions. By 9 April the majority of the French batteries were engaged and busily pounded the German lines. Between 1 April and 5 May Micheler's artillery would fire over 11 million rounds in the largest barrage yet seen. On 15 April, the day before the attack commenced, the artillery conducted barrages of chemical rounds. During the course of this barrage the artillery stopped firing altogether on several occasions to give the impression that the infantry assault was about to commence. The French guns then reopened their fire on the German defenders who had rushed to their positions expecting an imminent attack. As the main French attack was now expected daily, the Germans carried out their final defensive preparations. On 11 April General von Liebert tried to boost his troops' morale in his order for the day:

> The time has come for the decisive combat. The strengthening of the enemy fire tells of an imminent assault on our trenches. Our braves from the Rhineland, Hanover and, of course, the Guard regiments will fight dearly for their positions. I trust that not one man will give himself up.[9]

Following consultation with Haig, Nivelle delayed the date for the offensive until 16 April because of the bad weather. The deteriorating conditions had a major impact on the French preparations. In the final days of the lead-up, there were periods of freezing weather followed by torrential downpours of icy rain, sleet and even snow. Roads were washed away, resulting in delays in moving up men, supplies and ammunition. These problems caused delays in resupplying the artillery batteries with shells and in places the preliminary bombardment slackened. These pauses in the bombardment led officers on Nivelle's staff to have doubts about its effectiveness in cutting the enemy wire. One officer wrote, 'the preparation is not what we hoped, what we expected. The infantry will find itself facing strong resistance. They will find the breaches not made or repaired.'[10]

The terrain, which Nivelle had dismissed as being inconsequential, also had a major impact on the effectiveness of the bombardment. French artillery fire simply could not reach German positions on the reverse slope of the Chemin des Dames. As a result, German defences and troops on the far side of the ridgeline remained largely untouched. A dense freezing fog covered the battlefield on occasion, making artillery observation impossible. General Micheler commented that 'during the preparation and the day of attack, the observation of [artillery] fire, either by aerial observers or even by ground observers, was impeded considerably by very unfavourable atmospheric conditions'.[11]

In the run-up to the offensive, 14 April was the only day free from rain, snow, fog or strong winds. The weather gods were clearly not on Nivelle's side. As a result, reconnaissance flights were limited and those that did take place were largely ineffective. Alongside the weather issues, the German air service gained local superiority over the Chemin des Dames and this severely restricted French aerial reconnaissance. To be effective, the French artillery plan required coordination from the air; in the event, in the run-up to the attack, the French were not in a position to register and adjust their artillery properly.

For the troops on the ground, the build-up was dominated by the miserable weather. The men were constantly wet and cold and the colonial troops found these conditions particularly demoralizing. For the artillery, the frequent downpours often washed out their gun positions, thus requiring a period of frantic activity to rebuild the emplacements. The horses of the cavalry, artillery and supply units often became bogged down on the roads.

Before the attack the infantry were instructed to lighten their packs. Attacking troops were to carry their rifles, 120 rounds of ammunition, three hand grenades and two rifle grenades, two waterbottles, a spade, a gas mask, a food haversack, a tent section and a rolled blanket. All other equipment was to be left behind in order to facilitate the expected swift advance. The sodden terrain and prevailing weather conditions did not favour rapid movement, however.

Even so, Nivelle remained hopeful. On 4 April he issued his final instructions to his army group commanders. Characteristically, these concentrated on the planned movements that would follow the breakthrough. Nivelle reiterated that 'the objective remains the destruction of the principal mass of the enemy's forces on the Western Front'. This sense of optimism was somewhat downplayed by later tactical guidelines circulated by Nivelle's staff, which stated that 'the spirit of the offensive is not incompatible with caution'.[12]

On 15 April unit commanders received a manila envelope containing their final instructions. They were informed that the attack was set for the following day, with H Hour ('zero hour') planned for 6am. They passed on these orders to their men, and encouraged them to write a last letter home. After a meal they slept, or tried to, before being roused to begin assembling at 3.30 the following morning.

After weeks of political turmoil, contention and military preparation and planning, the much-delayed offensive began at 6am on the morning of 16 April. There were final orders groups during the night in the pouring rain as the troops assembled in the assault trenches. Now, as their officers blew their whistles, they clambered from the trenches and headed into no-man's-land. In some parts of the line regimental colours were held aloft by officers in the trenches as the troops advanced.

In retrospect, the taskings allocated to the attacking troops seem wildly optimistic. The troops of II Colonial Corps in Mangin's Sixth Army were expected to cover 6km within six hours and to cross over the top of the Chemin des Dames ridgeline. In reality they would achieve nothing like this. On the section of the front attacked by the Sixth Army, the advance encountered severe difficulties. Before the attack began, a French officer described a map brief on the German defences:

> There, between the two ink lines which define our sector, are exactly five lines of trenches that we must storm in one go: the Memel, Dresden, Brahms, Inglau and Kreutzer trenches. They are connected by a number of communication trenches; in between are printed

small crosses which represent wire lines and small arrows standing for machine guns are pointing in every direction. The whole thing looks unprepossessing enough. But probably nothing much of this remains?[13]

Mangin had thirty-seven infantry divisions under his command, with a cavalry division and two territorial divisions in reserve. In his first line of attack, he placed eight of his infantry divisions in four corps:

- I Corps Coloniale (2e and 3e Divisions Coloniale attacking towards Pinon)
- II Corps Coloniale (10e and 15e Divisions Coloniale attacking towards Vauclerc Plateau)
- VI Corps d'Armée (56e and 127e Divisions d'Infanterie attacking towards Chavignon)
- XX Corps d'Armée (39e and 153e Divisions d'Infanterie attacking towards Monampteuil)

Mangin's troops struggled forwards through a landscape that had been devastated by their own shellfire. The cratered terrain was simply impossible to cross at the rate set by Mangin, and the creeping barrage that was supposed to protect their advance moved ahead of them too quickly. For the colonial troops the icy weather made the experience even more horrendous. Edward Spears later described the misery of the Senegalese troops:

> We had been taught to believe that theirs would be a headlong assault, a wild savage onrush. Instead, paralysed with cold, their chocolate faces tinged with grey, they reached the assault trenches with the utmost difficulty. Most of them were too exhausted even to eat the rations they carried, and their hands were too cold to fix bayonets. They advanced when ordered to do so, carrying their rifles under their arms like umbrellas, finding what protection they could for their frozen fingers in the folds of their cloaks. They got quite a long way before the German machine guns mowed them down.[14]

Despite these difficulties, some initial progress was made. Units of II Corps Coloniale reached the ridgeline between 7 and 8am. Thereafter their attack stalled as they tried to take the ruined farm buildings at Hurtebise and Creute, which had been heavily fortified by the Germans. In the distance the officers of II Corps Coloniale could see the town of Laon – an objective that they were supposed to take within seven hours. Ultimately the town would not fall during the offensive.

The assault within the first two German defensive lines was intense and casualties were heavy as machine-gun and artillery positions, untouched by the French barrage, opened fire on the attacking waves from all directions. Officer casualties were especially high. Three of the four commanders of the Senegalese regiments, for example, were killed. As command and control broke down, the attacks ground to a halt around Hurtebise. The official history later summarised the action, stating that 'the two consecutive assault waves that attacked at an interval of thirty minutes mingled with the remnants of the foremost units and suffered their heaviest losses while retreating'.[15]

As the creeping barrage advanced uselessly onwards, artillery coordination officers with the attacking formations sent urgent messages to the batteries to have it readjusted. First it was brought back to the H+1.30 line and then to the H+0.30 line, demonstrating the lack of progress being made. An officer later outlined the initial phase:

> At H-hour the troops approach in order the first enemy positions. The geographic crest is attained almost without losses; the enemy's artillery barrage is not very brisk and is sporadic. Nevertheless our infantry advances with a slower speed than anticipated. The rolling barrage is unleashed almost immediately and steadily moves ahead of the first waves, which it quickly ceases to protect.[16]

The adjustments to the plans for the creeping barrage infuriated Mangin, despite the fact that his troops were not making progress. He responded: 'Resuming the [artillery] preparation is a mistake. It shows that our infantry hesitates to move on. Our artillery preparation can't have left the enemy with the means to set up a solid line of machine guns. We must take advantage of gaps and outflank the resistance pockets.'[17]

Such comments only reflect Mangin's lack of appreciation of the actual situation. Far from encountering 'pockets of resistance' his men were being drawn into the nexus of the German defence-in-depth positions. As they struggled to advance, they found themselves under intense machine-gun fire from the German MEBU positions. In several cases this fire came from *behind* the advancing troops. The Germans had also carefully planned their artillery support and the defenders signalled for artillery support using flares, calling in fire on the French attackers. Many of the initial French reports refer to the relatively light German artillery fire early in the attack. The Germans were, in fact, waiting for the French to advance further into their defences before bringing artillery fire to bear upon them.

In scenes familiar to those encountered on the Somme the previous year, the attackers also found that in places the barbed wire had not been cut by the artillery. As troops became bogged down opposite intact wire positions covered by machine guns, Mangin continually urged his divisional commanders to push forward: 'If the wire is not destroyed, have it cut by infantry; we must gain ground!'[18] By 10am it was obvious that a major breakthrough had not been achieved. The fighting was concentrated within the first two lines of German defences. Mangin still clung to the hope of getting the attack back on schedule, ordering his commanders to 'carry out artillery barrage according to schedule' and to 'try to catch up on the delay'.[19]

Back at GQG at Compiègne, Nivelle nervously awaited news. Staff officers later spoke of the subdued atmosphere in the operations HQ. Officers claimed that they did not have enough information, yet the lack of telegrams and reports of success were significant. Around 10.30am Nivelle received the first official progress report. Brigadier-General Maurice Gamelin, who was serving with the GAR, telephoned him with news of how the battle was progressing. It is now apparent that Gamelin tried to put the best possible gloss on rather bad news, giving a general enough account of the modest progress so far. Ominously, he reported that 'the battle is taking place on the first and second [German] positions'. By H+4.30 Nivelle had confidently predicted that his offensive would have passed these defences and would be gaining momentum. Instead, his Sixth and Fifth Armies were largely bogged down in the first German lines.

Similar scenes were played out all along the Sixth Army front. The 153e Division d'Infanterie's attack started well, only to grind to a halt outside the misnamed 'Paradise Wood'. Likewise the 56e Division d'Infanterie enjoyed initial success until it passed over the ridgeline at 'la Bovette Wood', where it was checked by machine-gun fire from concealed positions. The attacking troops had not only been left behind by the creeping barrage but they also found it extremely difficult to call in artillery support once they became bogged down. Despite the impressive number of guns that Nivelle had assembled, many of these fired on a flat trajectory and simply could not fire on the reverse slopes of the Chemin des Dames. Increasingly the infantry battle became more intense as the morning dragged on. A report from the 127e Division d'Infanterie described the fighting at Mont Sapin:

> The artillery barrage neutralizes the enemy's machine guns. The 25e BCP rushes at the Tirpitz trench, [taking] 30 prisoners but the slope is almost vertical, the ground is broken up. The barrage moves 100 metres away in three minutes; very soon German machine guns materialize again and fire violently at the chasseurs. The second waves, in small detachments, join in and manoeuvre cleverly. The German grenadiers are subdued, the machine guns captured in a fierce hand-to-hand fight, the minenwerfer servers are pinned down on their pieces. The capture of the caves of Mont Sapin gives us 300 prisoners, including eight officers.[20]

Similar desperate scenes were repeated throughout Sixth Army's zone. Worryingly for Nivelle and Mangin, it became increasingly obvious that further waves of their troops, which were tasked with exploiting the breach and advancing, were being dragged into the struggle for the initial lines of German defences. Not only had the first waves been unsuccessful, subsequent waves of troops were now being expended in trying to take the initial objectives. The later waves of attackers found the German resistance growing stronger and afternoon attacks in the Laffaux and Malmaison sectors suffered severe casualties.

On the front of General Mazel's Fifth Army the attack fared no better, despite having the assistance of tanks. For his attack Mazel had sixteen infantry divisions, two Russian brigades and a cavalry division, all supported by more than 3,800 guns.[21] A force of 128 Schneider tanks was to be deployed, split into two groups. (Some sources cite 132 Schneiders.) Another two St Chamond tanks were also deployed to carry ammunition forward. The tanks had not been deployed in the Sixth Army sector due to the terrain – one of the few sensible decisions to emerge from the planning process. In the flatter terrain around Juvincourt and Berry-au-Bac it was believed that the tanks could make progress, aiding the infantry attack and then advancing along surviving road systems beyond the first lines of defence. It was hoped that their deployment in this sector would be decisive.

The instructions to the tank force commander, Major Bossut, reflected the wild optimism that prevailed in the overall planning for the Nivelle Offensive:

> Tanks and infantry remain in close association during the combat but the tanks do not wait for the infantry if they see an opportunity for going forward. Once the attack has opened, the tanks advance on their objectives and halt only when they encounter obstacles which they cannot cross with the equipment available to them. When our infantry catch up with a tank which is detained in this way, they must do everything possible to help it overcome the obstruction. If the infantry are held up by enemy resistance before the tanks are on the scene, they must lie down and wait for the tanks to intervene. The tanks will roll through them and on against the enemy, suppressing hostile fire.[22]

Within these instructions we can see that the essential question of whether the tanks were supporting the infantry or *vice versa* had not been settled. Each tank group had an infantry company attached to it that was tasked with assisting the tanks over obstacles. In effect, this meant filling in both French and German trenches along the line of advance, under fire, until the tanks could make use of the roads behind the German front lines. In late March 1917 further instructions were issued to the tanks that made it clear they were not seen as potential breakthrough weapons. The first two lines of German trenches were to be taken by the infantry. The tanks would only take part in the attacks on the third and fourth lines of defences, where they would provide mobile artillery support as the infantry outpaced the artillery. On passing through the fourth line, the tanks were to exploit along road routes.[23]

While these plans were modest enough, they made few allowances for the slowness and associated vulnerabilities of the Schneiders. While it was acknowledged that they would follow the infantry formations, the attraction of slow-moving columns of tanks for enemy artillery was not appreciated. If the Germans could maintain artillery observation over the battlefield (and in this case they would) the result would be a veritable turkey shoot. Further, it was not appreciated how dangerous it would be for the accompanying infantry to try to assist stranded tanks.

The French tank force was split into two groups: 'Groupement Chaubès' (forty-eight tanks) and 'Groupement Bossut' (eighty tanks). Both groups set off at 6.30am but eight of the Groupement Chaubès tanks became bogged down and could not proceed. The remaining tanks of the Chaubès group then advanced in a single column towards Temple Ferme (Temple Farm), but almost immediately the column was observed by a German artillery-spotting aircraft and came under fire. It was found that the accompanying infantry had not filled in the trenches in order to allow the tanks to cross the battlefield, and while trying to cross various obstacles the leading Schneiders demonstrated their capacity for getting caught in a nose-down position in trenches. On reaching the German lines, a report later stated, it was found that 'work on the first German trench, 9 feet deep, was not complete when the first tank showed up. It nevertheless attempted to get through, tilted forward and obstructed the way.'[24] Chaos ensued as the column became bogged down behind the ditched tank. Some tanks tried to manoeuvre to clear the first line. The commander's tank was immobilised by a hit and, as the rear tanks came forward, it became extremely difficult to extricate the force. The German artillery had a field day. One tank officer later described the sickening feeling of being caught in such a predicament while under fire:

> There are some things that you'll never forget. Sights which will be for ever engraved on your mind, despite all the horror already burned there. The tank on the left suddenly becomes an inferno. In front of it is the shell which set it alight. Two torches get out, two torches making

a mad, frantic dash towards the rear, two torches which twist, which roll on the ground. A tank burns on the right; another one behind. And on our left; it looks as if someone is setting our line of steel alight like a row of floodlights.[25]

Unable to advance further than the first German line, the eight remaining tanks of Groupement Chaubès returned to their lines that evening, all in a damaged condition. Some of the surviving crews of the ditched and destroyed tanks removed the machine guns from their tanks and fought on alongside the infantry. Casualties for the Groupement Chaubès were fifty-one crewmen killed or wounded, with twenty-six of the force's Schneiders destroyed.[26]

Groupement Bossut's eighty tanks fared a little better although the 2km long column came under German artillery fire before it even left the French lines, when it reached the bridge over the River Miette west of the Cholera Farm position. One tank was hit and two others broke down. Having crossed the French trenches, the column was then delayed in no-man's-land for 45 minutes as the infantry struggled to fill in the German trenches while under fire. As had been the case with the tanks of Groupement Chaubès, there was an excruciating delay as the tanks tried to clear the German trenches. As they pushed through, some became stuck in shell holes, while German fire became increasingly accurate. Pierre Bossut, brother of the column's commander and also a tank officer, later wrote:

A few machines were stopped by enemy fire. Others, including mine, got into critical positions in shell holes and could only get out again after many attempts. For a few minutes as I was second in the column, I was terribly afraid of blocking the other seventy-nine tanks which, in that spot, had no way of getting through either on the left or the right. One of my steering mechanisms was broken and all I could do was to get out of the hole to clear the way. I cried with rage at our helplessness to repair the tank and it was difficult for me to follow the stages of the battle. I saw tanks catching fire all over the plain and the first wounded men walking past my vehicle. Some tanks were several kilometres ahead of me and pushing on.[27]

By 10.15am Groupement Bossut's leading tanks had reached the position at Cholera Farm but found that the attacking infantry had been broken up by German artillery. Shortly after, Major Bossut's tank was destroyed by a direct hit and he was killed, resulting in the already disorganised attack losing further cohesion. Tanks of the group continued to fight for the rest of the afternoon until around 5pm, when the surviving machines returned to their assembly area. In those few hours they had helped the infantry to take a key position known as Hill 78, while others had pushed on beyond the second German line. Some of Groupement Bossut's tanks also went to the aid of the 162^e Infanterie and assisted in beating off a German counterattack. They also backed up late afternoon attacks by the 151^e and 155^e regiments. Some tanks advanced as far as 5km into the German lines. Yet these small successes hardly made up for the overall cost. Of the eighty tanks of Groupement Bossut, thirty-one were knocked out by artillery while a further thirteen broke down or became bogged down. In all, 129 crewmen, including Bossut, were killed or wounded. Pierre Bossut later described how he found his brother's tank knocked out on the battlefield:

> I first saw the almost charred remains of Sergeant-Major Duyff, who had been able to crawl about twenty yards away from the tank before dying. Under the very tank's door was my poor brother, largely spared by fire, with a quiet composure on his face; his skull showed a number of wounds. A piece of shrapnel that had entered his chest near his heart and come out below his shoulder blade had certainly killed him instantly. There is no doubt that the Major, blown out of the burning tank by the explosion, would have tried to get away from the blaze had he still had a breath of life in him.[28]

The combat debut of the French tank force had been difficult and costly. Rather than a decisive new weapon, they had failed to live up to expectations. The Schneiders had demonstrated very poor cross-country capabilities, while cooperation from the infantry in clearing obstacles had proved problematic. Ultimately, they had shown that a tank that could not even clear trenches was a liability on the battlefield. While the tanks were impervious to small arms fire, they had proved to be incredibly vulnerable to direct and indirect artillery. Some German observers even claimed that some tanks had caught fire without even being hit by their artillery.[29] Against infantry in the open they had some effect, but they needed infantry support in the face of well dug-in opposition. Later in the evening of 16 April General Passaga noted that 'after this day, a very difficult one for the tanks, I am wondering whether I can count on them tomorrow for an efficient intervention'.[30]

Across the Fifth Army's front the attacking infantry found it tough going. The river and canal proved to be difficult obstacles and many units stopped on the canal line. The Germans also had several redoubt systems in the Fifth Army's sector. Luxembourg Redoubt was taken at around 2pm but the redoubt at Brimont proved impregnable and artillery on the rearward slope of the hill was able to shell the advancing French waves and also put down enfilading fire. There were similar mixed results across the entire sector. At Neuchatel the 151st Division enjoyed initial success and by 8am had pushed the Germans from their front lines. Almost immediately, the Germans brought up machine-gun teams to halt the French advance and then put in a counterattack. By the afternoon the French had been pushed back in the sector. The failure of the two columns of tanks on this front also meant that the infantry had to try to seize their objectives without the promised tank support. The exception was at Hill 108 where, after some delay, the tanks showed up and supported the infantry. For the infantry, there always seemed to be further lines of German defences as they tried to push forward, and as they persisted in their attacks the German artillery grew stronger. German machine-gun fire also became heavier and in the afternoon the Germans began a new series of counterattacks.

The vulnerability of the flanks of the attacking troops also became more apparent as the day wore on. For example, the attacks of the 1st and 2nd Divisions on the Californie Plateau towards Corbeny were stopped by enfilade German machine-gun fire from Hurtebise, which was actually in the Sixth Army's sector but had not been taken. The fighting around Craonne and the associated German positions at Hun's Wood and Buttes Wood was particularly severe. Craonne was seen as a key objective as it dominated the surrounding terrain. The 1st Division's report described the Craonne objective as 'a village hanging on the bluff, below the almost vertical wall of the Californie Plateau. The enemy has observation posts there with far-ranging views of the French positions.'[31] Given orders that Craonne simply had to be taken, the attacking *poilus* had to advance under heavy machine-gun and artillery fire. General Muteau later described the attack:

> The regiments set off exactly on time and were almost immediately submerged in the fire of the countless machine guns that concrete bunkers or natural caves had protected from our shelling. In the fields east of Craonne a large number [of bunkers] materialized in the middle of the fields; the photographs had not shown any evidence of them. This particular situation accounts for the high losses.[32]

The instruction manual procedure for clearing such bunkers was for infantry units to try to suppress the fire of the position with their Chauchat light machine guns and/or rifle fire. This would then allow soldiers with grenades, or better still rifle-grenades, to take out the bunker. Some units also carried the man-portable 37mm gun for this purpose. In reality, the sheer number of bunkers was totally unexpected and, with mounting casualties, the infantry struggled to clear these bunker systems. When they reached the German lines fierce hand-to-hand fighting and grenade exchanges developed. Then as the Germans withdrew within their trench system their artillery spotters called in fire to shut down the advance. This fighting decimated the French units and ensured that they could not continue the advance.[33]

Reserve units and units that had originally been tasked with taking part in one of the later phases of attack found themselves reinforcing those units that had suffered serious casualties. One I Corps officer reported that 'given the fierceness of the fight on the Vauclerc Plateau, we will have to replace the other infantry divisions by fresh units without delay if we want to push on or even hold the top of the plateau'.[34] Along the line, grim contests developed as the *poilus* tried to hold on to the limited gains that they had made at such terrible cost. Some of these positions fell to German counterattacks and by the end of the first day I Corps Coloniale had been pushed back to its starting line. Throughout the territory that had initially been overrun, German 'stay behind' units emerged from deep bunkers, cellars and caves and began to engage the French from the rear. Confusion reigned as the now exhausted troops struggled to combat this new development, while throughout the night the Germans signalled to their artillery with flares to coordinate bombardments.

Sadly for the attackers, once again they also found their medical services to be inadequate. In their optimism, the staff at GQG had planned for modest numbers of wounded and had assigned medical units and field hospitals in keeping with these predictions. The huge numbers of wounded overwhelmed the dressing stations and field hospitals and many wounded were left outside during the night awaiting treatment. On the battlefield itself lay thousands of wounded, who could not be evacuated due to a shortage of stretcher parties. The evening and night of 16/17 April saw further downpours of freezing rain and road transport ground to a halt.[35] Jean Ybarnégaray, a parliamentary deputy serving in the infantry, later decried the lack of adequate medical facilities:

> Why? Like everything else, it was because in this offensive we'd planned for everything but defeat. We began from the idea that the offensive would be a success. That's why nothing had been organised: no evacuation routes, too few aid posts, impossible to get the field ambulances to the wounded.[36]

By the end of the first day, therefore, the attacks of both the Fifth and Sixth Armies had made extremely limited gains. The most significant successes came in the Fifth Army's sector, with some units advancing a few kilometres into the enemy lines – a not inconsiderable feat given the strength of the opposition. Most units, however, were lucky if they had established footholds in the first and second German lines at most. Some German machine guns and artillery had been captured, as had more than 13,000 German soldiers. After-action reports made for grim reading, describing how units 'dissolved on the line of combat'. One report from II Corps Coloniale concluded that 'the enemy's reserves are in effect almost intact. Well-protected in holes on the northern slope or in very strong dugouts, they have not suffered from the bombardment.'[37] The cost in making even these limited advances had, however, been huge. The II Corps Coloniale (Sixth Army) had more than 3,800 casualties, whereas the 2nd Division (Fifth Army) had lost more than

3,700 killed, wounded or missing. At regimental and battalion level some units had effectively ceased to exist.

Within Nivelle's HQ it would seem that the atmosphere was subdued, indeed. Not even the most optimistic interpretation of these reports would suggest that the massive breakthrough had been achieved. Rather than passing through the German lines in a series of dramatic leaps, the attack had become bogged down. The communiqués issued for the benefit of the press were extremely circumspect; the communiqué issued at 2pm on 16 April did not even refer to the opening of the offensive but rather described the artillery battle that had developed in the days before the attack. Later communiqués were equally vague – none referred to the taking of any specific objectives or locations.

Nivelle's own mindset at this time is difficult to fathom. He had promised to call off the attack if success had not been achieved within 24 to 48 hours. Now, by the end of the first day, it was clear to any objective observer that the attack had stalled, despite the huge weight of artillery, manpower and other resources that been brought to bear. Yet Nivelle was in a far from objective frame of mind. Noting that the Fifth Army had made some gains and that opposition seemed to be lighter in its sector, he decided to renew the attack the next day by increasing the effort in the Fifth Army sector. His actions over the next few days suggest that he was increasingly desperate to try to fulfil at least some of his grandiose predictions of the previous months, rather than just calling off the attack.

It is difficult to create a true assessment of how Nivelle was processing the unit reports that came to his HQ during the evening of 16 April because he himself left little in writing about this crucial period. It is known that he tried to meet with Painlevé that evening in order to inform him of the situation, but exactly what he intended to tell the minister is unknown. Given his past performances and also later events, it is unlikely that he was planning to give Painlevé a true appreciation of the situation. The fact that Painlevé was unavailable to meet with Nivelle, or even talk with him on the phone, at this juncture is also significant and suggests that the Minister of War was trying to distance himself from the failure early on. Jacques Helbronner, the secretary to the war cabinet, suggests in his journal that Nivelle had already discussed the situation with the army group commanders and was considering calling off the attack.[38] If this is true, it would appear that by the next morning he had changed his mind. Rather than calling off the offensive, he ordered further attacks and tried to redirect the offensive in pursuit of some level of success.

Despite Nivelle's efforts to contain the situation, the extent of the failure was already becoming known. As early as 16 April Field Marshal Haig wrote:

> Nothing seems to have been gained. Reports were at first very favourable. Later it was said 'Enemy counterattacked very strongly and ground gained was lost'. French claim 10,000 prisoners but the attitude of French officers attached to my staff makes me think that they are not quite satisfied and that the much-talked-of victory has not been gained by the French up to date.[39]

On 17 April Haig wrote: 'I could get no details from the French as to the results of today's fighting, which is always a bad sign and I fear that things are going badly with their offensive.'[40]

Chapter 6

Reinforcing Failure

The battle began at 6.00am. By 7.00am it was lost. Fifteen minutes after the assault waves set out across the huge Aisne plateau, nothing could be heard but the stuttering of machine guns and a single cry escaping thousands of anguished breasts – 'the machine guns haven't been destroyed'. The victory we thought was in the bag was going to be a bloody reverse.

(Jean Ybarnégaray, 249th Infantry)[1]

One of the greatest criticisms that would later emerge about Nivelle was that he continued the offensive despite the fact that it was obvious quite early in the attack that the dramatic 'rupture' he had promised had failed to materialise. During the night of 16/17 April it continued to pour with rain, and this would have an impact on the fighting the next day. Due to the fact that the Fifth Army had made the better advance, Nivelle tried to re-orientate the battle to the north-east in the hope of profiting from their limited success. Mangin's Sixth Army, which had been driven back to its start line in some places, was ordered to attack the southern side of the River Ailette, while Mangin was also asked to try to increase his foothold on the Chemin des Dames. Significantly, the commander of the GAR, General Micheler, refused to release even one fresh division to reinforce Mangin's Sixth Army. In Micheler's estimation the army was exhausted and a breakthrough was not possible. To paraphrase the old military axiom, he was not prepared to reinforce failure.

The main effort on 17 April was made by the Fifth Army and there were limited successes, with features such as the Grinons ridgeline and the quarries at Cour-Soupier being captured. However, I Corps (Fifth Army) struggled to gain a foothold on the Californie Plateau and along the line gains were mostly limited to the taking of a trench here and there. Artillery support, due to the bad weather and poor visibility, was largely ineffective and the infantry had to fight on, trench by trench, in a bloody slogging match. An officer of I Corps later wrote:

> We are down to communication trench fights, to equally impossible choices; such convulsions cannot lead to anything decisive. Will the I Corps eventually be able on its own to take the Californie [Plateau] and the wood; that is to say, occupy the entire plateau? Quite sincerely, I doubt it and all the present artillery fire will not change that.[2]

By the end of 17 April the front remained largely unchanged, although some dramatic gains were made during the night of 17/18 April as the Germans withdrew from the 'elbow' in the lines opposite the Sixth Army. Made aware that the enemy was beginning a withdrawal, Mangin ordered a series of attacks. These were carried out in phases up to 20 April, keeping the Germans under constant pressure. The Sixth Army advanced up to 7km in places and took more than 5,000 prisoners.

Further to the east, General Anthoine's Fourth Army, part of Pétain's Groupe d'Armées du Centre (GAC), was ordered to attack on 17 April in the hope of increasing pressure on the Germans. These attacks would also continue until 20 April and again some limited gains were made. On the first day the Fourth Army advanced more than 2km in places and captured key German observation positions at Sans-Nom and Mont Blond. Pétain controlled the Fourth Army's advance closely, urging caution and a methodological approach. Pétain also contacted Nivelle and requested three fresh divisions to replace front-line units. It is likely that this was a ploy on Pétain's part. Had he been denied the reinforcements, he would have shut down his attack and this would have guaranteed the failure of the offensive. Ultimately Nivelle supplied the fresh divisions in order to retain some possibility of success.

However, by 17/18 April all talk of achieving a breakthrough had ceased at GQG at Compiègne and some of the cavalry divisions began to be relocated away from the front. They would not be needed for any exploitation phase. It is also significant that the battle had degenerated into a series of contests over terrain features. This is exactly what Nivelle had promised his offensive was NOT about, but his vision of clearing the German lines rapidly in a series of bounds and then overwhelming the enemy artillery and reserves was now laid bare for what it was – pure military fantasy. On being briefed on Nivelle's plans while still Minister of War some months earlier, General Lyautey had remarked 'It's a plan worthy of the Duchess of Gerolstein!' This caustic remark made reference to Offenbach's opera *La Grande-Duchesse de Gerolstein*, which was a satire on unfettered militarism.[3] A huge hit when first performed in 1867, the opera had been banned in France following the defeat of 1870. In many ways Lyautey's remark was an apt summation of the key problems with the whole offensive.

On 20 April Nivelle met Ribot and Poincaré in Paris to discuss the progress of the offensive – or lack thereof. Both the political leaders were acutely aware of the fragile state of the nation's morale and pleaded with Nivelle to avoid further losses. Despite the fact that the staff at GQG had been less than forthcoming about casualty figures, news had reached the government and the public that losses had been heavy. In an effort to assuage Ribot's and Poincaré's fears, Nivelle promised that only limited operations would be undertaken, preceded by heavy bombardment. By this stage in the operation the Tenth Army had been inserted in the line between the Sixth and Fifth Armies, relieving the pressure on both. It had been planned to use the Tenth Army as a major exploitation force, yet that plan was now clearly impractical; instead, the Tenth Army would now join the fighting for significant features on the Chemin des Dames front. Nivelle went on to assure the politicians that new operations would seize control of the entire Chemin des Dames ridgeline and push the Germans out of Laon, but in truth there was no basis for these predictions. These attacks would be supported by operations in the Alsace and Woëvre sectors, while Nivelle also promised to keep up the pressure to assist British operations in Flanders. In retrospect, the account of this meeting indicates a level of desperation on the part of Nivelle to downplay the failure of his attack, while also trying to misdirect Ribot's and Painlevé's attention to operations elsewhere.[4]

Considering the fact that Nivelle's offensive had obviously failed, it is unclear why the politicians did not sack him immediately. It would appear, however, that they were seeking a means of replacing him in the least dramatic way possible in order to maintain public support and also prolong the life of the Ribot ministry. Switching to a programme of limited offensives was a means to climb down more gracefully from the optimistic objectives set for the offensive. On 21 April Ribot, Painlevé and Nivelle met Lloyd George. Their assessment of the French offensive was modest, yet still support for wider British operations in Flanders was promised. This new policy of limited offensives was perhaps a wise course of action, as closing down all offensive action could have invited further German counterattacks. Previously in the war the German high command had shown an uncanny ability to recognise the loss of momentum and purpose in Allied offensives and had responded with timely counterattacks. They would do so again later in 1917 and in 1918.

On 21 April Micheler wrote to Painlevé outlining his concerns and listing reasons why the offensive should be halted. The German withdrawal to the Hindenburg Line had been decisive, while the attacks on Craonne and Sapigneul had failed, exposing the northeast flanks of the army. Infantry reserves (now only four divisions) and supplies of artillery shells were also not sufficient to permit further major actions. Micheler suggested limited operations towards Brimont, the Chemin des Dames, Sapin and Sapigneul in the hope of building on the limited gains in those sectors. He concluded: 'One may furthermore wonder whether, in the present circumstances, the front of attack of the GAR can possibly be exploited against a well-warned enemy who has had time to rally. Past experience should advise us against delusions in this respect.'[5]

In the days that followed, Nivelle made a humiliating tour of his army group commanders to appraise them of the switch to a programme of limited offensives. On 22 April he visited Pétain and Micheler, perhaps his two greatest critics, and outlined the new programme. As operational objectives, he instructed them to focus on clearing the Chemin des Dames of Germans. These meetings were frosty indeed. In the days that followed, the level of political anxiety about Nivelle increased, precipitated by intrigue within the staffs of the army group commanders. An officer (or perhaps officers) at army group level forwarded details of Nivelle's new plans to President Poincaré, who, fearful of further huge casualties, sent Nivelle a message of caution on 23 April. At this point Nivelle had not yet decided the date for his new phase of offensives, and it was clear that someone on one of the staffs was providing misleading information to politicians. Seizing the moral high ground, Nivelle went into a fury and insisted that the culprit be identified and punished.[6]

Despite such protestations, the government was by now aware of the extent of the failure. On 24 April Poincaré, Ribot, Painlevé and Admiral Lucien Lacaze, the Minister of the Navy, met to discuss how to replace Nivelle. All military logic suggested that this be done immediately, and Painlevé argued that Nivelle no longer had the respect of his subordinate commanders or the confidence of the army in general. Once again, however, the politicians wavered, fearful of what the political fallout and public reaction would be. As a compromise measure, Nivelle was called before them on 25 April to outline his new plans in further detail. At the meeting Nivelle briefed the political leaders on a series of four new attacks that he planned to initiate at the end of April. These would seize the Fort Brimont position and also clear the Chemin des Dames. Despite the alarming reports from the front, Nivelle had lost none of his former bravado, claiming that he had won 'the most brilliant of all strategic victories. We have the initiative in operations and will keep it.'[7]

During the course of the meeting, however, it also became obvious that Painlevé had been sounding out the army and army group commanders yet again. He announced to the meeting that both Pétain and Mazel had major reservations about the planned operations, which they had suggested to him would be 'hazardous, difficult and bloody'.[8] While the new plans were given outline approval, after the meeting Painlevé met privately with Nivelle and discussed the possibility of him being replaced. Realising that his position was becoming increasingly untenable, Nivelle agreed to resign if requested to do so by the government.

While operations continued at the front, the political and military wrangling continued. The political leaders met again on 26 April and discussed replacing Nivelle but yet again couldn't commit themselves to doing so. On the same day, in an effort at damage limitation, Nivelle transferred Mangin's Sixth Army to the GAN under the command of Franchet d'Espèrey. In the days since the offensive began, the relationship between Nivelle and Mangin had become increasingly strained and Nivelle had severely criticised the Sixth Army commander for his lack of success. In his search for someone to blame, Nivelle now focused on his former colleague and confidant. While

Mangin remains an unendearing and somewhat callous figure, the treatment now meted out to him by his chief can only be described as shabby. On 30 April Nivelle wrote to him:

> My dear Mangin,
> I am forced to take note of the fact that you no longer have your subordinates' trust and, in agreement with the war minister and to my deep regret, have no choice but to put you on the inactive list. It is sad and painful duty for me to have to cause a faithful comrade-in-arms so much sorrow.[9]

It was an obvious and clumsy attempt to scapegoat Mangin for the entire failure of the offensive. On being relieved, Mangin was forbidden from visiting Paris or even neighbouring departments. Showing a certain grim realism, Mangin remarked, 'I think General Nivelle thought he could make concessions by throwing me overboard.'[10]

The desperation and sheer lack of a grasp on reality displayed in Nivelle's ousting of Mangin are little short of breathtaking. The references to a 'loss of subordinates' trust' could so clearly have been applied to Nivelle himself even before the offensive began, and he seemed to display a dangerous lack of self-perception. Moreover, the reference to Painlevé indicates the complicity of politicians in yet another desperate move to save their government.

Throughout this period operations continued on the Fifth, Sixth and Tenth Armies' fronts. These were now much more modest in scope, but there was a series of fights to seize specific objectives. For Mangin's Sixth Army, the offensive degenerated into a series of tough battles to dislodge the Germans from prepared positions on the Chemin des Dames ridgeline. Objectives such as the Condé Redoubt and positions at Soupir, Chavonne and Vailly were overcome only with huge difficulty and high numbers of casualties. Other attacks were shut down in their opening phases. In the surviving reports phrases such as 'machine guns which had not been shelled out caused the attack to fail' appear with a depressing regularity.[11] The continuing poor weather made for tough going but on occasion the snow blizzards were actually advantageous as they concealed the advancing infantry. One junior officer from the Sixth Army later described his company's attack on the hamlet of Braye, giving a good indication of the difficulties in maintaining unit cohesion even in limited attacks:

> 5.30pm. The company sets off. They have never manoeuvred so well, it is superb. I weep with joy. Snow is falling but never mind; so much the better for us on the contrary. The 'tack-tack' begins. We can no longer advance in the open, only from one shell hole to another. Dead men of the 7th Company in the 'Unstrutt Trench'. So, they came as far as here yesterday morning. The Huns are shelling us. Each man [is] progressing on his own. 3 or 4 machine guns are firing at us, one kilometre away. I can see a few on the slopes, east of Braye. Our machine guns respond. On our right we can see men of the 20th Corps advancing. Sunshine again. We have reached our objective. Patrolling along the canal towards Braye. It is 7.45pm. Here are some Huns coming up with hands raised, carrying bundles and shoes on their backs. 51 of them. They make off quickly.[12]

Accounts of this period in late April make similar comments on the difficulties caused by terrain, weather, command-and-control issues and the very effective enemy opposition. In such a battle-space, plans for large formation manoeuvres and advances were obviously hugely over-optimistic.

One of the significant features overlooked by the planners was the abundance of underground shelters available to the Germans. In addition to the 'Stollen' that the Germans had built themselves, there were also numerous natural caves and large subterranean cellars and galleries associated with stone quarries in the region (referred to by the French as 'creutes'). These were largely invisible to aerial reconnaissance planes and therefore were not targeted during the artillery preparation. Some of the creutes had existed before the war and should have been known to the planning staffs, yet they were not factored into the operational plans. The Germans used them to shelter troops and machine-gun teams from the preliminary bombardment. These German units then emerged once the infantry attack began and caused much devastation to the advancing French formations.

One of the most significant was the 'Caverne du Dragon' ('Drachenhöhle' to the Germans). Situated to the west of Hurtebise Farm and dominating a section of the ridgeline, this underground cavern system was located in a stone quarry that had been in use since the sixteenth century. In some places it extended to a depth of 15m below the surface and the Germans seized it when they took control of the Chemin des Dames ridge in 1915. They quickly set about bringing in electricity and phone lines and fortifying the cavern. Apart from providing safe, underground living quarters, it housed signals and HQ positions. It also boasted sniper locations that dominated the French positions below, and machine-gun emplacements at each of the seven entrances. Its extensive galleries extended in various directions. The defenders likened it to a mythical beast, ready to breathe fire on anyone approaching it – hence its name: the Cave of the Dragon.[13]

The Caverne du Dragon was the biggest such system on the Chemin des Dames, but there were many smaller ones. They were the scene of fierce actions in late April and early May as the French needed to clear them in order to advance. These underground caverns became the setting for bitter hand-to-hand fighting. In the confines of the underground galleries soldiers of both sides fought it out with pistols, hand grenades and bayonets. The lighting was often poor but to carry a lamp or torch invited enemy fire. On occasion, flamethrowers were used to clear the galleries of Germans. Both sides hastily buried their dead within the galleries, adding to the fetid unhealthy stench.

Some of these positions, such as the 'Caverne du Elephant', were taken but the Caverne du Dragon was too well defended and did not fall. During the battles of early May German counterattack units emerging from the Caverne du Dragon and the 'Caverne du Saxons' shut down French attacks on the Vauclerc Plateau. One officer recorded: 'We advanced in the morning but, when we got through, the Huns were coming out of holes and shooting us in the back. Many were killed or wounded.'[14]

On 25 June 1917, after the Nivelle Offensive had actually ended, the French managed to gain a foothold in the Caverne du Dragon. Thereafter both sides strove to gain the advantage in the underground fight and a series of actions lasted until October. The fight for the cavern became an almost surreal subterranean battle, with both sides listening for the approach of the other in a prolonged battle that lasted several months.

On the surface, the units of the Fifth, Sixth and Tenth Armies continued the struggle to gain some significant battlefield advantage. From the surviving reports it is possible to get a sense of the difficulties faced by the attacking forces. Some points of the line were the focus of successive attacks and patterns similar to those seen during the first days of the offensive were repeated. Following yet another failed attempt at Mont Sapigneul in early May, one officer reported that 'countless machine guns have appeared, sometimes even in our men's backs, on very tricky terrain'. The Germans were, of course, fully alerted to French intentions by this stage and proved highly efficient at interrupting their preparations and the movement of assault formations with barrages of gas shells. In early May the 41st Division seized the village of Berméricourt but then lost it on the same day to a German counterattack. A similar pattern was repeated along the front, with hard-won gains being lost to lightning German counterattacks. After one such episode a despairing *poilu* wrote home: 'What a day, my Mimi! All our objectives had been reached by noon. This morning they were all lost again!'

The fighting at Craonne and Hurtebise continued into early May. For the soldiers involved, there was no sense that these were 'limited' attacks. Rather, the battle had degenerated into a series of costly slogging matches over points on a map, the value of which seemed to be apparent only to the generals. The German position at Hurtebise Farm proved to be particularly difficult, involving a tough fight to break into the position, followed by hand-to-hand fighting in the cellars of the former farm. The position at Hurtebise, centred on the ruins of a large farmhouse and its outbuildings, dominated the approach to the Californie Plateau. It was seen as a key objective. In 1814 Hurtebise had also been significant during the Battle of Craonne, one of Napoleon's last battles before his abdication and subsequent exile on Elba. In the fight for Hurtebise in 1917 casualties were heavy, XI Corps alone losing over 1,600 men in 24 hours. Using contemporary accounts, the French historian René Nobecourt later described the attack of the 102e Bataillon de Chasseurs à Pied:

They almost immediately came up against uncrossable wire networks. They were standing abreast, unprotected from the waist up, while the Germans were throwing grenades at them 'with extraordinary gusto' and machine guns, one every ten metres, kept them under continuous fire. The first wave was almost entirely mown down and the second whirled around; a hundred chasseurs were gone. The 102^e BCP was relieved on that very evening.[15]

There were some limited successes but they came at huge cost. The Moulin de Laffaux (Laffaux Mill) position was taken on 5–6 May after heavy fighting. In the April battles this objective had proved too difficult for the colonial troops of Mangin's Sixth Army. Now the Sixth Army attacked again, this time without Mangin in command and supported by tanks from the 'Groupe Lefebvre', which included both Schneiders and St Chamond tanks in three sections. This was the first time that the St Chamonds saw action and they displayed some significant problems, several suffering mechanical breakdowns. The crews also found that the St Chamonds suffered serious mobility problems and, like the Schneiders, had limited trench-crossing ability despite their large size. Nevertheless, the tanks provided the attacking infantry with valuable support and German reports later credited them with destroying several machine-gun positions.[16] At the end of five or six hours' combat, the tank crews were found to be exhausted due to the strain and physical effort of fighting in the cramped, lurching, fume-filled tanks. Losses among the tank sections were three Schneiders and three St Chamonds – a considerable improvement on their performance in the April attacks.[17] Despite the tank support, taking the Moulin de Laffaux proved difficult and it was finally seized by a regiment of dismounted cavalry (cuirassiers à pied).

In the final balance this later phase of 'limited offensives' was extremely disappointing. The troops were acutely aware that these attacks were, in a strategic sense, pointless. If the enemy had not broken in April, how could these limited operations against an enemy that daily grew stronger hope to achieve anything significant? There could be no decisive result from their sacrifices. Postal censors noted an alarming dip in morale as disaffection spread through the army. Printed tracts began to circulate among the troops bearing phrases such as 'Down with the war!' and 'Death to those in charge!'

As discontent spread through the French army in late April and May, General Nivelle found himself in an increasingly untenable position. He would survive in his role as commander-in-chief until May but this was only due to the gutlessness of the politicians, still clinging to the idea that they could limit the fallout caused by Nivelle's failure and his eventual removal. On 26 April the politicians had met yet again but only Painlevé pushed for Nivelle's immediate removal. Senior generals also did not emerge from this process creditably. To Nivelle's face, it would seem, several of them did not voice their misgivings with any forcefulness yet they were willing to complain in detail to the politicians. General Mazel, for example, has been criticised for his duplicity in assuring Nivelle that he would take Fort Brimont but then complaining to Painlevé that the attack would fail with high casualties. Premier Ribot later remarked that 'the deputies and Minister of War are destroying discipline by provoking such critiques'.[18]

Finally, in a face-saving measure, Painlevé suggested that Pétain be appointed as Nivelle's chief of staff and designated successor. Nivelle was in favour of such a move, but Pétain himself initially refused, being reluctant to prop up the Nivelle regime any longer than was necessary. On 29 April, however, Pétain was appointed as chief of staff of the army while Nivelle remained as commander-in-chief.

The final changeover in command was not a smooth process. There were some differences of opinion as to how long this interim arrangement would last. Nivelle evidently thought it would continue for some time in order to allow him to step back from command with his dignity intact. The government and Pétain obviously envisaged a much swifter transition. The process was not helped by doubts over Pétain's appointment as Nivelle's designated successor. From the British perspective there were concerns that Pétain would not pursue a policy of the offensive as his views on this type of warfare were well known. General Sir William Robertson, Chief of the Imperial General Staff, and Field Marshal Haig both voiced their concerns. Equally, there were doubts about Pétain within France. He was a Catholic, although not a very devout one, and had always shown disdain for politicians and their manoeuvrings. On 29 April Painlevé met with Ribot and told him that they needed to revive the office of 'Chief of the Army General Staff' – an appointment that had lain dormant for many years. Following further debate on Pétain's fitness for the role, Painlevé threatened to resign if he was not appointed and on 30 April, the appointment was formally announced in the *Journal Officiel*.[19] The news was greeted with public approval and within diplomatic circles it came to be known that Nivelle would soon be replaced and sent to North Africa.

Yet there were doubts as to the exact responsibilities of Pétain's new office. The government envisaged that he would act as an adviser to the Minister of War. On 3 May, however, Pétain wrote to Painlevé outlining how he saw his new duties. His vision was much more extensive, essentially commanding Allied armies on the Western Front and in other theatres while also acting as a delegate on the War Committee. In effect, Pétain was proposing that he run all military operations, while his proposed role on the War Committee would effectively make him an equal to the Minister of War. Still dealing with the fallout from Nivelle's military ambition, Painlevé was in no mood to countenance these new machinations and immediately put Pétain in his place. With a level of resolution and determination that had been lacking in recent weeks, Painlevé informed Pétain that he was subordinate to him and would merely act as an adviser to the government.

In the midst of these internal upheavals, a meeting of Allied leaders was scheduled to take place in Paris on 4 May. Whatever their actual feelings for one another, Ribot, Painlevé, Nivelle, Pétain and Admiral Le Bon met with the Italian, Russian and British leaders. During the morning meeting of military leaders, Pétain tried to downplay the failure on the Chemin des Dames but admitted that a breakthrough was no longer possible. In the afternoon meeting of military and political leaders, General Robertson summed up the military situation, stating: 'It is no longer a question of aiming at breaking through the enemy's front and aiming at distant objectives. It is now a question of wearing down and exhausting the enemy's resistance.'[20] While this seemed to mirror Pétain's ideas regarding limited objectives, it is also obvious that the Allied commanders found it difficult to abandon offensive operations entirely, no matter how sensible that course seemed. Robertson continued:

> In order to wear him down we are agreed that it is absolutely necessary to fight with all our available forces, with the object of destroying the enemy's divisions. We are unanimously of [the] opinion that there is no half-way between this course and fighting defensively, which, at this stage of the war, would be tantamount to acknowledging defeat.[21]

Lloyd George expressed his views that an offensive needed to be mounted against the German-held Channel ports in order to reduce U-boat activity. The French promised to assist in any such offensive and it was pointed out that America, now fully in the war, had made its Atlantic Fleet available for anti-U-boat operations. What emerged from this meeting was a tacit agreement between the French and British military commanders that the BEF would now take up the burden of offensive operations for the foreseeable future. Haig's subordination to the French, agreed at the contentious Calais Conference, was to end and the BEF would make the main effort during the summer of 1917 while the French would launch supporting operations. Also, both France and Britain would await the build-up of American troops. The level of distrust between the military and political leaders on both the French and British sides is also evident from this meeting. This was perhaps not surprising considering the recent political intrigues. Despite their many differences, Haig and Pétain agreed to cut the political leaders from the information loop as much as possible. Haig noted in his diary: 'Plan to be kept a perfect secret. Governments not to be told any details concerning the place or date of any attack, only the principles.'[22] Neither Haig nor Pétain was going to repeat Nivelle's mistake of revealing all his plans to the politicians, thus destroying any chance of operational security.

Having secured a successor, and having met with the other Allied leaders, Painlevé now set in motion the process to finally remove Nivelle. Throughout this period Nivelle furiously tried to shore up any remaining support within the government, the press and the army. He even went as far as writing to Joffre in the hope that the now sidelined former chief could bring some pressure to bear. Meetings with his critics did not go smoothly. Before the battle formally ended on 9 May, Nivelle travelled to Micheler's HQ at Dormans, where he castigated the commander of the GAR for not trying hard enough. Micheler ensured that the doors of his office remained open so that his staff could hear the exchange. Despite the presence of junior officers, the discussion rapidly became heated, with the two generals shouting accusations and recriminations at each other. Exasperated beyond endurance, Micheler finally shouted: 'You wish me to be responsible for this mistake. Me! Who never ceased to warn you of it! Do you know what such an action is called? Well – it is called cowardice!'[23] Nivelle, it was later reported, staggered to his car like a drunken man.

As the quarrelling with his subordinates increased, on 10 May the Council of Ministers agreed to Painlevé's request to have Nivelle removed. To the astonishment of both politicians and generals, Nivelle refused to go. He told the liaison officer to the government: 'They want my hide but neither my dignity, my conscience nor my sense of what I owe my country permits me to play their game'.[24] At a meeting between Nivelle, President Poincaré and Painlevé on 15 May the political leaders still refused to grasp the nettle and simply sack him. In their written communications they were, however, more courageous. On the same day Painlevé wrote to Nivelle in a rather businesslike manner:

> I have the honour to inform you that the government of the Republic has decided, as of May 15, 1917, to appoint Major-General Pétain at the head of the armies of the North and North-East. The decree dated December 12, 1916, by which you were given this command is therefore revoked. As a consequence you will please return the warrant of command which is now in your possession.[25]

President Poincaré also wrote to Nivelle on 15 May appointing him to the command of an army group on the north or north-eastern front; this would never actually come to pass and was obviously designed as a means of softening the blow. Pétain was appointed as Nivelle's successor and formally took command on 17 May. So Nivelle finally resigned – or perhaps it is more accurate to say he had been forced to resign.

The end of Nivelle's career – and this was effectively the end – was messy, which perhaps comes as no surprise. When Pétain arrived to take command on 17 May, he found that Nivelle was still in his office at GQG at Compiègne. This could be viewed as a courtesy, and it was fitting that there should be a formal handover between the incoming and outgoing commanders. Dinner that evening passed in silence. Later Pétain took over Nivelle's old room at the Compiègne Palace, which had once been occupied by Marie Antoinette. Surviving accounts suggest, however, that Nivelle lingered at GQG until 19 May, although what he hoped to achieve at this late stage remains unclear.

An officer on the staff later wrote that 'General Nivelle's departure was unceremonious. Rarely had a top-ranking general vanished from the scene in such indifference. While he was still in command, he had ceased to exist in everybody's eyes.'[26]

Nivelle went on leave. At the end of June Pétain wrote to inform him that:

> I have at the moment no particular mission to entrust you with. Nor can I foresee any vacancy in an army group command in the near future. In the circumstances, I therefore have to put you temporarily on the inactive list, until new developments in the war allow me to call on your collaboration and devoted service.[27]

In December 1917 Nivelle was appointed to a command in North Africa, removing him from any major theatre of operations for the remainder of the war. After so much confident bluster, the former commander-in-chief left the scene unnoticed by most and mourned by no one.

By mid-May 1917 the Nivelle Offensive had been wound down. There had been small territorial gains, and thousands of German soldiers and many artillery pieces had been captured. The cost, however, was huge. The immediate indications were that the French army had lost around 100,000 men wounded and more than 30,000 killed, with a further 4,000 missing or taken prisoner. In the months and years that followed, these figures were revised upwards.

While the politicians, military commanders and French public processed these casualty figures and the ramifications of yet another military failure, it became obvious that the army had been pushed beyond its breaking point. While the offensive was still under way, signs of discontent had begun to emerge. These soon degenerated into a large-scale collapse of morale and by late May the French army was no longer an effective fighting force. The 'brittleness' that many observers had noted within the army had been transformed into a state of collapse following the failure of Nivelle's plan. This rapidly deteriorating situation would preoccupy the new commander as he took command.

Chapter 7

The Mutinies

We refused to go up to the line on Tuesday night, we didn't want to march. You might almost say that we went on strike, and many other regiments have done the same thing. It'll be easier to explain when I come home on leave. They drive us like animals; they don't give us much to eat and they want us to get ourselves killed again for nothing. If we'd gone into the attack, only half of us would have come out alive and we refused to go forward.

(Private of the 36th Infantry)[1]

The final admission that the Nivelle Offensive had actually failed was to have drastic consequences that almost took France out of the war. In the weeks that followed the end of the offensive there were instances of what reports referred to as 'collective disobedience' across five army groups. Of these, four had been directly engaged in the Nivelle Offensive.

In retrospect, the mutinies should have come as no surprise. In the run-up to the attacks Nivelle had charmed politicians and, as news of his plans spread, the press had raised the public's expectations regarding the certain victory to come. The soldiers themselves had not been immune to this and the commanders of the various army groups, the regimental officers and Nivelle himself had assured the troops that victory was certain, within days and at little cost. By the end of May the grim reality of yet another costly failure had hit home. Morale within the French army, particularly in the infantry, plummeted.

There had been warning signs. By late 1916 morale within the French army was in a fragile state and the military censors noted an increased level of pessimism in letters home. December 1916 saw a mini-crisis. An announcement that the Ministry of War would improve conditions for the front-line troops resulted in a huge letter campaign, with hundreds of thousands of letters being sent from the front in protest, complaining about the harsh realities of the troops' lives. The rate of desertion within the army also soared. In late 1916 the average monthly desertion rate was 470 per month. By the end of April 1917 this had risen to over 600 per month, and no fewer than 1,291 men deserted in May. In June, at the height of the mutinies, 1,619 cases of desertion were reported. Perhaps the most surprising thing about these statistics is that they were not far worse. Battalion medical officers reported increased instances of shell-shock and insanity as soldiers broke down towards the end of what had been a brutal year of fighting.[2]

Perhaps even more worrying were the signs of sullen disobedience that began to emerge within the army. There had been instances of unauthorised retreats, mass desertions, large-scale surrenders and collective disobedience previously in the war. During 1916, in the Verdun sector, these became more common as the various bloody phases of that gargantuan battle played out. In May 1916 a small group of fifty men refused to return to duty in the trenches and were court-martialled. Throughout the summer there were signs of discontent in several regiments, and officers reported that in local counterattacks the troops left the trenches only reluctantly. In June 1916 the majority of one battalion surrendered to the Germans after a particularly heavy bombardment. Two junior officers were court-martialled and shot after ordering a withdrawal that had led to a minor local rout. In his fury, Joffre, then still commander-in-chief, ordered that both the regiments involved should be disbanded. By December 1916 it was reported that troops no longer sang while on the march. In some cases units on their way to the Verdun front bleated like sheep – like lambs being led to the slaughter. Cries of 'A bas la guerre!' ('Down with the war!') became common as troops were reviewed on their way to the front.

The hostility of the soldiers, especially the infantry, to rear echelon troops, referred to as '*embusqués*', became more noticeable. Staff officers, airmen and supply troops found themselves the focus of abuse and sometimes hurled stones. Even the artillery, which constantly frustrated the common infantrymen due to rounds falling short and tardy supporting fire, became the target for disgruntled *poilus*. And the medical services, which repeatedly came up short in the infantryman's point of view, were increasingly derided. A level of spite was also reserved for politicians: when President Poincaré visited one formation to hand out awards, the men hurled both abuse and stones at him.

Letters home became increasingly bitter, with soldiers referring to the generals as bunglers, fools and 'drinkers of blood'. The soldiers' news-sheets also became more critical. Their articles castigated not only army commanders and their staffs, but also politicians, journalists who wrote falsely about life at the front, war profiteers and the management of the war in general. The French army was in crisis even before the disaster of the Nivelle Offensive. By 1917 the army had lost more than a million men killed or missing. The French soldier had, just perhaps, enough resolve for one final offensive. When the failure of the latest venture became apparent at the end of April, before the offensive had finally been called to a halt, the army began to fall apart.

The mutinies of 1917 have remained a difficult subject in French history. The official files on this episode will remain closed until 2017. At the time a high level of secrecy was maintained in order to avoid panic. GQG staff were less than forthcoming to politicians about the extent of the problem, at least initially. Equally, French commanders did not discuss the mutinies in detail with their British counterparts. The true extent of the collapse of the army was not reported in the press in order to maintain public morale. Also, of course, it was desirable for the Germans not to get wind of this collapse.

The French historian Guy Pedroncini was allowed access to the relevant files in the late 1960s and his subsequent book, *Les mutineries de 1917* (Paris, 1967) has become the standard work on this subject. More recently, Denis Rolland, the distinguished scholar of France during the First World War, has published *La grève des tranchees: les mutineries de 1917* (Paris, 2005), which utilises other available sources. While some questions will remain unanswered until the files are released in 2017, it is possible to offer an account of what happened between April and June 1917.[3] It is possible to break down the mutinies into four distinct phases. Indeed, the term 'mutiny' is a much-debated one with respect to these instances. The military authorities at the time preferred to describe them as 'collective disobedience' and while it could be argued that this was an effort to downplay the serious of the situation, in many cases it would actually be an accurate description.

The first phase began on 16–17 April, at the outbreak of the Nivelle Offensive, and lasted until 15 May. During this initial phase there were twenty-six instances of collective indiscipline. The early incidents were, in general, low-key affairs compared to what was to follow and affected only a small number of units. They consisted of protests, a refusal to return to the line and a reluctance to obey orders in general. By 16 May the protests had spread, and between then and 31 May forty-six incidents occurred during the second phase of the mutinies. Whole units, including entire divisions, had become involved in acts of 'collective disobedience'. Protests were also becoming more violent.

The third phase, between 1 and 6 June, was the most alarming as the level of violence increased and it became obvious that the army was barely able to function. At the worst point, these incidents affected fifty-four divisions across five army groups, of which four had taken part in the recent offensive. Of these, Mangin's Sixth Army was the most heavily involved, with the Fourth, Tenth, Fifth and Second Armies also being affected in decreasing order of seriousness. In the final phase, to the end of June, order was restored. Some disturbances occurred in early July, but by then the worst of the crisis had passed.[4]

What form did these incidents take? In size, they ranged from just a few dozen soldiers to several thousand. In form, they ranged from demonstrations and vandalism of barracks and railway stations to a refusal to enter the trenches. In extreme cases the protests included assaults on officers and NCOs and the organisation of marches to eject the government in Paris. It is worthwhile discussing some examples.

There are various reports of disturbances and protests among troops from around 16 April, the opening day of the offensive. Five soldiers and an NCO of the 151st Infantry Regiment refused to leave the trenches to take part in the assault. The following day seventeen men of the 108th Infantry Regiment deserted their post *en masse*. On 21 April troops of the 1st Colonial Division of Mangin's Sixth Army, considered to be crack troops, engaged in a protest while being brought back from the front. As they moved to the rear in trucks they yelled to passing troops moving up to the line 'Long live peace' and 'We have had enough of killing'. Their officers watched, powerless to stop this demonstration by their men.

On 29 April the first major incident took place that involved a large number of troops. The 2nd Battalion of the 18th Infantry Regiment had suffered badly in the offensive, with only 200 men returning from the line. The battalion had lost a large number of officers and NCOs, and this was to prove significant in this and other incidents. The battalion was brought to a 'rest area' outside Soissons, and, due to the fact that the battalion had been decimated, rumours abounded that it would be sent to a relatively quiet sector in Alsace. Instead, replacements brought the battalion back up to strength. These replacements included new officers and NCOs, who were unknown to the men of the unit and therefore not respected or trusted. On 29 April, less than two weeks after being pulled out of the front line, the battalion was ordered back to the front. The scenes that followed were to be repeated across the army in subsequent weeks on an increasingly large scale.

Refusing to form up and march to the front, the troops of the 2nd Battalion proceeded to riot in the 'rest camp', which was, in reality, a miserable, rain-swept, tented encampment. Much alcohol was consumed; this was also a factor in later incidents. By evening the camp was no longer under control and the battalion was not under effective command. Yet this incident was dealt with relatively speedily. The battalion commander returned to the camp with a platoon of gendarmerie and order was restored. The troops, now sober and hung-over, were rooted out of their tents and hiding places and formed up and by 2am the battalion was marching towards the front. Some ringleaders were taken into custody and, in the *conseil de guerre* that followed, five were sentenced to death.[5]

The next major incident took place on 3 May. Troops of the 2nd Colonial Division of General Duchêne's Tenth Army were billeted in various villages around Soissons. On being ordered to return to the front, the men began to fall in but it was obvious to the officers and NCOs that a lot of the men were drunk and many were not carrying their rifles and packs. The scene soon descended into chaos with the men breaking ranks and protesting. A group of up to 200 men then went to divisional HQ to continue their protests, but were held back by a guard of gendarmes. It was only with difficulty that order was restored. Officers went round the groups of disgruntled soldiers and appealed to their sense of duty, and eventually convinced them to move to the front to hold the line but not to attack. While some ringleaders were detained, the regiments of the division moved out. Significantly, no courts-martial were held, and no large-scale punishments were meted out. This protest was far too large, affecting a whole division. This was something more than soldiers demonstrating, throwing stones, vandalising property and equipment or singing revolutionary songs. A whole division had effectively gone on strike, even if only briefly.

From mid-May the whole situation began to escalate and cases similar to that described above became the norm. There was also more destruction and violence. On 26 May, for example, four battalions of the 158th Division mutinied on being ordered to return to the front. One alarming feature was that the rebellious soldiers elected 'deputies' to represent them, following the pattern set in the Russian army after the February Revolution. The troops surrounded the HQ of the divisional commander and when a small column of the troops who had not mutinied began to move to the front, the mutineers followed them shouting pacifist slogans. As such disturbances increased in size and severity, it became obvious that regimental officers were increasingly powerless when it came to controlling their men. Also, as the discontent had spread to so much of the army, it was almost impossible to find reliable troops to put down the mutineers.

The town of Soissons became a particular focus of discontent. Located just over 100km northeast of Paris, it held depressing associations for the front-line infantry. It was through Soissons that hundreds of thousands of infantrymen passed on their way to the front; many of them never returned. It was also the location of various billets and 'rest camps' behind the lines where troops waited for their next spell in the line. The initial disturbance at Soissons took place on 15 May, when troops of XXI Corps mutinied and barricaded themselves in their barracks, taking pot shots at officers who tried to intervene. (It is interesting that in this second phase of the mutinies the soldiers retained and occasionally used their weapons, while in the earlier protests the tendency had been for them to throw their weapons away, thereby rendering themselves 'combat ineffective'.) Later in the evening a group of these troops headed to the railhead at Mercin in order to seize a train to Paris, but their plans were thwarted due to a lack of trains. Instead, they tried to reach other troops at Pernant, but were frustrated again due to the arrival of a regiment of territorials. They headed back to their barracks in Soissons but a few nights later trouble flared up again.

Troops of the 370th Infantry Regiment, on being ordered to the front, began to protest. After speeches made by the ringleaders, the men refused to board the trucks. By evening they were milling around in the streets of Soissons, many of them drunk on looted wine, when trucks arrived carrying mutinous troops from other regiments. Officers were assaulted in the streets, as were gendarmes who tried to intervene. This time the mutineers managed to seize a train in which they started out for Paris, waving red flags and singing revolutionary songs, but in the forest outside Villers-Cotterêts the train was intercepted by a unit of cavalry (the cavalry regiments were largely unaffected by the mutiny). An officer talked the men down and they were disarmed. Some who resisted were shot out of hand.[6] The preoccupation with the railway at Soissons also marked another new aspect of the mutinies. It became increasingly common for the rebellious soldiers to try to get to Paris in order to expel the government. They were no longer concerned with local protests but wished to end the war.

Similar protests occurred throughout the French army, with larger and larger formations becoming involved. In early June the 310th Infantry Regiment, based near Coeuvres, received orders to return to the front. The men rebelled. Refusing to recognise the authority of their officers, they took to the woods near Villers-Cotterêts and set up their own camp. They remained there for four days before surrendering to a regiment of cavalry. During their surrender they emerged from the woods washed, shaved and in perfect formation. The troops of the 298th Infantry Regiment carried out a similar protest, taking over the town of Missy-aux-Bois during the first week of June, until they too surrendered, in formation, to a cavalry regiment.

By the end of June sixty-eight divisions of the French army had been affected by the mutiny, with disturbances breaking out in 129 infantry regiments, 22 battalions of chasseurs à pieds (considered to be élite troops), seven artillery regiments, seven Coloniale regiments (also considered to be élite), one Somali and one territorial battalion. In all, it is estimated that some 40,000 men took part in the mutinies.

The causes of the mutinies of 1917 were numerous and were a mixture of long-term and immediate grievances. The immediate spark was, without doubt, the failure of the Nivelle Offensive. In the weeks preceding the attack the expectations of the troops had been raised to a high level. This time, they would defeat the Boche decisively and in short order. The reality had been yet another costly fiasco, with limited gains at high cost. The troops had endured similar failures since the beginning of the war but it became increasingly obvious that they had been pushed beyond endurance. Nivelle had planned his offensive on the assumption that the resolve and determination of the French *poilu* was limitless but he had succeeded in finding the breaking point of the army under his command.

The handling of the casualty issue fed the discontent further. In the aftermath of the offensive the staff officers at GQG tried to delay the publication of casualty figures; when they were released, they had been calculated downwards. This merely fed the army's rumour mill, which estimated that there had been some 100,000 fatal casualties, perhaps more. In the early days of the mutinies there was frequent criticism within the ranks about the carelessness of the generals, Nivelle in particular, with regard to the soldiers' lives.[7] This sentiment became more deeply entrenched in May and June. As Lord Bertie of Thame, the British ambassador in Paris, eloquently put it: 'they refuse to advance to be butchered'.[8]

Further long-term resentments also played into the mutinies of 1917. One of the most common complaints in soldiers' letters concerned the infrequency of home leave. In theory, each man was allowed three periods of seven days each year – essentially a week at home every four months. This was less than generous to begin with, but conditions at the front often meant that leave was delayed as commanders were reluctant to release men during crisis situations. Only 5 per cent of the troops could be on leave at any time, and on some occasions this was reduced to 2 per cent. Soldiers' leave was therefore rare, and there was also a conviction that rear-echelon types, the hated *embusqués*, were allowed to go on leave first. It was not uncommon for front-line troops to go without leave for five or six months and when soldiers were finally granted leave, they found the leave trains to be 'filthy, squalid and unimaginably slow'.[9] On the over-congested railways, leave trains were given low priority and were often shunted onto branch lines to wait for hours. Facilities on the trains and in the stations were lacking and soldiers faced long, uncomfortable trips home. On their arrival at home, they found that much of their leave allocation had been used in travelling and that they had little time remaining to spend with their families.

By 1917 the relationship between the French soldier and both his immediate officers and the higher command had been fundamentally damaged. Most soldiers felt themselves to have been ill-used and it cannot be over-emphasised how this reduction of their rights as citizens played in to the mutinies. French soldiers were, after all, citizen soldiers in that great French tradition. Just because they had donned uniform did not mean that they were abdicating their rights. So, French soldiers felt that they had a right to protest in the face of such treatment by their commanders. One postal censor noted:

> The soldiers are thinking like employees. They concern themselves with laws governing recruitment, pay, command structure, the guarantees afforded to them by the state. Moreover the soldiers are convinced that by acting collectively they can determine their own fate, if need be by imposing their will at the front as do workers in the rear by striking.[10]

Other immediate factors also played their part. Soldiers returning from leave told others of the difficult situation endured by their families at home. In some areas food was becoming scarce; the price of everything had become inflated due to the war, while at the same time wages were not matching this inflation. The practices of profiteers on the home front also fed the soldiers' discontent, as did rumours that rear echelon troops and colonial troops were seducing French women.

The mutinies occurred at a time of increased unrest on the home front. In the wake of the February Revolution in Russia and the failure of the Nivelle Offensive, the number of strikes and protest marches soared. In terms of industrial unrest, in 1916 there were 98 strikes in France. During 1917 there were 689 strikes and stoppages, involving over 300,000 workers.[11] As early as January 1917 some 400 women workers had staged an anti-war protest in Limoges. By May the authorities reported protests involving as many as 100,000 people in Paris. Reports of repressive measures by police and troops had, by the time they reached the front-line troops, been exaggerated into tales of the massacre of striking women workers. By May the rhetoric of the mutineers was becoming alarmingly revolutionary. One soldier of the 3rd Infantry wrote home: 'It's been like this throughout the war. It's the capitalists who aren't at the front and whose money brings in three times the interest it did before the war who keep it going to annihilate the workers.'[12] As the mutinies became larger and better organised, there was increased talk of soldiers' delegates and committees and, most alarmingly, soldiers' Soviets. The 'Internationale' became a popular song among the mutineers.

News of the February Revolution in Russia had reached the front by April 1917, but for the GQG the most alarming aspect concerned the four oversized Russian brigades, numbering more than 30,000 men, that had been sent to France in 1916. This was part of a scheme under which the Russians would be sent French weapons in exchange for sending troops to the Western Front. The one thing the Russian army was not short of was manpower. Two of these brigades were sent to shore up the Allied effort in Salonika but the 1st and 3rd Brigades remained in France and were fielded alongside the French army. In general they fought well but by the end of 1916 their morale was low, largely due to the poor performance of their own officers and also to supply problems – they disliked French food and mail from home was irregular. The activities of émigré Russians in Paris further complicated matters. Many of these were socialists or revolutionaries of other hues. There was even a Russian-language newspaper, *Nashe Slovo*, which had been founded by Leon Trotsky in Paris in 1914. By April 1917, as Richard M. Watt wrote, 'the Russian brigades in France reflected an accurate, and even slightly exaggerated, picture of the Russian army in its homeland. They had elected Soldiers' Councils, which the Russian officers were either too powerless or too negligent to suppress.'[13] This fervid atmosphere among the Russian formations affected the French units positioned alongside them.

Given the state of their morale, it was perhaps unwise for Nivelle to factor the Russians into his plans for the new offensive but by March–April 1917 the general was no longer attuned to such sensitivities. The Russian brigades were bolstered by the addition of French officers, who would lead them in the assault. Nevertheless, the Russian troops refused to take part without debating the merits of the assault among themselves, before putting the matter to the vote. Amazingly, they voted to take part in the offensive. They were ordered to put in an attack on a heavily defended position at

Fort Brimont, but it was futile and the Russians suffered more than 6,000 casualties, including half of the French officers assigned to them. They subsequently refused to take part in any further offensives.

The worsening situation in Russia was reflected within the Russian brigades and they ultimately broke down into factions – one side supporting the provisional government under Kerensky, the other supporting the Bolshevik cause. These tensions played out in a series of demonstrations and parades at the rest camp at Neuchâteau as Russian soldiers marched with red flags, singing the Internationale. As the camp was shared by French units, GQG staff feared that this revolutionary fervour would spread to the French army and thus the Russians were sent to a camp in the 'Zone of the Interior' at La Courtine. In the months that followed, the factionalism within the Russian brigades worsened and, despite the efforts of provisional government intermediaries sent from Russia, by September the majority of the Russian troops were not under effective command. They entrenched themselves within their new camp and, in what came to be known as the 'battle of La Courtine', they were suppressed using artillery fire in an action that lasted from 16 to 18 September.[14]

The role of the Russian troops in the mutiny is still much debated but what seems certain is that news of the February Revolution had an impact on the French soldiers and that this effect was exacerbated through the presence of the Russian brigades at the front. Certainly the language and symbols of the mutinies mimicked aspects of the February Revolution. Official reports tell of the appearance of red flags, the use of soldiers' councils, the singing of revolutionary songs. By May and June the GQG feared that the French army was about to descend into revolutionary chaos, just as had been the case in Russia.

The impact of America's entry into the war is also a moot point. On 6 April America had declared war on Germany, largely in response to the continued attacks by U-boats on US ships but also as a result of the 'Zimmerman Note' incident of the previous month. Reaction among French troops to this news was oddly mixed. Some soldiers, with good reason, felt that attacks should be delayed until American troops arrived in theatre. Others felt that the arrival of American troops would merely prolong the war, and the slaughter of Frenchmen would continue: French troops would continue to be killed at the front, while French workers would be replaced by Americans and sent to the trenches.[15] For many French troops, therefore, what should have been a piece of positive news was translated into another negative aspect of the war.

These various long- and short-term grievances distilled into the mutinies of 1917. The lot of the French soldier had pushed him to breaking point. This was compounded by other international factors, with the end result that by May 1917 the French army was no longer fit for purpose. On 20 May General Paul Maistre, who had just taken over command of the Sixth Army, postponed an attack because 'we risk having the men refuse to leave their trenches'. He requested fresh troops but there were no reliable units available to send. General d'Espèrey promised him five divisions, but commented that 'they are in a wretched state of morale'.[16]

Why the German army did not take advantage of this situation remains something of a mystery. If it is true that they were not aware of the collapse of morale, this would perhaps represent the biggest failure of German military intelligence in the war. It seems impossible that French soldiers taken prisoner at this time did not describe the dire situation within the French army. Perhaps German intelligence officers did not believe that the crisis could be so bad. It is possible that, due to their efforts in Flanders and also in carrying out counterattacks along the Chemin des Dames, the Germans simply did not have the capacity to mount a major offensive at this time. Moreover, while French soldiers may have refused to carry out further senseless attacks, would they really have allowed the German army to advance through their lines uncontested? As one soldier wrote, they must 'bar the way to the Boches, hard though it is'.[17] It does appear that by mid-July the Germans had acquired some intelligence of the nature of the crisis though spies in France, sources in Switzerland and captured French soldiers, but the full extent of the problem was either not clear to them or they disbelieved it and by the time they unleashed more vigorous attacks on the Chemin des Dames in July, the French army had been restored to order.

It fell to General Pétain to halt the process of the mutinies. Pétain, who had succeeded Nivelle as commander-in-chief in May 1917, faced a daunting prospect, taking over command at a time when the mutinies were increasing in number and severity. As military discipline collapsed and the military authorities looked increasingly ineffective, it must have seemed to many that Pétain could only look on as a bystander and watch the disintegration of the army. A great organiser and possessed of a monumental aura of imperturbableness, Pétain calmly set himself to repairing the army. This sense of calm control was conveyed first to his staff officers and then was communicated throughout the army. On 19 May Pétain issued his Directive No. 1, which was circulated throughout the army. In it, he set out his operational concept. Future offensives would be of a limited nature to ensure 'minimum losses'. There would be intensive artillery preparation, which would focus on the enemy's first line of defences. The infantry would then seize the enemy front line and consolidate the position. There were to be no successive operations and attacks. In short, the breakthrough concept was abandoned. This doctrine encapsulated Pétain's conviction that 'the artillery kills, the infantry occupies'. In the coming weeks, he would communicate this philosophy personally to the officers and soldiers under his command.[18]

Pétain utilised a combination of methods – accurately described by Robert M. Doughty as a 'carrot and stick' approach – to quell the mutinies.[19] With regard to the 'stick', Pétain immediately recognised that the rapid application of military justice would do much to calm the worst excesses of the mutineers, but the system of military law then current in the French army did not allow for this. At the beginning of the war the army had used a court-martial system (*cours martiales*) to try soldiers accused of breaches of discipline or cowardice. A conviction under this system could lead to a speedy execution *pour l'example*. This system was obviously open to abuse and misuse, and, following the bad publicity resulting from some cases of the seemingly hasty execution of soldiers, the French parliament pushed through reforms in late 1914. The new system was referred to as *conseils de guerre* and was designed to mirror certain aspects of the French civil law code. All soldiers convicted of a crime had the right of appeal to a higher court, while all death sentences had to be personally reviewed and approved by the president of the French Republic.

This system obviously denied the army the ability to mete out swift justice and summary executions, which Pétain believed were necessary to curb the rapidly spreading mutiny. Pétain applied himself to convincing the Minister of War, Paul Painlevé, that the *conseil de guerre* system must be relaxed in order to allow him to suppress the mutiny. To re-establish the *cours martiales* system would require approval in parliament but a modification of the *conseil* system was open to the minister. Painlevé took some convincing, but it seems Pétain was more forthcoming to him about the seriousness of the situation. Accordingly, on 9 June Painlevé issued a directive that removed the right of appeal in cases of 'collective disobedience'. He also convinced President Poincaré to give up his right to pardon in such cases. Finally, he instructed the military censors not to allow news of these changes to be reported in the press, while also forbidding the printing of an edition of the new code of military justice. In effect, Pétain had convinced Painlevé to reinstate the *cours martiales* system in all but name. Painlevé was fully aware of the enormity of what he had done, later stating 'when it is all over you may shoot me if you wish, but now only let me re-establish order'.[20] Military justice duly swung into action and some of the ringleaders of the early mutinies in May were executed in early June, shortly after these changes had been made in the military justice system.

The exact numbers of mutineers tried, convicted and executed remain a topic of debate. Pedroncini identified 3,427 cases of soldiers being convicted for offences during the mutinies. Of these, 554 were sentenced to death by firing squad but the majority received a presidential pardon and had their sentences commuted to periods in prison, usually with hard labour. The majority served their sentences in prison colonies in Algeria, Morocco or Indochina, with sentences ranging from three years to life, depending on the severity of their actions.[21] Pedroncini, who is the only scholar thus far to have had full access to the files on the mutinies, is certain that fifty-two men were executed by firing squad, while a further ten may also have been executed. According to Pétain himself, fifty-five were executed.[22] The French historian Denis Rolland identified twenty-seven executions.[23] There remains, therefore, a considerable level of doubt about the official statistics and many modern historians have come up with different totals. It is certain that Pétain was less than forthcoming with his own government at the time in an effort to play down the seriousness of the situation. It would seem that Painlevé did not see all of the dossiers of the men condemned to death and he later remarked that the mutinies had been suppressed 'at the price of twenty-three executions'.[24] The numbers of those shot on the spot by officers or gendarmes during the mutinies or summarily executed during the disturbances cannot be known for sure. As Richard M. Watt has remarked, 'Without doubt there were many more executions than the French army historians ever admitted – more, probably, than they ever knew about.'

The manner in which the new code of military justice was enforced was also interesting in its psychology. In some cases specific ringleaders were identified and sent to trial. In others, soldiers were picked out at random in a manner similar to the ancient Roman practice of decimation. In early June 1917 General Émile Taufflieb, the commander of XXXVII Corps, put down a mutiny within one of his battalions and, having harangued the mutinous unit on the parade ground, sent gendarmes into their ranks to pick out twenty men at random to go before the *conseils de guerre*. Yet despite the grave situation, Pétain refrained from over-using such tactics and did not sanction large-scale executions or the widespread use of decimation, unlike the practice within the Italian army following its collapse in October 1917. His mindset is reflected in a letter of 18 June:

> I have pressed hard for the repression of these grave acts of indiscipline; I will maintain the pressure with firmness but without forgetting that it is applied to soldiers who, for three years, have been with us in the trenches and are 'our soldiers'.[25]

The treatment of the mutinous Russian brigades was another matter entirely and it could be argued that the harshest punishment was meted out to them. It is unknown how many were killed or injured when the Russian camp at La Courtine was shelled in September. In total, eighty-one of the ringleaders were handed over to the Russian authorities at Bordeaux and it would seem that the majority of them were executed. A further 549 men were sent to prison or penal colonies in North Africa. After further unrest, the remainder of the rebels (more than 7,000 men) were sent to work in munitions factories or to North Africa.[26]

Pétain did not focus only on the rebellious enlisted men and NCOs. It became clear that he also felt that some officers had not done their duty. Some officers were immediately dismissed from their commands or units, but more than thirty later faced a *conseil de guerre*. These officers included three generals, eleven lieutenant-colonels and nine 'chefs de bataillon'. More junior officers were also included in these trials, but it was clear that the focus was on brigade, regimental and battalion commanders, who, it was felt, had not acted speedily and effectively to put down dissent within their commands.[27]

What then of Pétain's 'carrot' approach? The immediate grievances of the soldiers were all too apparent, and Pétain set about remedying them in a speedy and effective manner. The leave system, that perennial bugbear of the line infantryman, was overhauled. Furthermore, the army bulletin of 6 June made it obvious to the troops that the high command was actually aware of the problems with the leave system and was setting about rectifying them:

> The efforts of the high command have been directed towards ensuring seven days of leave every four months to everyone. The percentage of men allowed on leave at any one time, formerly fixed at 13% of effective strength, will be maintained. Nevertheless, as the situation permits, this may be increased to 25 or 50% in large units which have been taken to the rear to be reconstituted. The leave schedule is to be made up with the greatest of care and will be posted for inspection by those concerned.

This represented a huge change for the troops – more frequent leave and a system administered in an open and clear manner. Moreover, leave entitlement was later increased to ten days every four months. The organisation of leave trains was improved, with the YMCA, the French Red Cross and the *Foyers du Soldat* organisation asked to set up canteens at the railway stations used by the troops. Pétain also ordered that more gendarmes be posted at stations to cut down on drunkenness and also to discourage anti-war and socialist agitators who often targeted soldiers on leave. The rest camps, previously notorious as dreary places, were to be improved with the presence of barbers and proper washing facilities. Pétain also formalised a 'Zone of Rest' in the rear area where soldiers could actually enjoy their time out of the front line. New schools of instruction were set up to keep the soldiers engaged and efforts were made to cut down the supply of alcohol in order to try to reduce drunkenness.

Pétain emerged as a general in the Napoleonic mould and this unlikely figure showed a remarkable aptitude for connecting with the men under his command. He visited ninety divisions in person, talking with the troops, discussing their grievances and outlining the GQG's plans for the future. In this respect, he assured them that there would be no more senseless attacks. Any offensive action would be limited in nature and carefully prepared. In this, he adopted techniques that would later come to be associated with renowned Second World War commanders such as Montgomery and Eisenhower, among others. Pétain connected with the soldiers and explained to them the importance of their individual role. In terms of boosting morale, Pétain's visits to the troops were nothing short of masterful. He distributed decorations – most commonly the *Croix de Guerre* and also the newly instituted unit citation lanyard or *fourragère*. Troops had previously complained that it was only senior officers who got recognition and rewards. Pétain tried to convince them that this was not so.

Pétain concluded these visits by meeting the divisional officers, whom he usually addressed while standing on the hood of his car. In some cases the assembled officers found his words less than gentle. He reminded them of their duty as officers: 'Look at these men; there is nothing the matter with them. All they require is leading; all they need is example. Advance and they will follow you.'[28] Staff officers were also encouraged to visit the front lines more frequently.

Pétain later summarised the duty of the army in an article entitled 'Why we are fighting', which was published on the front page of most newspapers. Reprints were also distributed among the army. In simple terms, he tried to address the negative attitude that had recently emerged about the war and the alarming calls for peace: 'We fight because we have been attacked by Germany. We fight to drive the enemy from our soil. We fight with tenacity and discipline, because these are essential to obtain victory.' He concluded by stating: 'France can expect with reasonable confidence a victorious peace that is indispensable to it and that it deserves victory because of its heavy sacrifices.'[29]

It is now also clear that while Pétain was dealing with the mutinies, he was less than forthcoming to both his own government and his British allies about the true scale of the disturbances. The mutinies actually increased in severity from late May but Pétain clearly tried to downplay their seriousness in his communications with Painlevé. For instance, on 30 May Pétain was in possession of a report compiled by his staff that detailed instances of collective disobedience which had taken place from early May. Yet in his report to Painlevé he referred to incidents that had occurred during the past 'several days'. Despite his efforts, however, the scale of the problem became increasingly obvious to Painlevé and also to other deputies through reports from other officers and journalists, and also from letters that had been sent directly to them from the front. In an effort to counter the spread of this information, in early June the GQG put measures in place to reduce the flow of mail from the front. Pétain also severely criticised the press in a report to Painlevé. Yet despite the difficulties he faced in trying to control the flow of information, Pétain was reasonably successful in concealing the full extent of the disturbances until they had passed their worst phase.

With Field Marshal Haig, his British counterpart, he was equally coy. On 27 May he assured Haig that the French would keep their promise and provide six divisions in support of a planned British offensive in Flanders. However, Edward Spears, then the chief British liaison officer, knew that the situation was worse than was being suggested. By the end of May Haig was preparing contingency plans for holding Flanders without French support. On 2 June the situation worsened when Pétain's chief of staff, General Eugène Debeney, met Haig and explained that a planned offensive was being postponed. When Haig and Pétain finally met face to face on 7 June, the British commander found Pétain evasive. While the French commander admitted that there had been disturbances, court-martials and some executions, he implied that the mutinies had been confined to just two divisions. After the war, Pétain admitted to Haig that he had misled him. At the time Haig wrote:

> Pétain and I then had a private talk. He told me that 2 French divisions had refused to go and relieve 2 divisions in front line because the men had not had leave! Some were tried and shot. The French government supported Pétain. They also refused to allow the Socialists to go to

Stockholm for a conference with German Socialists. The situation in the French army was serious at one moment but is now quite satisfactory. But the bad state of discipline causes Pétain grave concern.

Thus informed of the French difficulties, Haig considered an even greater concern, writing 'if France drops out [of the war] we not only cannot continue the war on land but our armies in France will be in a very difficult position'.[30]

During his first weeks in command, therefore, Pétain was fully occupied in restoring order and addressing the immediate grievances of the troops, while making efforts to prevent both his own government and his British allies becoming too alarmed. He also needed to initiate a large-scale reform of the French army. The simple fact was that France was running out of men. The casualties inflicted on the French army since the beginning of the war were now having a major impact on the ability of the army to operate. And these casualties could no longer be replaced. As a report by the GQG concluded, 'the day is approaching when a large offensive by us must be curtailed because we cannot fill the vacancies in our units'.[31]

In recent months the practice had been to call up classes of conscripts early, bringing these recruits into the army before they reached the age of 21. The upper age limit was raised to 49. As was the case with all armies by this time, on both sides, the medical and physical standards were lowered. Men who would have been considered unfit for military service in 1914 were now taken into the army. Yet these measures, together with the use of troops and labourers from the French colonies, could still not make up the shortfall.

Therefore, the actual organisation of the army's units was reformed. Divisions were reduced in size from four to three regiments, while the establishment of infantry companies fell from 250 to 200 men. So, while the number of divisions may have appeared to be the same, they were now much smaller. In terms of actual strength, divisions shrank from around 15,000 soldiers to 13,000.

In order to preserve the army further, Pétain returned to a scheme originally initiated by Nivelle. In an effort to gather as many troops as possible to support offensive or counteroffensive action, Nivelle had commissioned General Roques to survey the French front line and report on ways in which it could be defended more effectively. This would reduce the number of troops needed to defend it and allow Nivelle to concentrate his forces and send reinforcements to any threatened sectors. Roques recommended that the fortifications be improved and suggested that the increased use of machine guns would be effective in allowing the front lines to be held by fewer troops. Further reforms, initiated by Joffre, also came to fruition after Pétain took command. In a system that paralleled the German defence-in-depth and the British 'redoubt' systems, it was decided that a continuous front line would no longer be maintained. Instead, the front would be held as a 'sentry line' by a relatively small number of troops. Behind this would be fortified centres of resistance incorporated within the defensive system using communication trenches. Any attacking German force would therefore eventually pass through the lightly held front lines, hopefully being heavily punished by the increased number of machine guns, only to be stopped by these fortified centres.

Throughout May and early June 1917, while mutiny spread through the army, Pétain and his staff were also hastily trying to improve the French defensive system. This urgent activity was prompted by Pétain's concern regarding German offensive intentions for 1917. He fully expected a 'combination of a frontal attack and a manoeuvre through Switzerland against France'.[32] In such an eventuality, it would be impossible for the French and British to successfully contest the front lines and hold their initial positions. The new defensive measures would allow the Allies to trade space for time, giving them the opportunity to launch counterattacks. For this, Pétain felt that the Allies needed a mobile reserve of forty divisions.

Alongside these measures, Pétain also knew that a huge rearmament programme was necessary. He drew on the immediate lessons of Nivelle's failed offensive. Early in the battle the French had lost control of the air, rendering Nivelle's army effectively blind during the preparatory artillery bombardment and also when the offensive began. Pétain urged Painlevé to speed up the aircraft production programme. The French *Service Aeronautique* simply needed more and better planes. In September Pétain initiated a programme for the construction of more than 2,800 new aircraft of improved designs.[33]

Although the tanks had been disappointing during the offensive, Pétain recognised that the central concept had potential. In an offensive, tanks could provide valuable mobile firepower in support of the attacking infantry. It was just that the Schneider and St Chamond were such poor designs. General Estienne had begun developing a new prototype light tank in late 1916 in cooperation with the Renault company. Various bureaucratic delays had stalled this project in the run-up to Nivelle's offensive. In some ways such delays were understandable, with a third tank development programme vying for funds and resources. After Pétain took command, Estienne's light tank project began to emerge as the best option. Of course, Pétain and Estienne knew each other, and this allowed Estienne to outline his 'bee theory' for the use of light tanks. Essentially, rather than using a relatively small number of heavy tanks, he proposed the use of hundreds of smaller tanks in attacks that would go forth like 'a swarm of bees'. For every heavy tank produced, they could produce five light tanks. A switch to light tanks would thus produce a fivefold increase in tank production. Each one would mount either a 37mm gun or a machine gun. The Germans had improved their defences and deployed more artillery, but attacks by swarms of the new tanks would present too many targets for the German artillery and they would be overwhelmed. Pétain agreed with this theory and in June increased the order for the production of light tanks to 3,500. These small, two-man light tanks, designated FT-17, were the first fighting vehicles to use a turret designed to traverse through 360 degrees.[34]

As an artilleryman, it was only natural that Pétain should focus some attention on reforming this arm of the service. In some ways he carried on reforms that had been initiated by Nivelle. Early in 1917 Nivelle had recognised the need for a mobile artillery reserve and had initiated a programme to create just such a reserve and also to supply it with tractor units to increase mobility. This concept was in accord with Pétain's own theories on the use of artillery in both offensive and defensive operations. If the mobility of the artillery could be enhanced, it could move speedily to sections of the line in order to subject the Germans to a sudden, intense barrage in the lead-up to a surprise offensive. Such a level of mobility would decrease the time needed to prepare offensives and thus reduce the chance of losing the element of surprise. If an advance were successful, tractor-drawn artillery could follow up infantry over broken ground more effectively than horse-drawn artillery could, and Pétain also planned for special pioneer units to be assigned to the mobile artillery to repair damaged roads if necessary. A mobile artillery reserve had advantages in defensive operations, too, and it was envisaged that it could be rushed to the location of German offensives to blunt such attacks.

If mobility were to be improved, some attention also had to be paid to the actual guns being used. Experience had shown that the French 75mm was simply not effective on the Western Front. What was needed was a heavier calibre, short-range cannon in order to tackle German entrenchments. In May 1916 a new programme had been initiated that facilitated a shift in artillery production priorities. Production of the 75mm was to be phased out, and the 155mm cannon was to take priority. By August 1916 French factories were producing around 180 cannon per month.[35] By the summer of 1917 this build-up of 155mm cannon was beginning to have a very real effect on the front line, and the increase in the number of short-range heavy guns would facilitate Pétain's plans for limited offensives. Within the artillery planning, he also increased orders for chemical shells and smoke rounds. He believed that the chemical rounds would be effective against German troop reserves, which were often protected in deep bunkers. They were also particularly useful in counter-battery barrages. Thousands of smoke rounds would be used to cover the advance of French infantry and tanks.

Pétain's philosophy of the offensive was, therefore, in direct contrast to the methods employed by Nivelle and, indeed, previous French commanders. By 1917 it was very apparent that French offensives were too reliant on the *poilu*. French commanders too often under-emphasised proper planning and the deployment of materiel, and instead relied on the efforts of the infantry to overcome all obstacles. For Pétain, it would be the other way round. Artillery, tanks, aircraft, chemical weapons and any other available technology would be employed to do the 'heavy lifting' in future attacks. He summed up his own offensive philosophy best with maxims such as 'lavish with steel, stingy with blood'.[36]

Also, the scope of future operations was to be severely curtailed. The army would only engage in limited offensives for specific objectives. Offensives would be of short duration and focused on attainable goals, and units would only be expected to carry out one assault before consolidating. Any further assaults would be carried out by fresh troops. All of these limited offensives would be supported with ample artillery and any other available assets, such as tanks. This philosophy simply turned the previous practice on its head. Gone were the days of the large-scale assault that hoped for a general breakthrough and exploitation, a method that required troops to carry out wave after wave of attacks. Formulating such a philosophy was one thing, but Pétain also communicated it to the officers and men of the army through his published directives and his personal visits during the summer of 1917.

Considering the state of the army when Pétain took charge in May, its return to a functioning state seems like little short of a miracle. The fact that it was able to undertake offensive operations by July seemed beyond belief to French generals and politicians and also to their British allies. An early indication that the army was returning to normal came in mid-July with the Bastille Day parade. Pétain selected a collection of units with good morale to take part in the parade, which had been carefully planned. The streets along the route from the Cours de Vincennes to the Place de la Nation were lined with seats for wounded soldiers. The population of Paris seemed to have turned out for the spectacle, while thousands of others travelled by train to be present. The whole affair was a demonstration of the type of military spectacle at which France so excelled. Regimental bands played their traditional marching songs as their battalions followed with colours held aloft. The colonial troops and cavalry looked particularly magnificent. As an exercise in the display of military strength and French *panache* it was masterful. President Poincaré distributed the new fourragères to deserving units, to a huge response from the crowd. The rather undemonstrative Pétain had pulled off a stunning public relations coup. The jittery nerves of the government and the French people in general had been calmed.

In the weeks that followed, the French army showed that it was capable of backing up this display. At the Paris conference on 4 May Haig and Pétain (who was then still only chief of staff) discussed plans for the summer. Given the failure of the Nivelle Offensive, it was mutually understood that the British would launch the next major offensive. In a memo the following day Haig outlined his intentions for an offensive to clear the Germans from several key ports along the Belgian coast. The first phase of the British offensive would take place in June and focus on the Messines–Wytschaete Ridge. This would be followed in July by a further offensive at Ypres. The British would provide the main effort, but French support would still be needed.

Having taken command, Pétain assured Haig at a meeting on 18 May that the French army would carry out supporting operations on the Chemin des Dames, at Reims and Verdun, and also in the Alsace sector. These would be on a 'considerable scale'. While Pétain questioned both the British methods and their objectives for the coming offensives, General Wilson reported that the French would carry out 'three or four small attacks for strictly limited objectives, and when the objectives were reached, the fighting would cease'. In principle, however, Pétain had agreed to support a British attack in Flanders, while also carrying out phased attacks on further positions along the German line.[37]

The British were understandably nervous as rumours of the mutinies spread. This was not helped when General Debeney met Haig on 2 June and told him that, while the promised six divisions would be sent to Flanders, the attack scheduled to take place on the Chemin des Dames on 4 June had been cancelled. Thereafter Haig and his staff viewed French promises with some scepticism.

Nevertheless, during June and July three of the French armies most damaged by the mutinies (the Fourth, Sixth and Tenth) took part in a series of actions in support of the British offensive and also to break up German operations along the French line. Limited offensives took place along a broad front, supplemented by flash barrages carried out by mobile artillery and also mine detonations. These operations were at their most intensive on a front stretching from the Lorraine to the Argonne. Gains were limited, in line with Pétain's intentions, and in mid-July the Fourth Army launched a spoiling operation to scupper German preparations for a local offensive.

The operations of the First Army in support of the British offensive in Flanders were particularly successful. The First Army, commanded by General Anthoine, had been badly affected by the mutinies but in early June it moved to positions north of Ypres in Flanders, where it slotted into the line between Belgian forces to the north and British troops to the south. To the First Army's front was the Yser Canal, running roughly north–south, and the Germans had gained a narrow foothold on the west side of the canal. In support of the left flank of the British attack, it was Anthoine's intention to push the Germans back across the canal as far as he could. The First Army had access to substantial firepower, with more than 900 guns in total; preliminary barrages began on 15 July and would carry on in phases and with shifting targets until the infantry attack began on 31 July. The French were meticulous in their preparation, constructing new roads and also a light railway in their rear area. Three complete surgical field hospitals were also established.[38]

The infantry attack on 31 July was a success, the French troops passing through the shattered German defences as far as the third line before digging in and consolidating. At the end of the day only 180 men had been killed, the majority of them by German artillery which shelled the captured positions. As an example of the application of Pétain's philosophy, it was an immense success but, as the Third Battle of Ypres ground on, Anthoine requested permission to call off further French attacks. Despite his own misgivings, Pétain felt obliged to support the British, especially as the promised Chemin des Dames offensive had been cancelled. As on the Somme the previous year, the Third Battle of Ypres, or Passchendaele as it is often known, dragged on until November, with the French First Army supporting Haig's misguided offensive. The hamlet of Passchendaele, just 8km from the offensive's starting line, was finally captured in early November, by which time the French had lost more than 1,600 men killed and 6,900 wounded. Total British casualties stood at more than 300,000 killed or wounded.

Further confirmation of the soundness of Pétain's approach came in August in the Verdun sector. In late June a German attack had seized terrain on the west bank of the Meuse near Hill 304. A mid-July counterattack by the French had recaptured the position, only to be ejected again by a new German attack. The commander of the Second Army, General Adolphe Guillaumat, planned his next counterattack operation meticulously. The French *Service Aéronautique* took control of the skies over Verdun so that artillery spotting could be carried out effectively. Artillery preparation began on 11 August and by 20 August more than 3 million rounds had been fired, including large numbers of gas shells. Machine guns were used to provide indirect fire in order to interdict German reinforcements moving up to the line. Guillaumat laid down strict instructions to his corps and divisional commanders, and objectives were to be strictly adhered to.

The infantry attack commenced on 20 August and was surprisingly effective, despite German counterattacks and artillery fire, and despite the fact that the Germans also retook control of the air during periods of this battle. By 26 August the French had succeeded in taking all of their operational objectives. These included Hill 304 again and also positions on Mort Homme, both scenes of costly battles in 1916 and 1917. The public and political reaction to these successes verged on the hysterical. Crowds celebrated the news in Paris, and on 25 August Pétain was awarded the Grand Cross of the Legion of Honour. On 29 August President Poincaré and Painlevé visited Verdun to present Pétain with his award. In his speech Poincaré remarked: 'Never has the army demonstrated more courage and more spirit. Three years of hard combat have neither altered its strength nor cooled its ardour.'[39] These remarks were reported widely in the press. The mutinies were not mentioned. Limited operations continued in the Verdun sector with limited success until September.

The months from May to July 1917 marked an extraordinary and potentially disastrous period in French history. Certainly, when Pétain took command in May he inherited an army that was dysfunctional, if not totally broken. His predecessor, Nivelle, had pushed the French army beyond its breaking point. As public and political morale also plummeted, the real possibility opened up of France suffering a major defeat in the field and then dropping out of the war. By introducing a combination of coercive measures and reforms, Pétain had effectively reversed this trend and returned the French army to a state in which it was 'fit for purpose'.

Pétain had been lauded as the 'Saviour of Verdun' in 1916 and would later be hailed as the 'médecin de l'armée' for his performance as commander-in-chief from the summer of 1917. He had effectively both repaired and rebuilt the army. The actual conditions of the troops had been improved and the army had been reorganised to take decreases of manpower into account. There had also been a fundamental shift in leadership ideology and this was personified in many ways by Pétain himself. He did not believe in wasteful offensives followed by successive attacks. He imposed this style of leadership on his army commanders, and even at the tactical level junior officers were encouraged to make judicious use of firepower rather than expending lives in wasteful attacks. For much of the remainder of the war French operations were characterised by limited attacks aimed at specific and attainable objectives. The French fighting doctrine factored in increased firepower, and the use of tanks and aircraft in support. Simply put, the 'l'offensive à outrance' concept, that relied so much on flesh and blood, was finished.

As the BEF and US forces increased in theatre, the French army found that it no longer carried the greater burden on the Western Front. French officers and instructors acted in a mentoring role for the newly arriving American troops, and the French army supplied much equipment to the American Expeditionary Force, including machine guns, artillery, tanks and aircraft. Since 1914 the French army had been engaged in continuous campaigning, either on the offensive or reacting to German attacks, as at Verdun in 1916. In the search for strategic alternatives, French troops were also sent to Salonika, Gallipoli, Egypt and Palestine. In 1918 France faced a further onslaught in a series of German offensives collectively referred to as the *Kaiserschlacht* ('Kaiser's Battle'). Comprising Operations Michael, Georgette, Blücher-Yorck, Gneisenau and Marne-Rheims, the Kaiserschlacht ran from 21 March to 17 July 1918. Having reached a position dangerously close to Paris, the German offensive stalled and the Allies went over to the attack. During the final months of the war the French army was almost continually on the offensive somewhere along its front.

On the day the Armistice came into effect, 11 November 1918, French troops were still active right up to the 11am ceasefire. Due to German hesitation in signing a ceasefire agreement during the negotiations at Compiègne, Foch insisted that offensive actions should continue. At Vrigne-sur-Meuse an operation was launched late on 10 November to cross the Meuse River. Around 700 French troops made the crossing, and more than 90 men were killed. The last of these is believed to have been Soldat Augustin Trebuchon, who was killed at 10.45am on 11 November 1918. He was an experienced soldier who served as a runner or messenger, and had been previously wounded. He was killed while carrying forward a message that read: 'Muster at 11.30 for food.' Trebuchon's memorial records the date of his death as 10 November, apparently due to the fact that senior commanders were ashamed that men had been killed so close to the armistice.[40]

Conclusion

Nivelle's failure was no greater than that of others, indeed rather less. He took more ground than Joffre did in his offensives or than Haig did at Arras. But Nivelle had promised more. Instead, he had carried the exhausted French army beyond breaking point.

(A.J.P. Taylor)[1]

Perhaps the most surprising aspect of the Nivelle Offensive was that, despite its failure, there were so few consequences for its instigator, Nivelle himself. Yes, his career as a commander was over, and for a man who was so ambitious and had such tremendous self-belief this must have been devastating, but, as was the case with so many failed First World War commanders, there would be no court-martial or further sanction.

There was, however, a Commission of Enquiry, which met in a series of sessions from August to October 1917. Its brief was to 'study the conditions in which the offensive of 16–23 April took place in the valley of the Aisne and to determine the role of the general officers who exercised command'.[2] It was an investigative commission only and had no power to impose any sanctions. It was headed by General Brugère and the other two members were Generals Foch and Gouraud. None of these officers had served under Nivelle during the offensive and were deemed suitable to carry out the inquiry due to their seniority. Nivelle did not attend all the sessions and submitted some of his testimony in a series of memoranda. Generals Micheler, Mazel and Mangin also attended to give evidence. Painlevé was deeply disappointed with the remit of the commission and later dismissed its report as mere 'rose water'.

Some time was spent considering Nivelle's overall principles, with Foch expanding on how Nivelle's concepts were flawed and how continuing the Somme offensive might have been more fruitful, perhaps even resulting in victory in 1917. The testimonies of Nivelle's subordinate commanders followed a pattern. Micheler, Mangin and Mazel all confessed to having had doubts about the plan and its operational security but they had ultimately felt obliged to follow orders. Mangin, now thoroughly disillusioned with his former chief, referred to Nivelle's Napoleonic attitude, while Mazel was described as 'cold and reserved' throughout the proceedings. Pétain, who had initially not been invited to attend, also obtained a hearing, during which he trotted out his previous criticisms. It seems that he was making an effort to disassociate himself from all blame, although it can be argued that he should have been more forceful in his opposition in March and April.

The commission also sought out the report prepared in early 1917 by Nivelle's former chief of operations, Colonel Renouard. This report had contained pessimistic predictions regarding the offensive's likelihood of success and several staff officers had read it. Interestingly, the members of the commission found that the report had been removed from the files.[3]

The commission's final thirty-page report is an excellent source for historians as it unpacks the development of Nivelle's plan throughout its span.[4] The role of the subordinate generals is also outlined and some, such as Mangin, are given credit for their performance. General Duchêne could not be criticised, it was stated, as his army's offensive had never truly got under way. Ultimate responsibility rested, the report concluded, with Nivelle.

Other aspects of the plan also drew severe criticism. The presiding generals concluded that the logistical measures necessary to maintain the artillery supply, and hence the barrage, had not been put in place. The medical services were singled out for particular criticism as they had inadequate personnel in place to evacuate wounded from the battlefield and then too few field hospitals and transport facilities.

Further points were also discussed that contributed to the offensive's failure. These included:

- inadequate artillery preparation;
- poor performance by the tanks;
- weather;
- lack of operational security;

- the German withdrawal to the Hindenburg Line; and
- the availability of German reserves.

Mention was also made of the activities of 'defeatist' and pacifist elements within France. The report made positive mention of the 'magnificent *élan*' and performance of the troops. The message was clear: the cause of the defeat lay not with the troops themselves but with their senior commanders.[5] It was perhaps the commission's president, General Brugère, who best summed up the main problem in a letter to Poincaré, in which he stated that Nivelle 'had not been up to' the demands of senior command.[6]

Paradoxically, the Germans also formed an investigative group to examine the French attack. It reached many of the same conclusions as the French inquiry. The Germans paid special attention to the deployment of the tank force, commenting, 'We can only conclude that the main striking force of an offensive resides in tanks and it is a question of developing the other arms in such a way that they can keep up with them.'[7] The German general staff would pay much attention to tank actions during the First World War as they developed new operational doctrines during the inter-war years. This process would ultimately produce the tactical methods of 'Blitzkrieg'.

The issue of casualties was a major feature of the French inquiry. In the offensive's early phases losses were being estimated at around 96,000 in total, killed, wounded or missing. It is now clear that these initial calculations were underestimated. During the worst phase of the army mutinies the losses were deliberately downplayed in the hope of minimising the public and political outcry. During wartime it was also difficult to get accurate casualty numbers due to various battlefield factors and the enormous pressures faced by administrative and medical staff. However, it would appear that there were some attempts to conceal the extent of the casualties. For example, casualties from the Russian brigades were not initially factored in, while lightly wounded who returned to their units were also not counted. Most modern accounts give the figure of 134,000 casualties, which includes 100,000 wounded, 30,000 killed and 4,000 missing or taken prisoner. A post-war study by the 1er Bureau of the GQG calculated the numbers to be much higher, and factored in losses for the whole of the operation from 16 April to 10 May and also included those who suffered light wounds. This gave significantly higher totals of 48,000 dead, 120,000 wounded and 4,500 taken prisoner or missing.[8] The Canadian historian G.W.L. Nicholson calculated as many as 187,000 losses in total. Such casualty rates represented the worst losses since November 1914.[9] The debate about the final casualty figures still continues. Due to the fact the GQG withheld the casualty figures at the time, the idea that the true total was much higher has endured. Some French sources claim 200,000–250,000 men *killed*.[10]

Can the Nivelle Offensive be considered anything other than a failure? In the light of such casualty figures it is obvious, by any sensible criteria, that it was a costly failure. Yet at the time there were attempts to cast it in a more positive light. Estimates of the numbers of German casualties vary but some sources claim as many as 163,000 total casualties, including more than 28,000 taken prisoner. More than 180 German artillery pieces and over 400 machine guns (some sources say 1,000) had been captured, along with 149 *Minenwerfer* and much other equipment. Some territorial gains had been made and key terrain features captured, while the Sixth Army's advance was one of the biggest French advances since the war had settled into trench warfare in 1914. The army was firmly rooted on the Chemin des Dames and these new positions would facilitate further actions in the summer of 1917. In the wider context of the French army's experiences in the First World War, this could be cast in a positive light. (*See* Map 4.) The wasteful offensives of 1915 had, for example, achieved less for similarly high casualties.

The key issue that made Nivelle's failure so disastrous in 1917 was the timing of it. The French army was on the brink of exhaustion at the beginning of the offensive and was then pushed beyond endurance to breaking point. And the suffering and sacrifice did not bring the promised victory. Such failures had been absorbed by the army and the French nation in 1914, 1915 and 1916, but by 1917 there was simply no room for further failure.

The aftermath of the events of 1917 also demonstrates that the ties binding the French government, army and people together in the war effort were in a critical state after this failure. In his classic study of military strategy,

On War, Carl von Clausewitz developed the concept of the 'trinity of war': the synergetic relationship between government, people and army that is necessary if a nation is to successfully conduct a modern war.

This principle was developed by later strategic theorists during the twentieth century and it remains largely true today. Alexandr Svechin, writing in the 1920s in the context of First World War and the recent Russian revolution and civil war, summed up this principle simply by stating that 'war may be waged only by the will of a united people'.[11] It is glaringly apparent that, at the time of the Nivelle Offensive, this 'trinity of war' had broken down in France. The relationship between the government and the military commanders was dysfunctional. The politicians were trying to exert more control over the military but their efforts were often ill-considered and largely ineffectual. Also, there was a lack of consistency; Painlevé found his efforts thwarted by colleagues within government, including Premier Ribot, who believed in Nivelle and his plans.

Within the military, the subordinate commanders never united in a concerted effort to oust Nivelle, despite their misgivings about him and his plans. He had his critics, yet the tendency was for generals to air their grievances privately to the politicians and the press while failing to present a united front at crucial meetings in order to have Nivelle removed. A greater loyalty to their own profession and the principles of command did not allow senior generals to unite and demand Nivelle's removal. Svechin later summed up the dysfunctional nature of the French political–military relationship during the run-up to the offensive:

> Officially the operation was greatly approved and everyone glorified the successes that would be achieved but then wrote confidential letters to influential politicians asking them to keep the army from launching an operation that had absolutely no chance of success. However, they did not have the civic courage to repeat these doubts in front of Nivelle at a special meeting called by Minister Painlevé.[12]

The mutinies that broke out in the wake of the failed offensive are ample proof that the rank and file of the French army had lost faith in their senior commanders. In this fractured relationship, command and control systems and military discipline broke down. The French public were also in a state of discontent with the politicians – all politicians, regardless of faction or party – and with how the war was being run. In the spring and early summer of 1917 this discontent erupted in strikes and protests that broke out across France. The French people sympathised with the *poilus* in the trenches and supported their mutinies as they had lost faith in the government and the military leaders. Ultimately, all the links within the crucial 'trinity of war' had broken down. By June 1917 France had ceased to function as a united nation at war.

In a wider context, the Briand government had also allowed itself to be drawn into a damaging political contest between British politicians, in particular Lloyd George, and senior British commanders. It could be argued that, like a contagion, the dysfunctional aspects of the French government and military also affected the political–military relationship of the British.

Alongside these wider ramifications, debate has continued as to why the offensive failed. The 1917 inquiry identified many of the key issues, which can be summed up as a combination of failings in leadership, choice of terrain, planning and preparation. Also, Nivelle had allowed himself to be drawn into what would now be referred to as 'mirror-imaging' – effectively, he expected the Germans to conform to his plans as to how the offensive would unfold. As A.J.P. Taylor put it, 'the Germans did not conform to Nivelle's requirements'.[13]

Perhaps inevitably, Nivelle himself has remained the focus of criticism. Yet even if one accepts that he was ultimately responsible for the failure, further questions remain as we are faced with a general who was demonstrably intelligent but who nevertheless acted in a seemingly irresponsible manner. Using modern 'Principles of War' criteria to examine the offensive, it can be shown that, in some respects, Nivelle can be considered to have performed well. The concept of 'Principles of War' has been in circulation since classical times and by the First World War had been codified by many armies. While there are variations in criteria in different nations, the modern US scheme identifies nine main principles:[14]

Principles of war	DEFINITION
Mass	Concentrate combat power at the decisive place and time
Objective	Direct every military operation towards a clearly defined, decisive and attainable objective
Offensive	Seize, retain and exploit the initiative
Surprise	Strike the enemy at a time, at a place, or in a manner for which he is unprepared
Economy of force	Allocate minimum essential combat power to secondary efforts
Manoeuvre	Place the enemy in a position of disadvantage through the flexible application of combat power
Unity of command	For every objective, ensure unity of effort under one responsible commander
Security	Never permit the enemy to acquire an unexpected advantage
Simplicity	Prepare clear, uncomplicated plans and clear, concise orders to ensure thorough understanding

It is possible to assess Nivelle's plan using these criteria. With respect to 'Mass', Nivelle had assembled a very large force and in that respect he scores well. Also, it is clear that he thought that he was fulfilling other criteria such as 'Objective', 'Initiative', 'Manoeuvre' and 'Economy of Force'. In reality, any objective analysis of these principles at the time should have made it clear to him that he was not planning comprehensively to fulfil these requirements. For example, his objective was the German reserve armies and their artillery, and while that may have seemed clear enough to Nivelle, he paid too little attention to the defences and forces that the French formations needed to fight through to reach this objective. Also, as the offensive stalled, new objectives in the shape of key terrain features began to dominate the battle in a classic example of 'mission creep'. This in turn affected the 'Economy of Force' principle as French formations became bogged down in these secondary fights.

It is possible to disassemble Nivelle's plan using other criteria to illustrate how operational realities contradicted elements of his plan. While he was confident that he was seizing the initiative and was convinced of the primacy of the offensive, he was not assessing the opposition or the battlespace correctly or objectively. His over-controlled approach to his staff and his intolerance of dissent exacerbated this lack of objectivity.

The principle of 'Surprise', in a First World War context, was simply not achievable for Nivelle due to the long preparatory barrage. In terms of 'Security', his plan was dangerously compromised owing to his own indiscretions and those of others, and also through the capture by the Germans of operational plans. Nivelle's difficulties with his subordinate commanders should have indicated that he was far from achieving 'Unity of Command'.

So, although Nivelle may not have assessed his situation using such precise criteria, it is still somewhat perplexing that he did not reflect on the viability of his plans at some point in an objective manner, especially given the increasing level of dissent among his army group commanders. It is difficult to explain. To an observer, it seems to be an example of what Norman Dixon, in his classic book *On the Psychology of Military Incompetence* (London, 1975), referred to as 'obsessional neurosis'. As Nivelle's plans advanced, he increasingly identified with them and became intolerant of dissent. His profound confidence and self-belief meant that he could not assess his own plans objectively, and his efforts to convince politicians and generals only served to increase his belief in his own abilities. As the offensive neared, he became increasingly inclined to assess intelligence and reach conclusions that fitted his own plans, and these assessments ran counter to the actual implications of the information being presented. While Nivelle had never been inclined to factor in others' opinions and assessments of his plan, by March 1917 it would seem that he had ceased to heed the opinions of his subordinate commanders. The one exception to this was, of course, Colonel d'Alançon, who was similarly obsessed with carrying out the plan. Equally, his close association with Mangin did not result in an objective assessment of the military situation. Mangin's 'can-do' attitude and his indifference to casualties only facilitated the process. Nivelle's mindset was neatly summed up by the historian Anthony Clayton:

> The undoubted virtues he had shown before 1917 turned to touchy, rigid, and over-controlled behaviour when under the stress of Supreme Command, with consequent errors of judgement, rejection of unpalatable information, stereotyping of outgroups, an authoritarianism based on a wish for showy assertion and, when failure became evident, scape-goating.[15]

Yet was Nivelle deserving of all the blame for this disaster? He was the architect of a military failure of vast proportions, but it could also be argued that the conduct of the politicians and also his subordinate commanders enabled his flawed military decision-making process. At a political level it is obvious that officials of both the Briand and Ribot governments had profound misgivings, yet they failed to remove Nivelle. This is particularly true in the case of Painlevé, who as Minister for War never believed in Nivelle's plan and yet, despite the fact that he sought the opinion of dissenting generals such as Pétain and Micheler, could not follow-through on plans to remove him. Accounts of the succession of meetings called to discuss the plan would make for comical reading, had this political indecision and lack of willpower not resulted in such tragic circumstances. The manner in which the subordinate commanders voiced their dissent also ensured that the plan went ahead. While they shared their doubts privately with politicians, especially Painlevé, there was a distinct lack of willingness to push the point forcefully at the various key meetings. Even Pétain would not openly support the last-minute attempt to oust Nivelle in April. Norman Dixon refers to this as 'a terrible crippling obedience'. Similar tendencies had been seen during the Boulanger and Dreyfus affairs: under pressure from politicians, the press or the public, senior commanders closed ranks. In this case, while senior commanders might have opposed Nivelle's plans, their loyalties to the army and their brother generals meant that they did not push the point as strongly as they should have done.

Ultimately the committee of inquiry would treat Nivelle quite lightly, perhaps due to the politicians and senior commanders being aware of their shared responsibility. An unpacking of the whole affair in an inquiry would have been messy indeed and no one would have emerged unsullied. For Nivelle, the sanction was reasonably light. In December 1917 he was appointed as commander-in-chief in North Africa and this role removed him from the Western Front for the remainder of the war. In July 1919 he was not invited to the official victory parade in Paris but remained in Algeria, presiding over victory celebrations there. Yet after the war he gradually returned to favour. He remained in touch with David Lloyd George and, in a somewhat surreal aside, the pair later exchanged photographs. Despite the events of 1917 and their consequences, the two men still seemed to share a level of regard for each other. The Australian historian Elizabeth Greenhalgh also noticed a peculiar entry in the index to Lloyd George's memoirs in which Nivelle is described as 'unfortunate as Generalissimo'.[16] This was an understatement indeed.

Nivelle was subsequently given two military commands within post-war France and in March 1920 was appointed as a member of the war committee (*conseil superior de guerre*). Due to his command of English, he was sent to America in 1920 as part of the French delegation to the tercentenary celebrations to commemorate the arrival of the *Mayflower* in America. During this tour he was well-received by the American public. In December 1920 Nivelle was awarded the Grand Cross of the Légion d'Honneur.[17]

Despite the interest of French scholars in Nivelle, he remains an oddly opaque figure. Denis Rolland, the premier French historian of the First World War, subtitled his biography of Nivelle 'L'inconnu de Chemin des Dames' ('The unknown of the Chemin des Dames'). This can be interpreted in various ways, yet it could be argued that Rolland has hit on one of the central paradoxes about Nivelle. At a certain level we know much about him – the formulation of his plan, his interactions with politicians and fellow-generals. Yet Nivelle 'the man' remains a total mystery. Behind the over-confident bluster, it is extremely hard to get a sense of the man or to hear his 'voice'. Accounts by third parties are largely unsympathetic and, although much of his correspondence survives in various archives, he never wrote a volume of memoirs. We are left considering a figure who showed promise and considerable ability in 1916 but who went on to plan what was arguably France's worst military disaster of the war. Surviving accounts of planning meetings suggest an over-confident general prone to bombastic outbursts and implausible promises. Yet he managed to convince a succession of political and military leaders of the soundness of his plans for a considerable period. It seems that Nivelle will remain a somewhat mysterious figure.

Nivelle died on 22 March 1924. In June 1931 his ashes were placed in the governor's crypt in Les Invalides in Paris. This commemorative ceremony for Nivelle and fifteen other marshals, generals and admirals included both Catholic and Protestant religious services, a military parade and a 75-gun salute and concluded with an address by the then Minister of War, André Maginot. Considering the damage caused by the Nivelle Offensive to the

French army and indeed to France itself, this rehabilitation of Nivelle was generous. However, he has yet to be commemorated with a statue in France and, given the painful associations with his period as commander-in-chief, it seems unlikely that this will change.

The figure perhaps best placed to shed real light on Nivelle, his close associate Colonel d'Alançon, died in September 1917. A bitterly disappointed man, d'Alançon had left the GQG along with Nivelle and returned home on sick leave. A few months later he was dead. Like Nivelle, he remains a largely silent figure. His impact on his brother staff officers was mixed. Perhaps Jean de Pierrefeu best summed up d'Alançon's complex character:

> Of all the actors in this war of position he was, in my eyes, the most original. He was a romantic figure, consumed with ambition, hardly to be measured by our ordinary standards. This silent man, for long modest and retiring, suddenly resolved to tempt Fortune with a spirit and a will worthy of the days when adventurers carved out kingdoms for themselves. By his strength of will, his inspired enthusiasm, his facility in dealing with great events, he always reminded me of a Napoleon devoid of genius.[18]

General Mangin remained remarkably tight-lipped about Nivelle after 1917, at least in public. Yet in many ways he fared better than his former commander. Despite his reputation as 'the Butcher' among French troops, Mangin returned to service in 1918 and took command of the Tenth Army. He later played a significant role in the Second Battle of the Marne (15 July–6 August 1918) and received a measure of political and public approval for his performance in the final campaigns of the First World War. His attitude remained grimly realistic. He could perhaps be given credit for summing up the battlefield experience of so many First World War generals when he stated: 'Whatever you do, you lose a lot of men.' Following the war, Mangin's Tenth Army occupied the Rhineland, where he created some controversy owing to his attempts to encourage the inhabitants to create a 'Rhenish Republic' separate from Germany. He also angered local mayors by pressuring them to establish official brothels for the use of his troops. Mangin died suddenly in Paris in March 1925, apparently the result of acute appendicitis combined with a stroke, although some alleged that he had been poisoned. He was buried in Les Invalides. When German troops entered Paris in 1940 Hitler ordered that his statue be destroyed. In 1957 it was replaced by a new statue.[19]

It is worth considering for just a moment some of the potential outcomes of the events in the summer of 1917. While the practice of engaging in counterfactual history is often problematic, if not a complete waste of time, it is interesting to reflect on the possible further ramifications of Nivelle's failure in 1917. This reverse pushed the army into a state of open mutiny and it ceased to function effectively. The collapse in military morale coincided with a period of public disillusionment and political turmoil. To suggest that France was in a state of near-collapse and as a result was close to dropping out of the war is not mere idle supposition. Indeed, Field Marshal Haig wrote of the possibility of France 'falling out' during the height of the crisis in 1917. The greatest fear of the Ribot government was that revolution would break out in France as it had done in Russia. This would in all probability have taken France out of the war and left Britain and Belgium to continue the fight alone in Europe while awaiting American support. In turn, the Americans would not have been in a position to provide meaningful support until 1918. Would such a strategic situation have forced the Allies into a negotiated peace with Germany and Austro-Hungary? Peace, yes, but on the terms of the Central Powers?

At the very least it can be seen that the French army's collapse came at a crucial moment in the wider strategic context. By May 1917 Russia's ability to assist in the war effort was looking increasingly doubtful. The October Revolution would move Russia towards a separate peace with Germany and Austro-Hungary. Despite British and French efforts to keep Russia in the war, this would become a reality with the Treaty of Brest-Litovsk in March 1918. By 1917 Italy was also in a state of near-collapse, while Romania had already dropped out of the war. The year 1917 had opened with a spirit of Allied optimism, but by the summer and autumn it was becoming increasingly obvious that there would be no Allied victory yet. The Nivelle Offensive was one of a series of Allied setbacks that would continue until the end of the year, with the British army suffering its own martyrdom at Passchendaele. Rather than emerging victorious, for the Allies 1917 became a period of grimly hanging on until the Americans could arrive in force and until war industry could provide more tanks, aircraft and other military materiel.

For France, the losses incurred during the offensive were significant, and it could be argued that in the final analysis they were also unnecessary. It was, quite simply, an offensive that should not have gone ahead. In this, it was in keeping with several other ill-conceived Allied efforts during the war. It added yet another large contingent to France's growing total of war casualties. By the end of the war France had suffered more than 1.3 million fatal casualties.[20] More than 3.2 million soldiers had been wounded, with more than a million of them permanently disabled.[21] More than 600,000 French soldiers were taken prisoner, some of who would return home and decrease the numbers of 'missing'. Thousands had been classed as missing, many of whom were, of course, dead. This pushed the total of fatal casualties higher. It is unlikely that the true number of casualties will ever be accurately calculated as proper figures were not kept during the war. Also, many of the wounded died from their injuries after the parliamentary report on casualties was completed in the summer of 1919 and so were not included in the figures. Whichever figure one chooses, the scale of French losses is depressingly large. After the war a French officer calculated that a formation of troops equalling the number of French war dead would take eleven days and nights to march past the Arc de Triomphe in Paris in parade formation.[22]

This number of casualties obviously had a major impact on France in the years after the First World War. In demographic terms, it resulted in a collapse in both marriage and birth rates. In the years up to 1914 France had been concerned that German births would ensure that the French would be outstripped in manpower terms. This now became an absolute reality. In military terms, it translated into a defensive mindset and later fostered the development of the Maginot system of fortifications. In any future war France would need to rely for its defence on a series of fortifications, on a grander and more modernised scale than the Verdun forts. From the 1930s it was also envisaged that this system of fortifications would be backed up by a scheme for mobile defence using tanks. While the development and basic wisdom of the Maginot scheme are still much debated, the impulse that drove it had a certain clear logic. France expected another war and from the 1920s found itself increasingly isolated and devoid of immediate allies. It seemed that it would face a future German attack alone, at a time when its supplies of manpower were finite. The Maginot plan, and a programme for acquiring allies in Eastern Europe, seemed like sensible policies. The manpower issue also resulted in a fall in the size of the French labour force, with corresponding falls in industrial production. This was particularly true in respect of iron and steel production, which had knock-on effects for weapons production.

The whole defence issue would remain a contentious subject for inter-war French governments, played out in national debates and contests between the right-wing *Bloc National* and the leftist *Cartel des Gauches*. The Poincaré government of 1922–24 took a hard-line stance regarding German war reparations and sent more than 40,000 troops to occupy the Ruhr in the hope of forcing payment. This resulted in the Dawes Plan, which made provision for phased payments by Germany. In 1924 a moderate socialist government was elected but proved to be disorganised and riven by internal factions. Poincaré was returned to office in 1926 and pursued a radical economic policy before retiring from politics in 1929. The post-war years saw much political turmoil in France, and in the early 1930s the factions of the extreme left and right flourished due to the difficulties of the Depression. This coincided with hugely differing views between political parties and factions as to how to approach strategic and defence issues. The short life of the leftist Popular Front government of 1936 was dominated by economic and labour issues, while its policy with regard to the civil war then raging in Spain served to further illustrate the fractured nature of French politics and society. The Daladier government of 1938 instigated new armaments programmes and also tried to accelerate existing ones but France still struggled to keep pace with German military expansion.

The political and economic turmoil of the 1920s and 1930s ensured that a long-term, coherent strategic policy was impossible. It should also be remembered that these events took place in a country that had been ravaged by war. Millions of francs needed to be spent on reconstruction owing to the fact that so much French territory had been devastated between 1914 and 1918. The evidence of war was apparent to all in the shape of destroyed towns and villages, ruined farms, the shell-damaged landscape and the dangers of unexploded ordnance. This damage needed to be repaired, and agriculture and industry needed to be re-established. Many people were unwilling even to imagine that another war was possible. Getting over the 'Grande Guerre' and trying to repair France would occupy not only the next few years but the next few decades.

Alongside the physical damage wrought on France, the human damage was also obvious to all. A whole generation had suffered in the war, and France had become a country with hundreds of thousands of widows and orphans. The war wounded, many of them showing evidence of terrible wounds, became a feature of French society. While most towns and villages soon had their own war memorials, they also had a grim reminder of the war in the shape of veterans who were limbless, sightless or otherwise maimed.

The war had created a scar across the French landscape and a wound deep within the psyche of the French people. The desperate years of 1914–1918 had been marked by grim defence against a series of German offensives. Equally costly had been the many futile offensives launched by French generals themselves. Indeed, the Russian strategist A.A. Svechin later singled out the French offensive strategy on the Western Front for particular criticism. During 1915 and 1916, Svechin argued, alternative strategies could have been pursued in Italy and the East, in what he referred to as the 'Paris–Salonika–Vienna–Berlin logic of attrition'.[23] Ultimately, the French allowed operational and tactical interests to supersede strategic imperatives. All the Allies were complicit in this to some degree but France, with the largest Allied army on the Western Front, had the most to lose by being drawn into this cycle of pointless and futile offensive actions.

Within the catalogue of failed French offensives, the Nivelle Offensive holds a special (but unenviable) place owing to its costliness and sheer futility. Quite apart from the dashed expectations of the French nation, the timing of the disaster caused huge concern. It seemed inconceivable, at this late point in the war, that senior generals could still plan and execute such disastrous attacks. Had no lessons been learned since 1914? One of the positive dividends of the failure of the Nivelle Offensive was the very clear signal sent to the army commanders by the government, the public and the soldiers themselves that this type of offensive had to stop. The crisis of 1917 signalled an end to a certain type of generalship. While there would be later failures and reverses, the strategy of limited offensives initiated by Pétain would become the norm for the French army for the remainder of the war. Nivelle's offensive marked the end of a particular, brutal learning curve.

Since the end of the war in 1918 generations of French scholars have studied the 'Grande Guerre' and its impact on France. They include figures such as Pierre Renouvin, Jean-Baptiste Duroselle, Jean-Jacques Becker, Denis Rolland, Guy Pedroncini, Nicholas Offenstadt and many others. Non-French scholars, such as Robert M. Doughty, Elizabeth Greenhalgh, Ian Sumner and Anthony Clayton, have also made the French army during the war the focus of their particular attention. While the Nivelle Offensive is not explored in huge depth in every case, a common feature is that it is singled out as a particular example of poor generalship resulting in needless losses. The works of French writers such as Jules Romains, Henri Barbusse and Gabriel Chevalier also provide powerful (and in some cases semi-autobiographical) accounts of the hardships faced by the *poilus* and the careless treatment of them by their generals. Jean Giono's *To the slaughterhouse* (1931) is a particular powerful account of the wastefulness of the war. In history, prose and poetry, therefore, the Nivelle Offensive is frequently discussed. The 'Song of Craonne' refers to the ill-fated offensive and is often sung at commemorations. Written in 1917, it has been referred to as the ultimate hymn of pacifism. The war also provided much inspiration for French artists such as Georges Edouard Darcy, Jean-Louis Forain and Jean Droit, among many others.

French cinema has also focused on the war, with films such as *Les Croix des Bois* (1932), *La Grande Illusion* (1937) and, more recently, *La vie et rien d'autre* (1989), *Captain Conan* (1996) and *La chambre des officiers* (2001). For many, however, the film most associated with France's experience during the First World War is Stanley Kubrick's *Paths of Glory* (1957). Starring Kirk Douglas, it is the tragic story of a misguided offensive against an impregnable German position known as the 'Ant Hill'. The movie was based on Matthew Cobb's novel of the same title, which was itself based on the real-life court-martial of six French soldiers in 1914.[24]

Released forty years after 1917, the parallels between the movie's subject and the Nivelle Offensive are also interesting. One of the principal characters is the ambitious General Mireau, played by George Macready, who continues to push for offensive action and is prone to chilling phrases such as 'the men died wonderfully'. In the film the failed offensive is followed by a series of courts-martial and in-fighting among the generals responsible. The movie's release in Belgium in 1958 resulted in protests from both French veterans and serving French military personnel. The parallels between the Nivelle Offensive and other French failures were equally obvious to officials in France at the time and although the film was not officially banned there, contrary to popular belief, diplomatic pressure was brought to bear on United Artists, the movie's distributor, and its release was delayed. As a result, *Paths of Glory* was not screened in France until 1975. Its release in Germany was also delayed for fear of offending French sensibilities but only for two years.[25]

The legacy of the Nivelle Offensive for France has been long and difficult. In the run-up to the centenary of the offensive in 2017 it will be fascinating to see how these painful events will be commemorated. In recent years efforts have been made to focus on the plight of individual soldiers, and to commemorate those involved in the army mutinies. The centenary will no doubt expose all the difficulties associated with commemorating lives lost in a military failure. For France, the Nivelle Offensive remains the epitome of military futility – a doomed plan driven by an overly ambitious and flawed general.

Appendix

Visiting the Battlefield

A visit to the battlefields of April 1917 is well worthwhile. Two roads (the D925 and the D18) run roughly east to west and north of the Aisne river through the Chemin des Dames zone. By using these roads and associated branch roads, it is possible to tour the battlefield and visit locations associated with the armies of Micheler's GAR army group. These were the Sixth Army under General Mangin and the Fifth Army commanded by General Mazel. Local towns such as Soissons and Fismes served as local army HQs.

The region is dotted with memorials, every town and village essentially having its own First World War memorial. As the region was also fought over by the British Expeditionary Force in 1914 there are a number of British cemeteries and memorials, in addition to the memorials associated with the Nivelle Offensive of 1917. At Berry-au-Bac is the French National Tank Memorial, located on the route taken by Commandant Bossut's group of Schneiders in 1917. Bossut was killed in this attack but the German position there, known as 'Ferme le Choléra', was taken by the 151st Infantry with the assistance of the tanks. The memorial was inaugurated in 1922 at a ceremony attended by Marshals Foch and Pétain, and Generals Estienne, Mangin and Weygand. The veterans' association of the French army's tank force holds a commemoration at the memorial every April. The locations of the fiercest fighting also have associated memorials. At Laffaux, the site of the 'Moulin de Laffaux' which witnessed fierce fighting in 1917, stands the national memorial to the 'Crapouillots' – the mortar artillery. In the form of a huge mortarbomb, this memorial was unveiled in 1958 to replace an earlier memorial that was damaged in fighting in 1940. There are other associated memorials here, including one to General Estienne, the tank pioneer.

Hurtebise Farm, so bitterly contested in 1917, is the site of an unusual memorial. In 1814 the location had been the scene of a battle between French troops under Napoleon and Prussian and Russian troops under Blücher. In 1914 a memorial was placed here to commemorate the centenary of the Napoleonic battle but this was destroyed in the intense fighting during the First World War. The modern memorial was unveiled in 1927. Designed by Maxime Real del Sarte, it depicts a 'Marie-Louise' soldier of the Napoelonic era and a *poilu* of the 1914–1918 period holding aloft a regimental colour. Nearby, there is a statue of Napoleon on the site of the windmill at Vauclair, his observation post in 1814.

Further memorials in the Chemin des Dames region focus on particular units, such as the Fusilier Marins memorial at Fruty, the Moroccan Regiment Memorial at Ferme de Bohéry and the memorial to the Basque troops of the 36th Division on the edge of the Californie Plateau. There are also several memorials to specific soldiers. The location of 'Old Craonne' village, which was totally destroyed in the war, is the site of a 7-hectare memorial arboretum. Throughout the region occasional German bunkers are dotted about the landscape, while the remains of some of the larger, pre-war forts also survive, such as the Fort de Malmaison and the Fort de Condé.

The majority of the memorials date to the immediate post-war years, but since the 1990s there have been further commemorative projects. In 1997 the Conseil Général de l'Aisne began a new programme of commemoration with associated educational projects. In 1998 a new memorial to the dead of the Chemin des Dames was unveiled by Prime Minister Lionel Jospin on the Californie Plateau near Craonne. Designed by Haim Kern, it depicts human heads entangled in barbed wire. The memorial was dedicated to all soldiers who died in the war and bears the poignant inscription 'Ils n'ont pas choisi leur sépulture' ('They didn't choose their burial place'). At the unveiling Jospin suggested that it was time to bring back into the public consciousness those men executed for mutiny. Shortly after the unveiling, this powerful monument was vandalised but it has since been repaired. This perhaps indicates the continued sensitivities surrounding the events of 1917 and the emotive subject of the army mutinies, and the difficulties associated with commemorating a costly failure.

The focal point for any visitor should be the Musée du Chemin des Dames at the Caverne du Dragon. The cavern itself was the location of heavy fighting in 1917, much of it underground. It is now the site of a visitors' centre and provides excellent background information. There are guided tours of the cavern, and guides can be hired to tour the surrounding battlefield. The Caverne du Dragon is also the location of some regimental memorials. In 2007 a new commemorative work to the Senegalese troops who fought and died in the battle was unveiled. Created by Christian Lapie, the 'Constellation de la Douleur' ('Constellation of Suffering') is an ensemble of nine statues of charred, untreated wood. Each figure is several metres high and they dominate the surrounding countryside to create a highly effective and somewhat eerie memorial. In the run-up to the centenary of the battle further events and memorials are planned, and a virtual memorial is currently being maintained online at Le Portail du Chemin des Dames (http://www.chemindesdames.fr/default.asp).

There are numerous war cemeteries in the area, not only French but also British, German and Italian. There are French and German cemeteries at Soupir, and French and Commonwealth War Graves Commission cemeteries at Vailly-sur-Aisne. Alongside the graves of the casualties of the Nivelle Offensive are laid to rest men who died in other battles in the war. The Italian cemetery at Chavonne, for instance, also holds casualties of the 2nd Italian Army Corps, which served in this zone in 1918. Some graves date from the Second World War and there is a German cemetery from that war at Fort de Malmaison, with over 11,000 burials. Further away, at St Hilaire le Grand in the Champagne region, are a Russian church, memorial and cemetery dedicated to the Russian troops who served in France between 1916 and 1918. The international aspects of the war are further commemorated at the Musée National de la Coopération Franco-Américaine at the Château de Blérancourt.[1]

Notes

Introduction
1. Richard Holmes, *The Western Front* (London, 1999), p. 157.
2. The military authorities had actually banned planes from flying through or over the Arc de Triomphe due to the dangers such a stunt could pose for the public. French airmen were supposed to parade on foot but Navarre was elected by a group of fellow-pilots to undertake this unofficial flight. A few weeks after the parade, Charles Godefroy flew a plane through the Arc.
3. *AFGG*, Tome 5, vol. 1, appx vol. 1, appx 446, pp. 774–6.
4. James L. Stokesbury, *A short history of World War 1* (New York, 1981), p. 197.
5. Charles Williams, *Pétain* (London, 2005), p. 149.
6. Elizabeth Greenhalgh, *The French Army and the First World War* (Cambridge University Press, 2014), p. 170.

Chapter 1
1. Gabriel Chevallier, *Fear* (1930), p. 7.
2. There is an excellent account of Nivelle's rise and fall in Robert Doughty's *Pyrrhic Victory: French strategy and operations in the Great War* (Harvard, 2005), especially pp. 311–54.
3. *Journal Officiel de la République française*, 1873, p. 451.
4. Douglas Porch, *The March to the Marne: the French Army, 1871–1914* (Cambridge University Press, 1981).
5. Ibid.
6. Piers Paul Reid, *The Dreyfus Affair: the scandal that tore France in two* (2012). See also Charles Sowerwine, *France since 1870: culture, society and the making of the Republic* (2009).
7. Anthony Clayton, *Paths of Glory: the French Army, 1914–18* (London, 2003), pp. 29–31.
8. Emmanuel Thiébot, 'L'affaire des fiches vue par les francs-maçons du Grand Orient de France en Basse-Normandie', *Revue historique des armées*, no. 241 (2005), pp. 106–21.
9. Porch, *The March to the Marne*. See also Clayton, *Paths of Glory*.
10. Greenhalgh, *The French Army and the First World War*, pp. 7–36.
11. Clayton, *Paths of Glory*, p. 33.

12. Doughty, *Pyrrhic Victory*, p. 22.
13. Jérôme ann de Wiel, 'The French invasion that never was: the Deuxième Bureau and the Irish republicans, 1900–04' in Nathalie Genet-Rouffiac and David Murphy (eds), *Franco-Irish military connections, 1590–1945* (Dublin, 2009), pp. 238–52.
14. Douglas Porch, 'French War Plans, 1914: the "Balance of Power" Paradox', *Journal of Strategic Studies*, vol. 29, No. 1, pp. 117–18.
15. Robert Doughty, 'French Strategy in 1914: Joffre's Own', *Journal of Military History*, vol. 67, No. 2 (Apr. 2003), pp. 437–41.
16. Greenhalgh, *The French Army and the First World War*, pp. 7–36.
17. Michael Howard, 'Men against fire: the doctrine of the offensive in 1914' in Peter Paret (ed.), *Makers of modern strategy: from Machiavelli to the Nuclear Age* (Princeton, 1986), p. 515.
18. Robert M. Citino, *Quest for decisive victory: from stalemate to Blitzkrieg in Europe* (2002).
19. Ferdinand Foch, *Des Principes de la Guerre* (Paris, 1903) and *De la Conduite de la Guerre* (Paris, 1904).
20. François Cochet, 'The French Army between tradition and modernity: weaponry, tactics and soldiers, 1914–18' in Matthias Strohn (ed.), *World War 1 Companion* (Oxford, 2013), pp. 94–106.
21. *Règlement sur la conduite des grandes unites* (Paris, 1913), p. 6.
22. Howard, 'Men against fire', p. 515.
23. Ibid., p. 512.
24. G.F.R. Henderson, *The science of war* (London, 1905), pp. 372–3.
25. Citino, *Quest for decisive victory*.
26. Joseph Joffre, *The memoirs of Joseph Joffre* (London, 1932), vol. 1, pp. 26–7.
27. Howard, 'Men against fire', p. 519.
28. Douglas Porch, 'The French Army in the First World War' in Allan R. Millett and Williamson Murray (eds), *Military Effectiveness. Vol. 1: The First World War* (Cambridge University Press, 2010), pp. 190–228.
29. John Sweetman, *Tannenberg 1914* (London, 2004). See also Richard W. Harrison, 'Samsonev and the Battle of Tannenberg, 1914' in Brian Bond (ed.), *Fallen Stars: eleven studies of twentieth-century military disasters* (London, 1991).
30. John Keegan, *Opening moves: August 1914* (London, 1973).
31. Barbara Tuchman, *The Guns of August* (New York, 1962).
32. Ian Sumner and Gerry Embleton, *The French Army, 1914–18* (London, 1995). See also Greenhalgh, *The French Army and the First World War*, pp. 37–69.
33. The Lebel was gradually phased out during the course of the war and was replaced with the Berthier rifle, which was loaded using clips of ammunition. See Ian Sumner, *French poilu, 1914–18* (Oxford, 2009), pp. 23–6.
34. Terence Zuber, *The Battle of the Frontiers: Ardennes, 1914* (London, 2013).
35. Ian Senior, *Invasion 1914: the Schlieffen plan to the Battle of the Marne* (Oxford, 2014).

36. Denis Rolland, *Nivelle: l'inconnu du Chemin des Dames* (Clamecy, 2012). Nivelle's father, Marie Jacques Nivelle, had served with some distinction during the campaign of 1870. His mother was Theodora Louisa Sparrow, daughter of Robert George Sparrow, formerly an officer of the 45th Foot.
37. Ibid.
38. Ibid., pp. 61–76.
39. For further comment on Nivelle at Verdun, see Alastair Horne, *The Price of Glory* (London, 1963).
40. Louis-Eugène Mangin, *Le Général Mangin* (Paris, privately published, 1990).
41. E.L. Spears, *Prelude to Victory* (London, 1939), p. 131.
42. Rolland, *Nivelle*, pp. 335–6.
43. Jean de Pierrefeu, *French Headquarters, 1915–18* (Paris, n.d. General Books imprint), p. 77.
44. Jean-Pierre Turbergue (ed.), *Les 300 jours de Verdun* (SHD, Paris, 2006).
45. In French, 'niveleur' means to level. The French press made a play on this to refer to 'Nivelle le niveleur' – 'Nivelle the leveller'.

Chapter 2

1. Gary Sheffield and John Bourne (eds), *Douglas Haig: war diaries and letters, 1914–1918* (London, 2005), p. 261.
2. Doughty, *Pyrrhic Victory*, p. 311.
3. Ibid., p. 313.
4. Guy Pedroncini (ed.), *Journal de marche de Joffre, 1916–1919* (Paris, 1990), pp. 160–1.
5. David Lloyd George, *The war memoirs of David Lloyd George* (London, 1934), vol. 1, p. 547.
6. Ibid.
7. Doughty, *Pyrrhic Victory*, p. 316.
8. Ibid., p. 320.
9. Briand gives a highly edited account of these events in his journal of this period. See Georges Saurez (ed.), *Briand: sa vie, son oeuvre, avec son journal et de nombreux documents inédits* (4 vols, Paris, 1938–40).
10. Rolland, *Nivelle*, pp. 79–84.
11. Greenhalgh, *The French Army and the First World War*, pp. 170–219.
12. Rolland, *Nivelle*. See also Doughty, *Pyrrhic Victory* and Greenhalgh, *The French Army and the First World War*, pp. 170–219.
13. Anthony Clayton, 'Robert Nivelle and the French Spring Offensive' in Brian Bond (ed.), *Fallen Stars: eleven studies of twentieth-century military disasters* (London, 1991), pp. 52–64.
14. Archives Nationales, Paris, 475AP/194, 'Nivelle, note pour la ministre de la guerre, 1916'.
15. Pierrefeu, *French Headquarters, 1915–18*, p. 76.

16. National Archives, Kew, War Office Papers: WO 158/37: 'Correspondence between General Robert Nivelle and Field Marshal Sir Douglas Haig', Nivelle to Haig, 21 December 1916.
17. Robert Blake, *The private papers of Douglas Haig, 1914–1919* (London, 1952), pp. 187–8.
18. Doughty, *Pyrrhic Victory*, p. 329.
19. Spears, *Prelude to Victory*, p. 65.
20. Ibid.
21. Gary Sheffield, *The Chief: Douglas Haig and the British Army* (London, 2011), p. 201.
22. Blake, *Private papers of Douglas Haig*, p. 192.
23. William Robertson, *Soldiers and Statesmen, 1914–1918* (2 vols, New York, 1926), vol. 2, p. 208.
24. Blake, *Private papers of Douglas Haig*, p. 201.
25. Ibid., pp. 201–2.
26. Spears, *Prelude to Victory*, p. 67.
27. National Archives, Kew, War Office Papers: WO 158/37: Correspondence between General Robert Nivelle and Field Marshal Sir Douglas Haig, 19 December 1916 to 17 April 1917.
28. Pierrefeu, *French Headquarters, 1915–18*, p. 77.
29. Paddy Griffith and Peter Dennis, *Fortifications on the Western Front, 1914–18* (Oxford, 2004), pp. 30–3.
30. Douglas Porch, *The French secret services: a history of French intelligence from the Dreyfus affair to the Gulf War* (1995), p. 104.
31. Doughty, *Pyrrhic Victory*, p. 335.
32. Cyril Falls, *History of the Great War: Military operations in France and Belgium, 1917: the German retreat to the Hindenburg Line and the battle of Arras* (London, 1940), p. 126. See also Pierrefeu, *French Headquarters, 1915–18*, pp. 71–3.
33. Ian Jones, *Malice aforethought: the history of booby traps from World War 1 to Vietnam* (London, 2004), pp. 51–82.
34. Ian Sumner, *They shall not pass: the French Army on the Western Front, 1914–18* (Barnsley, 2012), p. 144.
35. David Dutton, 'Paul Painlevé and the end of the sacred union in Wartime France', *Journal of Strategic Studies* (1981), pp. 46–59.
36. Spears, *Prelude to Victory*, p. 338. See also Richard M. Watt, *Dare call it treason: the true story of the French army mutinies of 1917* (New York, 1969), p. 162.
37. For an insight into Painlevé's relationship with his British allies, see Elizabeth Greenhalgh, 'Paul Painlevé and Franco-British Relations in 1917', *Contemporary British History* (2011), pp. 5–27.
38. Watt, *Dare call it treason*, p. 163.

Chapter 3

1. Yves Buffetaut, *The 1917 Spring Offensives: Arras, Vimy, le Chemin des Dames* (Paris, 1997), p. 102.
2. Ibid.
3. Rolland, *Nivelle*, pp. 106–10.
4. Griffith and Denis, *Fortifications on the Western Front*.
5. Ibid. See also Anthony Clayton, 'Robert Nivelle and the French Spring Offensive' in Brian Bond (ed.), *Fallen Stars: eleven studies of twentieth-century military disasters* (London, 1991), pp. 52–64.
6. Buffetaut, *The 1917 Spring Offensives*, p. 116.
7. Doughty, *Pyrrhic Victory*, pp. 311–54. See also Greenhalgh, *The French Army and the First World War*, pp. 170–220.
8. Buffetaut, *The 1917 Spring Offensives*, p. 116.
9. Sumner, *They shall not pass*, p. 146.
10. Erich Ludendorff, *My war memories, 1914–1918* (London, 1919).
11. Ludendorff, *War memories*.
12. Porch, *French secret services*, pp. 104–6.
13. Watt, *Dare call it treason*.
14. For further details of the French army build-up, see Clayton, *Paths of Glory* and Greenhalgh, *The French Army and the First World War*.
15. Buffetaut, *The 1917 Spring Offensives*, p. 104.
16. Nicholas Offenstadt (ed.), *Les Chemin des Dames* (Paris, 2013).
17. Buffetaut, *The 1917 Spring Offensives*, p. 102.
18. Ibid.
19. Ibid., p. 103.
20. Paul Painlevé, 'La verité sur l'offensive du 16 avril 1917', *La Renaissance* (1919), p. 20.
21. Ibid.
22. Jean de Pierrefeu, *L'offensive du 16 avril: le verité sur l'affaire Nivelle* (Paris, 1919), pp. 61–5.
23. Commandant de Civrieux, *L'offensive de 1917 et le commandement de General Nivelle* (1919), p. 77.
24. Ibid.
25. *AFGG*, Tome V, vol. II, p. 193.
26. Ibid.
27. SHD, Vincennes, 5N255: Commission d'enquête réunie en execution de la note ministérielle no. 18194 du 14 Juillet 1917. 'Pièces remises par le Général à la commission', pp. 17–27.
28. Ibid.
29. Watt, *Dare call it treason*, p. 170.
30. Pierrefeu, *French Headquarters, 1915–18*, p. 63.

174   Breaking Point of the French Army

31. David Lloyd, *War memoirs*, vol. I, p. 901.
32. Sumner, *They shall not pass*, pp. 147–8.
33. Ibid., p. 148.
34. *Journal Officiel*, 24 June to 1 July 1922, p. 333.
35. Buffetaut, *The 1917 Spring Offensives*, p. 103.

Chapter 4
1. Sumner, *They shall not pass*, p. 150.
2. Citano, *Decisive victory*.
3. Steven J. Zaloga, *French Tanks of World War 1* (Oxford, 2010). See also Richard M. Ogorkiewicz, 'The French tank force' in Bernard Fitzsimons (ed.), *Tanks and weapons of World War 1* (London, 1973), pp. 95–101.
4. Zaloga, *French Tanks*. See also Jean-Gabriel Jeudy, *Chars de France* (Paris, 1997).
5. E.G. Ramspacher, *Le Général Estienne: Père des Chars* (1983).
6. Iain Gougaud, *L'Aube de la Gloire, Les Autos-Mitrailleuses et les Chars Français pendant la Grande Guerre* (Musée des Blindés, 1987), p. 111.
7. François Vauvillier, 'Et vint le Schneider: Brillié, Estienne et la chenille Holt', *Tank Zone* (Dec. –Jan. 2008/9), pp. 24–36.
8. J.F.C. Fuller, *Tanks in the Great War* (London and New York, 1920).
9. Lloyd George, *War memoirs*, vol. I, p. 385.
10. Zaloga, *French Tanks*.
11. Rolland, *Nivelle*.

Chapter 5
1. Sumner, *They shall not pass*, p. 146.
2. For concise accounts of the Vimy and Arras actions, see Nigel Cave and Jack Sheldon, *The Battle of Vimy Ridge, 1917* (Barnsley, 2007) and Pierre Berton, *Vimy* (Barnsley, 2012).
3. John Terraine, *Douglas Haig: the educated soldier* (London, 1963), p. 282.
4. Terraine, *Douglas Haig*, pp. 282–3.
5. Alexander Turner, *Vimy Ridge 1917: Byng's Canadians triumph at Arras* (Oxford, 2005).
6. As is the case with all First World War battles, some sources suggest even higher casualty rates on the German side.
7. Ludendorff, *War memories*, pp. 421–2.
8. Doughty, *Pyrrhic Victory*, p. 348.
9. Buffetaut, *The 1917 Spring Offensives*, p. 126.
10. *AFGG*, Tome 5, vol. I, annexes vol. II, annex 1338, pp. 841–2.
11. Ibid., annex 1896, p. 1507.
12. SHD, Vincennes, 16N1686, 'GQG. Note sur l'organisation du terrain dans la bataille offensive', 12 April 1917.

13. Buffetaut, *The 1917 Spring Offensives*, p. 138.
14. Spears, *Prelude to Victory*, p. 490.
15. Buffetaut, *The 1917 Spring Offensives*, p. 132.
16. Pierrefeu, *L'offensive du 16 Avril*, pp. 83–4.
17. Buffetaut, *The 1917 Spring Offensives*, p. 133.
18. Ibid., p. 134.
19. Rolland, *Nivelle*, p. 182.
20. Buffetaut, *The 1917 Spring Offensives*, p. 136.
21. Heinz Guderian, *Achtung! Panzer* (1937), p. 60.
22. Ibid., p. 61.
23. Ibid., p. 62.
24. Buffetaut, *The 1917 Spring Offensives*, p. 153.
25. Sumner, *They shall not pass*, p. 151.
26. Zaloga, *French Tanks*, p. 12.
27. Buffetaut, *The 1917 Spring Offensives*, p. 151.
28. Ibid., p. 152.
29. Guderian, *Achtung! Panzer*, p. 65.
30. Buffetaut, *The 1917 Spring Offensives*, p. 150.
31. Ibid., p. 156.
32. Ibid.
33. Clayton, 'Robert Nivelle and the French Spring Offensive', pp. 52–64.
34. Buffetaut, *The 1917 Spring Offensives*, p. 152.
35. Greenhalgh, *The French Army and the First World War*, pp. 188–93.
36. Sumner, *They shall not pass*, p. 153.
37. Pierrefeu, *L'offensive du 16 avril*, pp. 83–4.
38. Rolland, *Nivelle*, p. 179.
39. Blake, *Private papers of Douglas Haig*, p. 217.
40. Ibid., p. 218.

Chapter 6

1. Jean Ybarnégaray was a parliamentary deputy serving in the infantry. Quoted in Sumner, *They shall not pass*, p. 153.
2. Buffetaut, *The 1917 Spring Offensives*, p. 160.
3. Watt, *Dare call it treason*, p. 163.
4. Greenhalgh, *The French Army and the First World War*. See also Pierrefeu, *French Headquarters, 1915–18* and *L'offensive du 16 Avril*.
5. Buffetaut, *The 1917 Spring Offensives*, p. 174.
6. While there had been leaks from within his own staff and also those of the other army group commanders before the offensive, it is now clear that this process accelerated in light of the failed attacks and also Nivelle's refusal to stop the offensive.
7. Buffetaut, *The 1917 Spring Offensives*, p. 177.

8. Raymond Poincaré, *Au service de la France* (10 vols, Paris, 1926–33), vol. IX, p. 122.
9. Buffetaut, *The 1917 Spring Offensives*, p. 176.
10. Ibid.
11. Ibid., p. 171.
12. Ibid., p. 165.
13. For the homepage of the Caverne du Dragon visitors' centre, see http://www.caverne-du-dragon.com/fr/default.aspx.
14. Buffetaut, *The 1917 Spring Offensives*, p. 180.
15. René Nobecourt, *Les Fantassins du Chemin des Dames* (1983).
16. Zaloga, *French Tanks*, p. 18.
17. Ibid.
18. Alexandre Ribot, *Journal d'Alexandre Ribot et correspondances inédites, 1914–1922* (Paris, 1936), p. 82.
19. Williams, *Pétain*, p. 151.
20. Robertson, *Soldiers and Statesmen*, vol. II, p. 235.
21. Ibid.
22. Blake, *Private papers of Douglas Haig*, p. 227.
23. Watt, *Dare call it treason*, p. 174.
24. Émile Herbillon, *Souveniers d'un officier de liaison pendant la guerre mondiale* (2 vols, Paris, 1930), vol. II, p. 84.
25. Buffetaut, *The 1917 Spring Offensives*, p. 177.
26. Pierrefeu, *French Headquarters, 1915–18*, p. 82.
27. Buffetaut, *The 1917 Spring Offensives*, p. 177.

Chapter 7
1. Sumner, *They shall not pass*, p. 162.
2. Guy Pedroncini's *Les mutineries de 1917* (Paris, 1967) remains the standard work on this subject. Pedroncini's account was based on official files which are, at the time of writing, closed. Denis Rolland's *La Grève des Tranchées: les mutineries de 1917* (2005) has re-examined the events of 1917 using other available sources.
3. Watt, *Dare call it treason*, is also a useful study of the events of 1917 and addresses the subject of pacifist elements within French politics and society.
4. Greenhalgh, *The French Army and the First World War*, pp. 201–19.
5. Watt, *Dare call it treason*, p. 179. See also Greenhalgh, *The French Army and the First World War*, and Williams, *Pétain*.
6. It is unclear how many were summarily executed this way. See Clayton, *Paths of Glory* and Doughty, *Pyrrhic Victory*.
7. Sumner, *They shall not pass*, p. 162.
8. Williams, *Pétain*, p. 141.
9. Sumner, *They shall not pass*, p. 163.
10. Ibid., p. 168.

Notes   177

11. Jean–Jacques Becker, *The Great War and the French people* (Oxford, 1985), pp. 205–35.
12. Sumner, *They shall not pass*, p. 167.
13. The history of the ill-fated Russian troops in France is addressed in Jamie H. Cockfield, *With Snow on Their Boots: The Tragic Odyssey of the Russian Expeditionary Force in France During World War 1* (London, 1999).
14. Pierre Poitevin, *La Mutinerie de la Courtine. Les régiments russes revoltés en 1917 au centre de la France* (Paris, 1938).
15. SHD, Vincennes, 16N1485. 'Contrôle postal: rapport sur la correspondance des troupes du 25 avril au 10 mai, 1917'.
16. *AFGG*, Tome 5, vol. 2, annexes vol. 1, annex 412, pp. 691–2.
17. Sumner, *They shall not pass*, p. 169.
18. Williams, *Pétain*.
19. Doughty, *Pyrrhic Victory*, pp. 355–404.
20. Paul Painlevé, *Comment j'ai nommé Foch et Pétain* (Paris, 1923), p. 147.
21. Scholars of this episode such as Pedroncini, Rolland and Offenstadt, among others, have arrived at different totals for the numbers executed.
22. Philippe Pétain, *Une crise morale la nation française en guerre, 16 Avril–23 October 1917* (Paris, 1966), p. 97.
23. Rolland, *La Grève des Tranchées*.
24. Painlevé, *Comment j'ai nommé Foch et Pétain*, p. 147.
25. *AFGG*, Tome 5, vol. II, annexes vol. 1, annex 526, p. 870.
26. Poitevin, *La Mutinerie de la Courtine*.
27. For details of the officer trials, see Pedroncini, *Les mutineries de 1917*.
28. Watt, *Dare call it treason*, p. 223.
29. *AFGG*, Tome 5, vol. II, annexes vol. I, annex 426, p. 719.
30. Blake, *Private papers of Douglas Haig*, p. 247.
31. Doughty, *Pyrrhic Victory*, p. 368.
32. Ibid., p. 369.
33. Ibid. These new aircraft included updated versions of the SPAD fighter that had proved increasingly successful against the German air service.
34. Zaloga, *French Tanks*.
35. Doughty, *Pyrrhic Victory*, p. 369. See also Greenhalgh, *The French Army and the First World War*, pp. 220–70.
36. Henri Carré, *Les grandes heures de Pétain et la crise du moral* (Paris, 1962), p. 176.
37. Blake, *Private papers of Douglas Haig*, p. 232.
38. See Doughty, *Pyrrhic Victory*, pp. 378–9. See also Watt, *Dare call it treason*, pp. 244–5.
39. Poincaré, *Au service de la France*, vol. IX, pp. 305–6.
40. American historian Joseph E. Persico has calculated that there were over 11,000 casualties on 11 November 1918. See J.E. Persico, *Eleventh month, eleventh day, eleventh hour: Armistice Day 1918 – World War 1 and its violent climax* (2005).

Conclusion

1. A.J.P. Taylor, *The First World War* (London, 1963), pp. 176–7.
2. Elizabeth Greenhalgh, *Foch in command: the forging of a First World War general* (Cambridge, 2011), p. 237.
3. Watt, *Dare call it treason*, p. 163.
4. SHD, Vincennes, 5N255: 'Commission d'enquête réunie en execution de la note ministérielle no. 18194 du 14 Juillet 1917'.
5. Ibid.
6. Greenhalgh, *The French Army and the First World War*, p. 217.
7. Quoted in Guderian, *Achtung! Panzer*.
8. Buffetaut, *The 1917 Spring Offensives*, p. 183.
9. G.W.L Nicholson, *Canadian Expeditionary Force 1914–1919: official history of the Canadian Army in the First World War* (Ottawa, 1962), p. 243.
10. Guéno, Jean-Pierre and Yves Laplume (eds), *Paroles de poilus: letters de la Grande Guerre* (Paris, 1998), p. 9.
11. A.A. Svechin, *Strategy*, edited Kent D. Lee (Minneapolis, 1991), p. 103.
12. Ibid., p. 312.
13. Taylor, *The First World War*, p. 167.
14. http://www.wpi.edu/academics/military/prinwar.htmlf.
15. Clayton, 'Robert Nivelle and the French Spring Offensive', p. 63.
16. Greenhalgh, *The French Army and the First World War*, p. 216.
17. Nivelle had been made a chevalier of the Légion d'Honneur in 1895 and had been promoted through different grades of the order during the course of his career. In September 1916 he had been made a Grand Officer of the Légion d'Honneur. During the course of the war he had also been decorated by various Allied governments and had received awards from Britain, Belgium, Russia, Italy, Serbia, Japan, Romania and America. Mount Nivelle in the Canadian Rockies was named in his honour in 1918.
18. Pierrefeu, *French Headquarters, 1915–18*, p. 83.
19. Mangin, *Le Général Mangin*, is a useful study of this fascinating but controversial general.
20. Depending on the sources used, French fatal casualties are calculated at between 1,357,000 and more than 1,397,800.
21. Some sources put the figure for the wounded at more than 4 million. See Doughty, *Pyrrhic Victory*, p. 508.
22. This statistic features in Bertrand Tavernier's film *La vie et rien d'autre* (1989). The central character, Comdt Dellaplane, played by Philippe Noiret, is responsible for identifying the missing and calculating casualty numbers.
23. Svechin, *Strategy*, p. 248.
24. In December 1914 six French soldiers were executed at Vingré for supposedly disobeying orders. They were chosen for execution by drawing lots in what can

only be described as a dubious judicial process. Following a long campaign by their former comrades, they were vindicated in 1921. They are commemorated on a memorial at Vingré.
25. David Hughes, *The Complete Kubrick* (2000). See also Paul Duncan, *Stanley Kubrick: the complete films* (2003).

Appendix
1. The best guide for anyone planning to visit the battlefield is *Major and Mrs Holts concise illustrated battlefield guide to the Western Front – South* (Barnsley, 2nd edition, 2011). Filled with information and maps, it is simply a 'must have' piece of equipment for any tour of the region. Richard Holmes, *Fatal avenue: a traveller's history of the battlefields of Northern France and Flanders, 1346–1945* (London, 2008) gives a good overview of the military history of this region.

Bibliography

Due to the size of the French army during the First World War, and the extent of its operations, the archival sources for this subject are, quite simply, vast. The main archives for the records of the French army during the war are held at the Service Historique de la Défense at Château de Vincennes near Paris. The holdings for the war period are measured, quite literally, in kilometres of archival space (http://www.servicehistorique.sga.defense.gouv.fr/?lang=en).

With respect to published sources, in the early 1920s the French General Staff began publishing an official history of the war (Imprimerie Nationale, *Les Armées Françaises dans la Grande Guerre*, Paris, 1922–1939). This series would eventually number more than a hundred volumes in eight 'tomes'. These official history volumes include copies of original documents and maps, and they remain an invaluable resource for anyone researching the activities of the French army during the war. In the notes for this volume the title has been shortened to the standard abbreviation *AFGG*.

Due to the close relationship between the French army and the British Expeditionary Force, records are also held in the National Archives in Kew and in other archives in the UK and provide details not only of the Nivelle Offensive of 1917 but also other Allied operations of the First World War.

Service Historique de la Défense, Vincennes (SHD)
5N255: Commission d'enquête réunie en execution de la note ministérielle no. 18194 du 14 Juillet 1917 (Nivelle Inquiry)
1K/113: General Micheler papers
16N1485: Rapport sur la correspondence des troupes du 25 Novembre au 10 Décembre 1916
16N1485: Rapport sur la correspondence des troupes du 10 au 25 Décembre 1916
16N1417: Commission de contrôle postal de la VIe Armée, 1916–17

National Archives, Kew
War Cabinet Papers, 1916–1917 (CAB series). In particular:
    CAB/23/1: Cabinet Minutes, 11 January 1917
    CAB/23/1: Cabinet Minutes, 13 February 1917
    CAB/24/7: Copy of letter from French ambassador in London to General Nivelle, 7 March 1917
    CAB/23/3: Cabinet Minutes, 6 June 1917

CAB/24/9: Copy of letter from General Nivelle to General Cadorna, March 1917
CAB/24/11: Cabinet Minutes, 30 April 1917
CAB/24/18: Copy of letter from E.L. Spiers to Major-General F. Maurice on the morale of the French army, 29 June 1917
War Office Papers:
WO 158/37: Correspondence between General Robert Nivelle and Field Marshal Sir Douglas Haig, 19 December 1916 to 17 April 1917

Liddell Hart Centre for Military Archives, King's College, London
GB0099 KCLMA Spears: Papers of Major-General Sir E.L. Spears.
(Author's note: E.L. Spears changed his name from 'Spiers' to 'Spears' in 1918.)

Contemporary Newspapers and Magazines
Le Figaro
L'Humanité
L'Illustration
Le Journal
Le Matin
La Renaissance
The Times
Illustrated London News

Published Sources
Bach, André, *Fusillés pour l'example* (Paris, 2003)
Barnett, Correlli, *The Swordbearers* (London, 1963)
Becker, Jean-Jacques, *The Great War and the French people* (Oxford, 1985)
Blake, Robert, *The private papers of Douglas Haig, 1914–1919* (London, 1952)
Bond, Brian (ed.), *Fallen Stars: eleven studies of twentieth century military disasters* (London, 1991)
Brown, Malcolm, *Verdun 1916* (Stroud, 2000)
Buffetaut, Yves, *The 1917 Spring Offensives: Arras, Vimy, le Chemin des Dames* (Paris, 1997)
Bull, Stephen, *World War 1 trench warfare*, parts 1 and 2 (Oxford, 2002)
Chevalier, Gabriel, *Fear* (Paris, 1930; London, 2011)
Clayton, Anthony, *Paths of Glory: the French Army, 1914–18* (London, 2003)
Cooper, Bryan, *Tank battles of World War 1* (London, 1974)
David, Saul, *100 days to Victory: how the great war was fought and won, 1914–1918* (London, 2014)
Doughty, Robert M., *Pyrrhic Victory: French strategy and operations in the Great War* (Harvard, 2005)
Dutil, Léon, *Les chars d'assaut: leur création et leur rôle pendant la guerre 1915–1918* (1919)

Fitzsimons, Bernard, *Tanks & weapons of World War 1* (London, 1973)
French General Staff, *French trench warfare 1917–1918: a reference manual* (English translation, Imperial War Museum, 2009)
Fuller, J.F.C., *Tanks in the Great War, 1914–18* (London, 1920)
George, David Lloyd, *War Memoirs*, 2 vols (London, 1938)
Giono, Jean, *To the slaughterhouse* (Paris, 1931; London, 1969)
Greenhalgh, Elizabeth, *Foch in command: the forging of a First World War general* (Cambridge, 2011)
Greenhalgh, Elizabeth, *The French Army and the First World War* (Cambridge University Press, 2014)
Griffith, Paddy and Denis, Peter, *Fortifications of the Western Front, 1914–18* (Oxford, 2004)
Guderian, Heinz, *Achtung Panzer! The development of tank warfare* (English translation, London, 1992)
Guéno, Jean-Pierre and Yves Laplume (eds), *Paroles de poilus: letters de la Grande Guerre* (Paris, 1998)
Hellot, Frédéric, *Le commandement des généraux Nivelle et Pétain* (Paris, 1936)
Herbillon, Colonel E., *Du general en chef au gouvernement: souveniers d'un officier de liaison pendant la guerre mondiale*, 2 vols (Paris, 1930)
Holmes, Richard, *The Western Front* (London, 1999)
Holmes, Richard, *Fatal avenue: a traveller's history of the battlefields of Northern France and Flanders 1346–1945* (London, 2008)
Holstein, Christina, *Verdun: Fort Douaumont* (Barnsley, 2002)
Holt, Valmai and Tonie, *Major and Mrs Holt's Battlefield Guide to the Western Front – South* (Barnsley, 2005)
Horne, Alastair, *The price of glory: Verdun 1916* (London, 1964)
Jeffery, Keith, *Field Marshal Sir Henry Wilson: a political soldier* (Oxford, 2006)
Joffre, Joseph, *The memoirs of Joseph Joffre* (London, 1932)
Jones, Ian, *Malice aforethought: a history of booby traps from World War One to Vietnam* (London, 2004)
Jurkiewicz, Bruno, *Les chars français du combat 1917–1918* (2008)
Keegan, John, *The First World War* (London, 1998)
Liddell Hart, B.H., *A history of the First World War* (London, 1970)
McPhail, Helen, *The long silence: the tragedy of occupied France in World War 1* (London, 2014)
Michelin & Cie, *Le Chemin des Dames* (Clermont-Ferrand, 1920)
Millett, Alan R. and Murray, Williamson (eds), *Military effectiveness. Vol. I: the First World War* (Cambridge, 2010)
Neillands, Robin, *The Great War Generals on the Western Front 1914–1918* (London, 2004)
Nobécourt, R.G., *Les fantassins du Chemin des Dames* (1983)

Offenstadt, Nicholas (ed.), *Les Chemin des Dames* (Paris, 2013)
Painlevé, Paul, 'La vérité sur l'offensive du 16 avril 1917' in *La Renaissance* (November 1919)
Painlevé, Paul, *Comment j'ai nommé Foch et Pétain* (Paris, 1923)
Paret, Peter (ed.), *Makers of modern strategy: from Machiavelli to the Nuclear Age* (Princeton, 1986)
Pedroncini, Guy, *Les mutineries de 1917* (Paris, 1967)
Pierrefeu, Jean de, *L'offensive du 16 Avril: la verities sur l'affaire Nivelle* (Paris, 1919)
Pierrefeu, Jean de, *French Headquarters, 1915–1918* (Paris, n.d.[1923?])
Poincaré, Raymond, *Au service de la France*, 10 vols (Paris, 1926–1933)
Porch, Douglas, *The March to the Marne: the French Army, 1871–1914* (Cambridge University Press, 1981)
Porch, Douglas, *The French secret services: a history of French intelligence from the Dreyfus affair to the Gulf War* (1995)
Porte, Rémy, *Joffre* (2014)
Rolland, Denis, *La Grève des Tranchées: les mutineries de 1917* (2005)
Rolland, Denis, *Nivelle: l'inconnu du Chemin des Dames* (2012)
Romains, Jules, *Verdun* (Paris, 1938; London, 1962)
Saurez, Georges, *Briand: sa vie, son oeuvre, avec son journal et de nombreaux documents inédits*, 5 vols (Paris, 1938–1941)
Serman, William and Bertaud, Jean-Paul, *Nouvelle Histoire Militaire de la France, 1789–1919* (Paris, 1998)
Sheffield, Gary, *The Chief: Douglas Haig and the British Army* (London, 2011)
Sheffield, Gary and Bourne, John (eds), *Douglas Haig: war diaries and letters, 1914–1918* (London, 2005)
Smith, Leonard V., *Between Mutiny and Obedience: the case of the French Fifth Infantry Division during World War I* (Princeton, 1994)
Spears, E.L., *Prelude to Victory* (London, 1939)
Strohn, Matthias (ed.), *World War 1 companion* (Oxford, 2013)
Stokesbury, James L., *A short history of World War 1* (New York, 2002)
Sumner, Ian, *French Poilu 1914–18* (Oxford, 2009)
Sumner, Ian, *They shall not pass: the French Army on the Western Front, 1914–1918* (Barnsley, 2012)
Svechin, A.A., *Strategy*, edited by Kent D. Lee (Minneapolis, 1991)
Taylor, A.J.P, *The First World War* (London, 1963)
Terraine, John, *Douglas Haig: the educated soldier* (London, 1963)
Watt, Richard M., *Dare call it treason: the true story of the French Army mutinies of 1917* (Barnes & Noble, 1969)
Williams, Charles, *Pétain* (London, 2005)
Zaloga, Steven J., *French tanks of World War 1* (Oxford, 2010)

Journals
Journal of Military History
Journal of Strategic Studies
La Journal Officiel
La Renaissance
Revue historique des armées

Index

Académie des Sciences, 76
'Affaire des Fiches', 4–5
Allenby, Sir Edmund Allenby, 85, 89
Alsace-Lorraine, 6, 8, 9, 15
America, 51, 64, 66, 131–2
American Expeditionary Force (AEF), 147
   AEF museum, 168
André, General Louis, 4–5
Anthoine, General François, 44, 107, 144–5
ANZAC forces, 85, 88
Asquith, Herbert H., British PM, 30
Aubriot-Gabet prototype tank, 74

Barbusse, Henri, soldier and writer, 164
Basque Memorial, Chemin des Dames, 167
Battles and Campaigns:
   1st Aisne, 18, 19
   Alsace Offensive, 19
   2nd Anglo-Boer War, 12
   Arras, 84–8
   Artois Offensive, 20
   Boxer Rebellion, 19
   Brusilov Offensive, 28
   Bullecourt, 88
   Charleroi, 76
   1st Champagne, 20
   2nd Champagne, 20
   Colenso, 12
   Craonne (1814), 114
   Fashoda Expedition, 22
   Flers Courcelette (Somme), 79–80
   Franco-Prussian War, 1–2, 15
   Frontiers Campaign (1914), 17
   'Kaiserslacht' (1918), 147
   La Courtine, 131, 135
   Loos, 73
   1st Marne, 14, 18
   2nd Marne, 159
   Mudken, 13
   Mulhouse, 16–17
   Neuve Chapelle, 20
   Russo-Japanese War, 13
   Salonika, xvii, 29, 32–3
   Scarpe, 87–8
   Somme, xiv, 21, 27, 28, 30
   Tannenberg, 15
   Verdun, xiv, 1, 21, 23, 27, 28, 29, 30, 35, 36, 39, 40, 54, 122
   Verdun Offensive (1917), 145–6
   Vilnius Offensive, 21
   Vimy Ridge, 87–8
   Vrigne-sur-Meuse, 147
   2nd Ypres, 73
   3rd Ypres, 143–5, 160
Becker, Jean-Jacques, historian, 164
Belgian army, 17, 89, 90
Belgium, 8–9, 15, 18, 72, 143, 160, 165
Berry-au-Bac tank memorial, 166
Bloc des Gauches, 4
Bloc National, 162
Bloch, Ivan S., strategic theorist, 13
'Bloody April' (1917, RFC), 86
Boehn, General Max von (German Seventh Army), 60
Boirault, Louis, tank designer, 74–5
Bonaparte, Napoleon, 114, 167
Bonnamy, Georges, 131st Infantry, 84
Bonneau, General Louis, 16–17
Booby-traps (German), 49
Bossut, Major Louis, French tank commander, 97, 98–100, 166
Bossut, Pierre, 99–100
'Boulanger Affair', 2–3, 157
Boulanger, General Georges, 2–3
Breton, Jean-Louis, tank designer, 75
Breton-Prétot machine, 74–5, 80
Briand, Aristide, French premier, 21, 25, 28, 30, 32–5, 41, 47, 49–50, 154, 157
Brillié, Eugène, 75–8
British alliance, 7–8
British cemetery, Chemin des Dames, 168
British Expeditionary Force (BEF), 17, 21, 30, 38, 39, 41–4, 47, 57, 64, 70, 84–9, 118, 143–5, 166

British Formations (within BEF):
  First Army, 20, 65
  Third Army, 85, 87
  Fifth Army, 85
British supporting attacks (Arras sector), 84–9
British tank programme, 79–81
Brugère, General Henri Joseph, 149, 151
Bulgaria, 21, 29, 30

Calais Conference, 41–4, 46, 118
Canadian Corps (BEF), 87, 88
Cartel des Gauches, 162
Castelnau, General Edouard de, 34, 38, 66, 68
Caverne du Dragon, 112–13, 167–8
Chemin des Dames, 55–6 (topography), 89–91, 112–13 (caves), 167–8, 168 (cemeteries), museum, 167–8
Chevalier, Gabriel, soldier and writer, 164
Churchill, Sir Winston, 68, 80
Clausewitz, Carl von, Prussian officer and strategic theorist, 153
Clayton, Anthony, historian, 4, 156, 164
Cobb, Matthew, writer, 164
Combes, Émile, French premier, 4
Conseil Général de l'Aisne, 167–8
Creusot engineering works (Schneider), 75

Daladier, Edouard, French premier, 162
D'Alançon, Lt-Col. Audemard, *chef de cabinet* to Nivelle, 23–4, 36, 44, 51, 69, 86, 159, 159
Darcy, Georges Edouard, artist, 164
Dawes Plan, 162
Debeney, General Eugène, chief of staff to Pétain, 138, 144
Delcassé, Théophile, foreign minister, 21
D'Espèrey, General Franchet, 34, 38, 47–8, 52, 56–7, 64, 66, 89, 90, 110, 132
Diaz, General Armando, Italian chief of staff, xiv
Dixon, Norman, writer, 156, 157
Doughty, Robert M., historian, 133, 164
Douglas, Kirk, actor, 164
Dreyfus Affair, 3–4, 157
Dreyfus, Captain Alfred, 2–4
Droit, Jean, artist, 164
Duchêne, General Denis Auguste, 57, 126, 150
Duroselle, Jean-Baptiste, historian, 164

École de Guerre, 10, 11
École Polytechnique, 8, 19
Entente Cordiale, 6–8

Estienne, Jean-Baptiste Eugène, pioneer of French tank forces, 76–82, 141, 166

Falkenhausen, General Ludwig von, 87, 89
Ferry, Jules, educationalist, 6
Foch, General (later Marshal) Ferdinand, xiv, 5, 10–11, 34, 38, 39, 147, 149, 166
Forain, Jean-Louis, artist, 164
Forts:
  Belfort, 17
  Brimont, 55, 101, 109, 110, 116, 131
  De Condé, 167
  De Malmaison, 55, 96, 167
  Douaumont, 24–5, 35
  Vaux, 24, 25, 35
France, post-WW1, 161–3
French Army:
  Army Technical Services, 78, 81
  Casualties, 14, 20–1, 31, 161
  Colonial troops, 22–3, 25, 62, 93–4, 115
  Desertion rates, 122
  Deuxième Bureau (military intelligence), 46–7, 60–1
  Executions, 134–5
  Grand Quartier Général (GQG), 8, 27, 34, 36–7, 40, 41, 43, 58, 69, 95, 103, 107, 108, 119, 123, 128, 130, 137, 138, 139, 151, 152
  Leave system, 128–9, 136
  Lebel rifle, 17
  Medical services, 103, 122, 150
  Military justice system, 133–5
  Morale, 26–7, 63, 115, 120–3
  Mutinies, 121–48
  Plan XVI, 8–9
  Plan XVII, 8–9, 14, 16–18
  Post-mutiny reforms, 139–43
  Pre-war and early campaigns, 1–26
  Section technique du genie, 74
  Service Aeronautique, 61–2, 91, 140, 145
  Tank programme, 57, 72–83
  Uniforms (1914), 16
French Army Groups:
  Groupe d'armées du centre (GAC), 22, 30, 48, 52, 56, 107
  Groupe d'armées du nord (GAN), 30, 47, 56, 89, 40
  Groupe d'armées de reserve (GAR), 51, 52, 56, 89, 95, 106, 109, 166
French Armies:
  First Army, 16, 144–5
  Second Army, 20, 22, 26, 124, 145

Index

Third Army, 89
Fourth Army, 107, 124, 144
Fifth Army, 57, 60–1, 70, 95, 96–7, 101, 103, 104, 106–7, 108, 111, 114, 124, 166
Sixth Army, 57, 60–1, 92, 93, 95, 96, 97, 101, 103, 106–7, 108, 110, 111, 114, 115, 124, 132, 144, 152, 166
Seventh Army, 90
Tenth Army, 57, 60–1, 108, 111, 114, 124, 125, 144, 159
French Formations:
   I Corps Coloniale, 102
   II Corps Coloniale, 92–3, 103
   VII Corps (First Army), 16
   I Corps (Fifth Army), 106–7
   XI Corps (Sixth Army), 114
   XXI Corps, 126
   XXXVII Corps, 135
   1st Colonial Division (Sixth Army), 124
   2nd Colonial Division (Tenth Army), 125–6
   1st Infantry Division (Fifth Army), 101
   2nd Infantry Division (Fifth Army), 103
   41st Infantry Division, 114
   56th Infantry Division, 96
   127th Infantry Division, 96
   151st Infantry Division, 101
   153rd Infantry Division, 96
   158th Infantry Division, 126
French Units:
   25th Bn Chasseurs à Pied, 96
   102nd Bn Chasseurs à Pied, 114–15
   3rd Infantry Regiment, 130
   18th Infantry Regiment, 125
   57th Infantry Regiment, 70
   89th Infantry Regiment, 70
   131st Infantry Regiment, 84
   151st Infantry Regiment, 124, 166
   155th Infantry Regiment, 100
   162nd Infantry Regiment, 100
   249th Infantry Regiment, 106
   298th Infantry Regiment, 127
   310th Infantry Regiment, 127
   370th Infantry Regiment, 127
   4th Artillery Regiment, 19
   5th Artillery Regiment, 19
   22nd Artillery Regiment, 76
   Artillerie Speciale units (tanks), 82
   Groupement Bossut (tanks), 98, 99–100, 166
   Groupement Chaubès (tanks), 98–9
   Groupement Lefebvre (tanks), 115
   5th Aviation Group, 76
French Cemeteries (Chemin des Dames), 168
French WWI films, 164
Freycinet, Charles de, French premier, 2, 52

Gallieni, General Joseph, 18
Gamelin, General Maurice, 95
German Armies:
   First Army, 18
   Second Army, 18
   Seventh Army, 17, 60
German casualties, 152
German cemeteries (Chemin des Dames), 168
Giono, Jean, writer, 164
Gouraud, General Henri, 149
Grandmaison, Lt-Col. Louis Loyzeau de, 10
Greenhalgh, Elizabeth, historian, xvii, 158, 164
Gullaumat, General Adolphe, 145–6

Haig, Field Marshal Sir Douglas, xiv, xvi, 20, 26, 28, 35, 38, 39, 40, 41–4, 46, 47, 64, 79–80, 84–9, 90, 105, 116, 118, 138–9, 143, 145, 160
Hankey, Col. Sir Maurice, secretary to the British war cabinet, 42
Helbronner, Jacques, secretary to the French war cabinet, 104
Henry, Major H.J., 4
Hentsch, Colonel Richard, German staff officer, 18
Hindenburg, Field Marshal Paul von, 45, 60
Hindenburg Line, 44–6, 56, 84, 89, 109, 151

Industrial unrest (France), 5, 129–30
Ireland (French invasion plans), 7
Italian cemetery, 168
Italy, 29, 40, 52, 64, 66, 135

Janin, General Maurice, staff officer to Joffre, 77
Joffre, General (later Maréchal) Joseph, xiv, xv, 6–9, 10–15, 16, 18–22, 27, 28, 29, 20, 31, 32–6, 38, 42, 47, 71, 77, 78, 122
Jospin, Lionel, French premier, 167

Kerensky, Aleksandr, Russian leader, 131
Kern, Haim, artist, 167
Kiggell, Lt-Gen. Sir Lancelot, chief of staff to Haig, 42
Kluck, General Alexander von, 18
Kubrick, Stanley, film director, 164

Lacaze, Admiral Lucien, 110
Langlois, General Hippolyte, 12–13
Lanrezac, General Charles, 11
Lapie, Christian, artist, 168
Liebert, General Eduard von, 90
Lloyd George, David, British minister and later PM, 28, 30, 39, 40, 41–3, 47, 70, 80, 109, 118, 154, 157–8
Ludendorff, Field Marshal Erich, 45, 59, 60, 89
Lyautey, General Hubert, minister for war, xv, 33, 36, 41, 49–50, 108

Macready, George, actor, 164–5
Maginot, André, soldier and minister, 34, 64, 158
Maginot Line, 161
Maistre, General Paul, 132
Mangin, General Charles, 22–3, 38, 57, 63, 92–6, 106, 110–11, 115, 124, 144–50, 159–60, 166
Mazel, General Oliver Charles, 57, 58, 96–7, 116, 149–50, 166
Messimy, Adolphe, minister for war, 8, 16, 65
Michel, General Victor (and Plan XVI), 8
Micheler, General Joseph Alfred, 24, 51–2, 56–7, 60, 64–7, 89, 90, 106, 109, 118–19, 149–50, 166
Moltke, General Helmuth von, 18
Moroccan Crisis, 2, 5, 6
Moroccan regimental memorial, 167
Musée du Chemin des Dames, 167–8

Navarre, Jean, French air ace, xiv
Nicholson, G.W.L., historian, 152
Ninet, Jules, 89th Infantry, 70, 72
Nivelle, General Robert: xiv–xvii, 1; origins and early war career, 19–26; success at Verdun, 22–6; public acclaim, 25–6; rise to commander-in-chief, 27–35; qualities for command, 34–5; initial plans, 35–6; initial relations with staff, 36–7; meets Lloyd George, 39; relationship with Haig, 38–44; Calais Conference, 41–3; reaction to German withdrawal, 44–9; negative reports from staff and army commanders, 51–2; offensive plans and assumptions, 54–71, 82, 84, 86–7, 89–90; his offensive, 90–120; fall from grace, 115–20; plans for reform, 139, 141, 146; Commission of Inquiry, 149–52; analysis of military decision-making process, 154–6; post-war career, 157–8;
American tour, 158; death, commemoration and legacy, 158–9, 165
Nivelle Inquiry, 149–52
Nivelle Offensive, 1, 14, 54, 72, 83, 84–120, 120, 121, 128, 143, 149–52, 151–2, 160–1, 163–4
Nivelle Offensive, operational and tactical objectives:
Berméricourt, 114
Berry-au-Bac, 97
Bovette Wood, 96
Braye, 111
Buttes Wood, 101
Californie Plateau, 101, 106–7, 114, 167
Caverne du Dragon, 112–13
Chavignon, 93
Chavonne, 111
Cholera Farm, 99, 166
Condé redoubt, 111
Cour-Soupir, 106
Craonne, 101–2, 109, 114, 167
Creute, 94
Hill 78, 100
Hill 108, 101
Hun's Wood, 101
Hurtebise Farm, 94, 101, 112, 114, 166–7
Juvincourt, 92
Laffaux Mill, 95, 115, 166
Luxembourg redoubt, 101
Malmaison, 96
Monampteuil, 93
Mont Blond, 107
Mont Sapin, 96, 109
'Paradise Wood', 96
Sans Nom, 107
Sapigneul, 109, 114
Soupir, 111
Temple Farm, 98
Vailly, 111
Vauclerc Plateau, 93, 113

Offenstadt, Nicholas, historian, xvii, 164
Operation Alberich (German withdrawal to the Hindenburg Line), 45–50

Painléve, Paul, French minister for war, xv, 50–3, 64–8, 86–7, 104, 109–10, 116–19, 133–4, 138, 153, 157
Passaga, General Fénelon, 101
Paths of Glory, war movie, 164–5
Pedroncini, Guy, historian, 123, 134, 164
Pershing, General John J., 39

Pétain, General Philippe, xiv, 11, 20, 25–6, 34, 44, 48, 52, 56–7, 65–8, 70, 76, 107, 109, 116–20, 132–48, 150, 157, 166
Picq, Col. Ardant du, 10–11
Pierrefeu, Jean de, French staff officer, 24, 44, 68, 159
Poincaré, Raymond, president of France, 34, 66, 108–10, 119, 122, 134, 143, 146, 151, 162
Popular Front government, 162
Prince of Wales (later Edward VII), 58

Renault, Louis, vehicle designer and manufacturer, 77
Renault FT17 tank, 141
Renouard, Col. Georges, 51, 150
Renouard report, 51, 150
Renouvin, Pierre, 164
Ribot, Alexandre, French premier, 50, 51–2, 64–7, 108–10, 116, 117, 153, 157
Richthofen, Manfred von, German air ace, 86
Robertson, General Sir William, chief of the Imperial General Staff, 40, 41–4, 47, 116, 117–18
Rolland, Denis, historian, xvii, 123, 134, 158, 164
Romains, Jules, writer, 164
Romania, 29, 30, 32
Roques, General Pierre, 32, 139–40
Rouvier, Maurice, 3
Royal Flying Corps (RFC), 85–6, 87
Russia, 6–7, 29, 30, 32, 40, 51, 52, 64, 66, 160
Russian brigades, 97, 130–1, 135
Russian cemetery, 168
Russian memorial and church, 168
Russian revolutions, 126, 130, 160

St Chamond tanks, 74, 81, 97, 115, 141
Sarte, Maxime Real del, artist, 167
Schlieffen, General Alfred von, 8
Schlieffen-Moltke Plan, 8–9, 13–14, 15, 18

Schneider & Cie, 75, 77–8
'Crocodile', prototype tank, 74
tanks, 57, 74–83, 97–100, 115, 141
Serrail, General Maurice, 32, 43
SOMUA factory, 78, 79
'Song of Craonne', 164
Souain tank trials, 77
Spears, Edward, British liaison officer and writer, 23, 40, 93, 138
Stockholm Conference, 138–9
Stokesbury, James L., historian, xvi
Sumner, Ian, historian, 164
Svechin, Alexandr, Russian strategist, 153, 163
Swinton, Ernest, engineer and tank designer, 80
Switzerland, 18, 32, 60, 72, 132, 140

Taufflieb, General Émile, 135
Taylor, A.J.P., historian, 149, 154
Thame, Lord Bertie of, British diplomat, 128
Trebuchon, Augustin, last French casualty of WW1, 147
Trotsky, Leon, 130
Turkey, 29

Union Sacrée government, 17, 49–50

Victory Day parade, 1919, xiv
Viviani, Réné, French premier, 17, 21

Watt, Richard M., historian, 130, 135
Weygand, General Maxime, 166
Wilhelm, Crown Prince, 55, 59, 60
Wilson, General Sir Henry, 43, 144

Ybarnégaray, Jean, soldier and deputy, 103, 106

Zola, Émile, writer, 3